MW00694483

THE JEAN BAUDRILLARD READER

European Perspectives

European Perspectives

A Series in Social Thought and Cultural Criticism
Lawrence D. Kritzman, Editor

European Perspectives presents outstanding books by leading European thinkers. With both classic and contemporary works, the series aims to shape the major intellectual controversies of our day and to facilitate the tasks of historical understanding.

For a complete list of books in the series, see pages 227–8.

The Jean Baudrillard Reader

STEVE REDHEAD

COLUMBIA UNIVERSITY PRESS

NEW YORK

Columbia University Press
Publishers Since 1893
New York

Copyright © 2008 Steve Redhead, editorial matter and organization
All rights reserved

First published in the United Kingdom by Edinburgh University Press

Library of Congress Cataloging-in-Publication Data

A Cataloging-in Publication record for this book is available from the Library
of Congress

ISBN 978-0-231-14612-8 (cloth)
ISBN 978-0-231-14613-5 (pbk.)

⊗

Columbia University Press books are printed on permanent and durable
acid-free paper.

This book is printed on paper with recycled content.

Printed and bound in Great Britain.

c 10 9 8 7 6 5 4 3 2 1

Contents

Acknowledgements

Grateful acknowledgement is made to the following sources for permission to reproduce material previously published elsewhere. Every effort has been made to trace the copyright holders, but if any have been inadvertently overlooked, the publisher will be pleased to make the necessary arrangements at the first opportunity.

'Mass Media Culture', from *Revenge of the Crystal*, Jean Baudrillard, translated by Paul Foss and Julian Pefanis, London: Pluto Press, 1990.

'The Linguistic Imaginary', from *Symbolic Exchange and Death*, Jean Baudrillard, translated by Iain Hamilton Grant, London: Sage, 1993.

'The Ecliptic of Sex', from *Seduction*, Jean Baudrillard, translated by Brian Singer, London: Macmillan, 1990.

'The Beaubourg Effect: Implosion and Deterrence', from *Simulacra and Simulation*, Jean Baudrillard, translated by Sheila Faria Glaser, Ann Arbor, MI: University of Michigan Press, 1994.

'Please Follow Me', from *Please Follow Me*, Jean Baudrillard. *Suite Venitienne*, Sophie Calle, translated by Dany Barash and Danny Hatfield, Seattle, WA: Bay Press, 1988.

'The Evil Demon of Images', from *The Evil Demon of Images*, Jean Baudrillard, translated by Paul Patton and Paul Foss, Sydney: Power Institute of Fine Arts, 1988. © Jean Baudrillard and Power Institute 1987.

'The Gulf War: Is It Really Taking Place?', from *The Gulf War Did Not Take Place*, Jean Baudrillard, translated by Paul Patton, Sydney: Power Institute of Fine Arts, 1995, English translation and introduction © Power Institute and Paul Patton 1995.

Originally published in French as *La Guerre du Golfe n'a as eu lieu* © Editions Galilée.

'Pataphysics of the Year 2000', from *The Illusion of the End*, Jean Baudrillard, translated by Chris Turner, Cambridge: Polity, 1994.

'Impossible Exchange', from *Impossible Exchange*, Jean Baudrillard, translated by Chris Turner, London: Verso, 2001.

'The Millennium, or the Suspense of the Year 2000', from *The Vital Illusion*, Jean Baudrillard, translated by Julia Witwer, New York: Columbia University Press, 2000.

'Truth or Radicality? The Future of Architecture', full version of 'Truth or Radicality? The Future of Architecture', *Blueprint*, No. 157, 1999, Jean Baudrillard, translated by Chris Turner, London: Blueprint, 1999.

'The Art Conspiracy', from *Screened Out*, Jean Baudrillard, translated by Chris Turner, London: Verso, 2002.

'Requiem for the Twin Towers', from *The Spirit of Terrorism*, Jean Baudrillard, translated by Chris Turner, London: Verso, 2003, 2nd edition.

'Pornography of War', full version of 'Pornography of War', *Cultural Politics*, Vol. 1, No. 1, 2005, Jean Baudrillard, translated by Chris Turner, Oxford: Berg.

'Contemporary Art: Art Contemporary with Itself', from *The Intelligence of Evil or The Lucidity Pact*, Jean Baudrillard, translated by Chris Turner, Oxford: Berg, 2005.

'The Pyres of Autumn', full version of 'The Pyres of Autumn', *New Left Review*, 37 Jan./Feb. 2006, translated by Chris Turner, London: New Left Review.

'What I am, I don't know. I am the simulacrum of myself.'
Jean Baudrillard

CHAPTER ONE

On Non-Postmodernity
by Steve Redhead

This *Reader* will be of interest to students and staff in the human and social sciences in a range of university courses across the globe and to those general readers interested in contemporary public intellectuals like Jean Baudrillard and to some extent those he specifically selected as influential and important such as Giorgio Agamben, Slavoj Žižek and Paul Virilio. It is modelled on the author's already published *Reader* on Paul Virilio, Baudrillard's long-time friend and compatriot (Redhead 2004b). Virilio is still, after all these years, the closest theorist to Jean Baudrillard, personally and politically, symbolised in all sorts of connections. For instance, a photograph from Jean Baudrillard's extensive portfolio adorns the front cover of Paul Virilio's book of interviews on the 'accident of art' (Lotringer and Virilio 2005). However, as this book demonstrates, there should be no confusion between the two of them. Baudrillard and Virilio should always be seen as separate. A couple of years before he died (MacFarquhar 2005) Baudrillard insisted 'what I am, I don't know. I am the simulacrum of myself'. Jean Baudrillard, the simulacrum, is certainly a singular object. As Baudrillard has emphatically stated in discussion, 'you must create your underground because now there's no more underground, no more avant-garde, no more marginality. You can create your personal underground, your own black hole, your own singularity'.[1]

The previous book, *The Paul Virilio Reader*, which complemented a companion book *Paul Virilio: Theorist for An Accelerated Culture* (Redhead 2004a), where Baudrillard was also compared in a detailed consideration of Virilio and French social theory, is the model for *The Jean Baudrillard Reader* in design, format and intended readership. *The Jean Baudrillard Reader* is conceived as a teaching book on Baudrillard, an enterprise once labelled in academia as something of a contradiction in terms. The original Jean Baudrillard writings in this *Reader* are presented in the chronological order in which Baudrillard's books were published in French because English translations over the years have been undertaken in a very different time scale and misunderstandings and misinterpretations of Baudrillard's ideas have resulted. A further complicating factor is that his books were often made up of disparate articles published on a different time scale. The readings are chosen from a number of different sources. A range of international publishers of the English translations of Baudrillard's original French are represented in the *Reader* including Polity Press, Blueprint magazine, Verso, Sage, Macmillan, Pluto Press, Power Institute of Fine Arts in Sydney, University of Michigan Press and Columbia University Press. One major theme, which is supported by a close reading of Baudrillard's texts featured in the book, as well as the bibliographical introductions to each chapter, is that the work of Baudrillard has been frequently mistakenly associated with the label postmodern, postmodernity or postmodernism. The book asserts that to properly situate Baudrillard in the pantheon of critical thinking it is better to understand his work outside of debates about postmodernism as he himself was wont to do. This *Reader*, through its carefully chosen extracts which mention other key thinkers pervasively, also helps to accurately place Jean Baudrillard in the historical continuum of post-war public intellectuals.

It was felt that now is the time for the publication of a representative *Reader* of Jean Baudrillard's writings from the 1960s to the present day, set in a more accurate context than previous books. In the course of the author preparing the materials for this book, Jean Baudrillard sadly died from cancer after a long illness. Ever generous with his time, he was even kindly awarding permissions for publications of extracts from his work in his last weeks of life. Baudrillard's profound legacy suddenly loomed large as obituaries appeared all over the world. The present book is a timely collection of extracts ('fragments' to echo the oft used label for Baudrillard's work, used twice in English translation of titles of his many books) of writings by Jean Baudrillard. Baudrillard was unarguably a major international theorist who into his eighth decade boasted a back catalogue stretching over six decades and an incisive, energetic online journal devoted to situating and analysing his work as well as hundreds of thousands of webpages in cyberspace concerned with his name in some form or other. There is a great advantage in collecting together in one volume extracts from various writings of Jean Baudrillard, demonstrating what he has written over the years and exactly when he wrote it. This book does just that at a time when global interest in Baudrillard's writings has, justifiably, never been higher. Once the rather ghoulish media fascination with his death has died down it is surely the case that, for decades to come, Baudrillard will be studied even more avidly than when he was alive.

Even before his death, Baudrillard's own disappearance was characteristically set up. In late 2006 Baudrillard was due to speak in Britain twice within a couple of months. In the event his serious illness prevented Baudrillard from travelling from France to the UK. The media reception of his impending appearances was telling. Reporting his agreement to engage in conversation with Semiotext(e)'s Sylvere Lotringer on the subject 'Art Beyond Art' at the annual Frieze Art Fair in London the organisers noted that Baudrillard

> is the most important intellectual working today: an icon. If you ask any young artist who is the most important writer on sociology or philosophy, they will tell you Baudrillard. He is very au courant, from what he says about politics to what's happening in art practice. (Higgins 2006: 15)

At the same time Baudrillard's attendance at an international academic conference at Swansea University in Wales was eagerly anticipated. 'Engaging Baudrillard', a title replete with double meaning, was massively subscribed with over a hundred speakers from all over the world representing various disciplines and theoretical persuasions. Topics for sessions ranged from 'Baudrillard and the Art Conspiracy' through 'Baudrillard's Taste' to 'Baudrillard's Sense of Humour'. Unfortunately a seriously ill Baudrillard had to apologise in advance for his absence and the Jean Baudrillard Plenary session had to be presented (by a prominent academic commentator on Baudrillard, Mike Gane) *in absentia*. The topic? 'On Disappearance'! Baudrillard, as ever, remained enigmatic and elusive.

Jean Baudrillard, in death as well as life, was perhaps the most controversial of all social and cultural theorists. In 2001 he was nominated for 'Most Despicable Quote in the Wake of September 11' (Goldblatt 2001). He has been described as merely 'an over-rated French theorist' (Cohen 2007: 110), a 'political idiot', and a 'philosopher clown', worshipped as the high priest of postmodernism and, more caustically, vilified as one of the notorious 'intellectual imposters' (Sokal and Bricmont 2003) who write 'fashionable nonsense'.[2] In his seventies he survived global fame and local dishonour, and contracted cancer. The appeal of Jean Baudrillard is global. Apart from the likes of Zygmunt Bauman, Paul Virilio, and Slavoj Žižek, Jean Baudrillard arguably has been the most prominent contemporary global theorist in the short twenty first century. Jean Baudrillard's work is taught in all nooks and crannies of the world in many different humanities and social science courses, especially media studies, cultural studies, philosophy, sociology, popular culture, political theory, literary theory, art history and art criticism. Baudrillard, followed subsequently by Žižek, has an online journal dedicated to the study of his life, work and death entitled the *International Journal of Baudrillard Studies*. The *IJBS*, organised by founder Gerry Coulter, featured Jean Baudrillard himself on the editorial board. It is freely available by clicking on the URL for the website which is provided by Bishop's University in Canada (http://www.ubishops.ca/BaudrillardStudies) and hosts some of the most affecting and engaging obituaries of Baudrillard as well as translations of his work and stimulating, critical essays on Baudrillard and many of his associates. Baudrillard's comments on events like 9/11, the burning vehicles in Paris streets or the torture at Abu Ghraib have been voraciously sought and digested. However, his translated publications since 1968 have left a trail of confusion and misinterpretation: Marxist, post-Marxist, post-history, post-modernist, post-structuralist, post-culture, post-theory; even 'post-everything' as Simon Frith once put it having just read the poetic, aphoristic portrait of 'Amerique' in Baudrillard's *America* (Baudrillard

1988; Gundersen and Dobson 1996) in the late 1980s. There is now, though, sufficient evidence in Baudrillard's multiple texts, and increasingly excellent translations into English, for a cool re-assessment to be made. This book is a central part of that re-assessment. It is the representative, accessible collected Baudrillard. It concentrates on what Jean Baudrillard has written and the order in which he wrote it. *The Jean Baudrillard Reader* comprises sixteen sections, with this editorial introduction and a concluding innovative reading guide making eighteen chapters in all. Each section has an extract of one of Jean Baudrillard's writings already translated into English, prefaced by a short bibliographical intro-duction setting the context of the piece. These cryptic contextual and bibliographical prefaces seek to put the debates about Baudrillard over the years into sharp perspective, clearing up, where possible, confusion and mistaken interpretations, but also provoking new controversy and intellectual and political debate.

This book is aimed at students and teachers, some of whom may be coming to the writing of Jean Baudrillard for the first time. The bibliographical prefaces by the author are intended to be a guide but there is no substitute for reading, and re-reading, the extracted Baudrillard texts themselves. There is, however, a never ending Baudrillard studies beyond these core extracts. An innovative guide by the author to reading the entire work of Jean Baudrillard, and of his interpreters, completes the book, together with various suggested ways to follow up the readings collected here. Arranged chronologically in order of first publication in French, the *Reader* illustrates the development and interconnect-edness of Baudrillard's work since the 1960s. It collects in one accessible volume for the first time extracts of Baudrillard's work from the 1960s through the 1970s, 1980s and 1990s and into the 2000s. Baudrillard's first book in 1968 eventually translated into English as *The System of Objects* (originally his doctoral thesis) is left out of these extracts. Baudrillard himself felt that it was some-what unrepresentative. The readings begin with an extract from Baudrillard's second full length book, *The Consumer Society*, written in the late 1960s in the wake of situationist politics spilling onto the Paris streets, which concentrates on Pop art, consumption, advertising and the mass media. This is followed by extracts from *Symbolic Exchange and Death* and *Seduction*, two 1970s 'lost' treatises which contain much of the 'secret' of Baudrillard's theorising of symbolic exchange (which includes seduction) as opposed to simulation or the semiotic order. The next extracts are diverse cultural commentaries on the architecture of the Pompidou Centre (Beaubourg) in Paris, Sophie Calle's provocative photography and the 'evil demon of images' in the cinema. These are followed by extracts on the cultural politics of the first Gulf War in the early 1990s, the 'pataphysics' of the millennium, the theory of impossible exchange, the countdown to the end of the century, the future of architecture, the US art world, the event of 9/11 in New York, the degradation of inmates in Abu Ghraib, and the 'contemporariness' of modern art. The extracts end with Baudrillard's acute observations on the nightly burning of cars in French suburbs (*banlieues*) in late 2005 when he was already seriously ill but still as prescient as ever.

Baudrillard had in fact begun writing twenty years before the first extract in this book. In 2005 Jean Baudrillard published, in co-operation with the London Institute of Pataphysics, a fourteen-page, fifty-five-year-old text by his younger self from 1952. It was put out in a limited edition (177 numbered copies, forty-four signed by Baudrillard) entitled *Pataphysics*, packaged in a special handmade cover. *Pataphysics* was a text he had actually penned in the early 1950s when he was in his early twenties, which has also now been collected with other writings less expensively and extravagantly elsewhere (Baudrillard and Lotringer 2005). Pataphysics, defined by its late nineteenth-century founder Albert Jarry as the science of imaginary solutions, has always been a thread in Baudrillard's thinking from young man to old, and Jarry's pranksterism endured for Baudrillard who has admitted to occasionally using completely imaginary quotations in his writings and finding such practice hilariously funny. Rather than accepting a division between a young and old phase in his life, Baudrillard seemingly regarded himself as forever young. In answer to a questioner at a reading in New York in November 2005 (when he was actually seventy-six years old) who after noting that Baudrillard had 'spent a great deal of time writing a great many books' asked how old he was, Baudrillard retorted 'very young!'

(MacFarquhar 2005). More seriously, there is no simple, radical 'epistemological break' between the 'young Baudrillard' (or the 'early Baudrillard') and the 'mature Baudrillard' (or 'old Baudrillard') evident in the massive body of Jean Baudrillard's work covered by this book. Attempts to set up an epistemological break between an 'early writings' and a 'late writings' in Baudrillard, as with Karl Marx a century previously, are ultimately doomed to failure and the interest in pataphysics, as with philosophers such as Friedrich Nietzsche, is consistent throughout his life. Twenty-five years after Baudrillard's first, short, unpublished text on Albert Jarry, Antonin Artaud and pataphysics, a Cleveland punk band emerged with the name Pere Ubu to popularise globally the drama of Jarry from the late nineteenth century which had so fascinated the 'young Baudrillard'. As popular music historian Clinton Heylin (Heylin 2007: 219) notes, David Thomas in 1975 in Cleveland, Ohio named his band Pere Ubu 'after Albert Jarry's caricature king because … it would be an added texture of absolute grotesqueness … a darkness over everything'. Baudrillard had never shown any awareness of this 'low culture' connection, though he did once appear in a 'punk' costume of his own (a gold lame jacket with mirrored lapels) reading the text of his self-penned 1980s song ('Motel-Suicide') backed by a rock band at the 'Chance Event' held at Whiskey Pete's in Las Vegas in November 1996.

Jean Baudrillard was in many ways an unusual recruit to the diverse parade of French social theory partly because of his social and cultural background. He was born in Rheims in north east France on July 29, 1929, a few months before the great stock market crash. He died on March 6, 2007 at seventy-seven years old, survived by two children and his second wife Marine. His grandparents were peasants. His own parents worked as civil servants. From a background in literature and languages he worked as a teacher of German in a Lycee (high school) from the mid 1950s to the mid 1960s, eventually also conducting extensive editorial and translation work (German into French) for publishers. Finding it difficult to enter the university milieu, having tried and failed to get into the Ecole Normale Superieure by taking the aggregation, Baudrillard was a late comer compared to his contemporaries in French social theory (Foucault, Derrida, Deleuze, Althusser, Guattari) and always regarded himself as something of an outsider. Once installed in the mid-1960s at Nanterre (University of Paris X) he taught uninterrupted from 1966 to 1986 within the Nanterre university campus, nominally as a sociologist. In 1986 he moved to the University of Paris IX Dauphine but by this time had become a notorious internationally known academic and provocative thinker and his university career was effectively over by 1987. He spent some of the subsequent twenty years of his life travelling abroad, especially to the USA and within Europe, but remained Parisien. He lived in an apartment in Paris, in the rue Sainte Beuve, where he took many of his photographs, right up until he died in March 2007. Self-consciously wary and private until after death but admired and praised by those who actually met him, Baudrillard was described rather bizarrely in an obituary published by the *West Australian* newspaper in Perth, Australia as having lived in a Paris home with '50 television sets' and many images of America, and as being 'one of the most important philosophers of the last fifty years … a stocky, rumpled, bespectacled figure who smoked fat hand-rolled cigarettes … a simple man whose basic impulses were a dislike of culture and a love of fast cars'.

To place Jean Baudrillard in any theoretical or political pigeon hole has always been a difficult enterprise. It remains so today, even after his death. Although Baudrillard was influenced by Marxists like Jean-Paul Sartre, Herbert Marcuse and Henri Lefebvre his work has always born a tangential relationship to any brand of Marxism, neo- or otherwise. Philosophical antecedents of Baudrillard's work are complex and for sure Marx and Engels are present but so too is Mani, the Persian Gnostic prophet writing nearly 2000 years ago. In particular, this book questions the idea that Baudrillard is a postmodernist in any sense and challenges the reader to find evidence for the supposition in the texts extracted. The *Reader* highlights the term 'non-postmodernity', used by the author in other contexts, parodying French social theorist Bruno Latour's concept of 'non-modernity' (Latour 1993) in order to help situate Baudrillard and his writings in the lineage of key contemporary thinkers. It is meant to suggest that it would be better to concentrate on 'modernity' in all its aspects, however extreme, if Baudrillard's work on the nature of the contemporary world is to be properly appreciated. The moral relativism often connected to postmodernism is actually nowhere to be seen in Baudrillard. Nevertheless, from the 1970s onwards, Baudrillard, as a figure and as the head of a body of knowledge, became integrally associated with terms like postmodernism, postmodern sociology/art/architecture and postmodernity, and the general issues surrounding media and screen culture and virtual cyberspace which seem, inevitably, to attract the label 'postmodern'. It should be said that this process of linking Baudrillard with the idea of the 'post' was mainly through dubious labelling by others and not through Baudrillard's own words. Partly it has been a consequence of commentators using the term 'postmodern' to cover anything recent or contemporary especially in the rapidly changing world of new media. In some ways, in any case, Baudrillard is a quite perverse choice of theorist of the new media technologies, or commentator on their future potential. He was stubbornly 'old media' writ large. He admitted, in 1996, that he did

> not know much about this subject. I haven't gone beyond the fax and the automatic answering machine. I have a very hard time getting down to work on the screen because all I see there is a text in the form of an image which I have a hard time entering. With my typewriter, the text is at a distance. With the screen, it's different ... That scares me a little and cyberspace is not of great use to me personally.[3]

Baudrillard also always preferred photography to digital video.

The rethinking of the work of Jean Baudrillard around the notion of 'non-postmodernity' (rather than postmodernism, postmodernity and the postmodern) which this book promotes is, in part, a matter of implied critique of two theoretical constituencies which have interpellated Baudrillard for many decades. Both of these traditions in social science and the humanities invoked him, at least initially, as a postmodernist, and both, self-consciously, on the left of the political spectrum cast him as something of a lapsed Marxist. These theoretical constituencies which constructed Baudrillard as a postmodernist had to come to terms with the international crisis in Marxism, and Marxist theory, in the 1970s and 1980s, something Baudrillard had already resolved some years previously. One constituency is the 'historical materialism plus postmodernity' perspective best exemplified by Fredric Jameson (Jameson 1991) and David Harvey (Harvey 2001) which had considerable influence in the USA. The other constituency is the perspective developed around the *Theory, Culture and Society* (TCS) journal and book series by Mike Featherstone (Featherstone 1991) and Scott Lash (Lash 1991), 'postmodernism in sociology (without the historical materialism)', which made its mark mainly in the UK. In recent years a new international constituency has emerged which has moved away from these conventional interpretations of Baudrillard and taken more seriously the words of Baudrillard himself rather than his myriad interpreters. In some aspects of this work it is not even thought relevant to mention that once upon a time Baudrillard was regarded as a Marxist or a postmodernist. This book solidifies this new global constituency by providing comprehensive evidence of what Jean Baudrillard wrote and precisely when he wrote it. The idea that Baudrillard was essentially a 'postmodern sociologist' is still pervasive in much commentary, much of it stemming from those orthodox 1970s and 1980s readings of Baudrillard, but it is ultimately, in the last instance, an unhelpful notion. Politically as well as intellectually these fixed perspectives have done no favours to Baudrillard or, ultimately, his readers. For instance, from the early 1960s Baudrillard and his friend Félix Guattari were regarded, confusingly, as Maoists. Later Baudrillard himself wrote books debating strands of Marxist theory in the early 1970s (Baudrillard 1975; Baudrillard 1981) but his relationship to Marx and Marxism is certainly no one way street and after the mid-1970s there is little serious engagement on Baudrillard's part. Further, the period Baudrillard spent around the influential *Utopie* journal in France beginning in the mid 1960s and continuing until the late 1970s, was undoubtedly evidence of his involvement in ultra-leftist politics in France but Baudrillard clearly broke with much European 'leftism' in the late 1970s and 1980s for being insufficiently radical. His future thinking was a perspective some way 'beyond' Marx. Baudrillard was also present, as a lecturer, at the Nanterre campus when it became the spark for May '68. However, Baudrillard was never a paid up member of left organisations and ploughed a very individual furrow throughout his life and work. Still the labelling, and myths, persisted. Situationist? Though sympathetic to the situationists he was never a member of the Situationist International, or ever even met Guy Debord. New Philosopher? In the 1970s the Nouveaux Philosophes movement of Andre Glucksmann and Bernard-Henri Levy (former leftists who publicly renounced leftism) left Baudrillard untouched but he became guilty by association in the minds of some Trotskyists when he later published with Grasset, Bernard-Henri Levy's publishing house, and wrote in journals in France in the 1980s that were regarded as on the 'new right'. In 2006 Bernard-Henri Levy published a book of his diaries written while travelling in the USA entitled *American Vertigo* (Levy 2006) which was compared favourably by the *International Journal of Baudrillard Studies* to the mid 1980s book by Jean Baudrillard published in English as *America* (Baudrillard 1988) but 'left' criticism of Baudrillard's politics (and even sexual politics) persisted in Europe right up until his death.

Playing on Bruno Latour's idea that 'we have never been modern' (Latour 1993) it could conceivably be argued instead that 'we have never been postmodern' and that 'non-postmodernity' is truly the condition that we inhabit today. In what might be called a commitment to a critical poetics of the modern object, Jean Baudrillard consistently strived to produce a theorisation of modernity, of the up to the minute contemporary state, the non-postmodern condition. But this is a modernity that has changed over the years he has been writing since the early 1950s and particularly in the period since the publication of his first books in the late 1960s. His conception is that 'the real' has become transformed in such a way in this era that as the virtual takes over, the real, in its simulation, has hoovered up its own images. The process means for Baudrillard that the real can no longer be thought separately from the image and that the reality of the modern world of the 1950s is radically different from the reality of the modern world of the early twenty-first century and beyond.

Notes

1. See an open discussion forum in June 2002 with Jean Baudrillard after a reading at the European Graduate School: http://www.egs.edu/faculty/baudrillard/baudrillard-between-difference-and-singularity-2002.html.
2. *Fashionable Nonsense* is the US title of the risible book by Sokal and Bricmont (2003) in which Jean Baudrillard features prominently alongside other 'French theorists', including Paul Virilio, as, apparently, one of the intellectual imposters who 'abuse science'.
3. See 'Baudrillard and the New Technologies: an interview with Claude Thibaut', 6 March 1996, at: http://wwww.egs.edu/faculty/baudrillard/baudrillard-baudrillard-on-the-new-technologies.html.

References

Baudrillard, Jean and Lotringer, Sylvère (2005) *The Conspiracy of Art: Manifestos, Interviews, Essays*. Los Angeles and New York: Semiotext(e).

Baudrillard, Jean (2005) *Pataphysics*. London: Institute of Pataphysics and Atlas Press.

Baudrillard, Jean (1988) *America*. London: Verso.

Baudrillard, Jean (1981) *For a Critique of the Political Economy of the Sign*. St Louis, MO: Telos.

Baudrillard, Jean (1975) *The Mirror of Production*. St Louis, MO: Telos.

Cohen, Nick (2007) *What's Left? How Liberals Lost Their Way*. London: Fourth Estate.

Featherstone, Mike (1991) *Consumer Culture and Postmodernism*. London: Sage.

Goldblatt, Mark (2001) 'French Toast', *National Review Online*, 13 December, at: http://www.nationalreview.com/comment/comment-goldblatt121301.shtml.

Gundersen, Roy and Dobson, Stephen (1996) *Baudrillard's Journey to America*. London: Minerva.

Harvey, David (2001) *A Singular Modernity*. London: Verso.

Heylin, Clinton (2007) *Babylon's Burning: From Punk to Grunge*. London: Viking.

Higgins, Charlotte (2006) 'Baudrillard to Appear at London Art Fair', *The Guardian*, 3 August.

Jameson, Fredric (1991) *Postmodernism, Or, The Cultural Logic of Late Capitalism*. London: Verso.

Lash, Scott (1991) *Sociology of Postmodernism*. London: Routledge.

Latour, Bruno (1993) *We Have Never Been Modern*. Cambridge, MA: Harvard University Press.

Levy, Bernard-Henri (2006) *American Vertigo*. London: Grange Baker.

Lotringer, Sylvère and Virilio, Paul (2005) *The Accident of Art*. Los Angeles and New York: Semiotext(e).

MacFarquhar, Larissa (2005) 'Baudrillard on Tour', *The New Yorker*, 28 November.

Redhead, Steve (2004a) *Paul Virilio: Theorist for an Accelerated Culture*. Edinburgh: Edinburgh University Press/Toronto: University of Toronto Press.

Redhead, Steve (2004b) *The Paul Virilio Reader*. Edinburgh: Edinburgh University Press/New York: Columbia University Press, European Perspectives Series.

Sokal, Alan and Bricmont, Jean (2003) *Intellectual Impostures: Philosophers' Abuse of Science*, 2nd edn. London: Profile.

CHAPTER TWO

Mass Media Culture

In the late 1960s Jean Baudrillard was in many ways in the right place at the right time. Baudrillard's initial book was his doctoral thesis published in French as *Le Système des Objets* in 1968, the year of the May events. In the early 1960s he had published some literary reviews for *Les Temps Modernes*, the journal founded by Jean-Paul Sartre. There were also many translations which Baudrillard conducted in this period, from German into French, mainly of key figures like Karl Marx and Bertolt Brecht. He then studied for a PhD in sociology. Working under the tutelage of Henri Lefebvre, with whom he collaborated on the journal *Utopie*, Baudrillard subsequently took up a teaching post in sociology at the small University of Nanterre in 1966 where Lefebvre was based and had just publicly broken with the situationists. The second book by Jean Baudrillard was *La Société de la Consommation*, a work strictly written to the order of the publisher, effectively made up of essays and published in France by Gallimard in 1970. Sage published the whole book in English translation twenty-eight years later as *The Consumer Society*. 'Mass Media Culture', a section from *La Société de la Consommation*, was included in a collection of Baudrillard's writings in 1990 by Pluto Press entitled *Revenge of the Crystal: Selected Writings on the Modern Object and Its Destiny 1968–1983* edited and translated by Paul Foss and Julian Pefanis. The extract here is a section from the 1990 translation of 'Mass Media Culture'. It concentrates on Pop as an art form and displays Baudrillard's persistent connection to the Pop artist Andy Warhol. Warhol's 1960s idea that everyone has their fifteen minutes of fame enticed Baudrillard and he continued to quote it in interviews right up until his death. The piece also reveals Baudrillard's earlier influences such as the Canadian media theorist Marshall McLuhan and demonstrates his interest in the theme of the intertwining of the contemporary media and advertising industries.

'Mass Media Culture', from *Revenge of the Crystal*, trans. Paul Foss and Julian Pefanis, London: Pluto Press, 1990.

Pop: An Art of Consumption?

As we have seen, the logic of consumption can be defined as the manipulation of signs. The symbolic values of creation, and the symbolic relations of interiority are absent here: it is pure exteriority. The object loses its objective finality and its function to become a term in a much wider combinatory or series of objects, in which its value is purely relational. In another sense, it loses its symbolic meaning, its millennial anthropomorphic status, and tends to disappear in a discourse of connotations, which are also relative to one another in the framework of a totalitarian cultural system, which is to say one capable of integrating all significations whatever their origin.

We have based our analysis on *everyday* objects. But there is another discourse on the object: the discourse of art. A history of the changing status of objects and their representation in art and literature would be revealing on its own. Having played a minor symbolic and decorative role in all traditional art, objects in the 20th-century ceased to be tied to moral or psychological values, ceased to live in the shadow of man as his proxy, and began to take on extraordinary importance as autonomous elements in an analysis of space (Cubism, etc.). By the same token, they became fragmented to the point of abstraction. Having celebrated their parodic resurrection in Dada and Surrealism, and their decomposition and volatilisation through Abstraction, we now find them in Neo-Figuration and Pop apparently reconciled with their image. This raises the question of their contemporary status; in any event, it is forced upon us by this sudden elevation of objects to the pinnacle of artistic figuration.

In a word: Is Pop an art form contemporaneous with this logic of signs and of consumption under discussion? Or rather, is it not simply an effect of fashion, and thus a pure object of consumption itself? The two are not mutually exclusive. It could be argued that, whereas Pop Art turns this object-world upside down, it still ends up (according to its own logic) in objects pure and simple. Advertising shares the same ambiguity.

Let us pose the problem another way: the logic of consumption eliminates the traditionally sublime status of artistic representation. Strictly speaking, the object is no longer privileged over the image in terms of essence or signification. One is no longer the truth of the other: they coexist in the same physical and logical space, where they 'operate' equally as signs[1] (in their differential, reversible, and combinatorial relations). Whereas all art before Pop was based on a vision of the world 'as depth',[2] Pop claims to be at one with that *immanent order of signs*, with their industrial and serial production, and thus with the artificial or manufactured character of the whole environment, with the physical saturation as well as culturalised abstraction of this new order of things.

Does it succeed in 'rendering' this systematic securalisation of objects, in 'rendering' this new environment of signs in its total exteriority – in such a way that nothing remains of that 'inner light' which once constituted the mystique of all earlier painting? Is it an *art of the non-sacred*, which is to say an art of pure manipulation? Or is it itself a non-sacred art, which is to say productive of objects and thus non-creative?

Certain people will say (including Pop artists themselves) that things are much simpler, that they make their art because they feel like it, that they're basically having a good time, that they simply look around, paint what they see, and that it's a spontaneous form of realism, etc. But this is mistaken: Pop signifies the end of perspective, the end of evocation, the end of testimony, the end of the expressive gesture, and, last but not least, the end of the subversion and malediction of the world through art. It not only aims at the immanence of the 'civilised' world, but at its total integration into this world. It reveals an insane ambition: to abolish the annals (and foundations) of an entire culture of transcendence. Perhaps it is also simply an ideology. Let us dispense with two objections: 'It is American art', in its subject matter (including the obsession with 'stars and stripes'), in its optimistic and pragmatic empirical practice, in the incontestably chauvinistic infatuation of certain patrons and collectors who 'identify' with it, etc. Even though this objection is tendentious, let us reply objectively: if all this is *Americanism*, then Pop artists, according to their own logic, cannot but adopt it. If manufactured objects 'speak American', it is because they have no other truth than the mythology that inundates them – so it is only logical to integrate this mythological discourse, and to be integrated into it oneself. If consumer society is engulfed by its own mythology, if it has no critical perspective on itself, and if *this is its exact definition,*[3] then there can be no contemporary art that is not, in its very existence and practice, a compromise with and an accomplice of this manifest opacity. Indeed, this is why Pop artists paint objects according to their real appearance, since *it is how they function mythologically – as readymade signs, 'fresh from the assembly line'*. It is why they prefer to paint the logos, trademarks, or slogans transported by these objects, and why they can only finally paint these things (like Robert Indiana). This is not due to chance, nor to 'realism', but to the recognition of an obvious fact about consumer society – namely, that the truth of objects and products is their *trademark*. If this is 'Americanism', then such is the very logic of contemporary culture, and Pop artists can hardly be reproached for bringing it to light.

No more than they can be reproached for their commercial success, and for accepting it without shame. The worst thing would be to damn them, and thus to reinvest them with a sacred function. It is logical for an art that does not contradict the world of objects, but explores its system, to become itself part of the system. It is even the end of hypocrisy and total illogicality. Unlike the early painting of the 20th-century, whose inventive and transcendent spirit did not prevent it becoming a *signed* object and being commercialised in terms of its signature (Abstract Expressionists carried this triumphant inventiveness and shameful opportunism to new heights), Pop artists reconcile the object of painting with the painting as object. Is this coherent or paradoxical? Pop, as much in its commercial success as in its predilection for objects, in its infinite figuration of 'trademarks' and consumables, is the first movement to explore the very status of art as a 'signed' and 'consumed' object.

Yet this logical enterprise – whose extreme consequences, were they to contravene our traditional *moral* aesthetic, could not but meet with our approval – is coupled with an ideology into which it is in danger of sinking: the ideology of Nature, Revelation ('Wake Up!') and authenticity, which evokes the better moments of bourgeois spontaneity.

This 'radical empiricism', 'uncompromising positivism' and 'anti-teleologism' (Mario Amaya, *Pop as Art*) sometimes begins to look suspiciously like a form of *initiation*. Oldenburg: 'I drove around the city one day with Jimmy Dine. By chance we drove along Orchard Street, which is crowded with small stores on both sides. As we drove I remember having a vision of *The Store*. In my mind's eye I saw a complete environment based on this theme. It seemed to me that I had discovered a new world. Everywhere I went I began wandering through the different stores *as if they were museums*. I saw the objects displayed in windows as precious works of art.' Rosenquist: 'Then suddenly the ideas seemed to flow toward me through the window. All I had to do was seize them in mid-air and start painting. Everything spontaneously fell into place, the idea, the composition, the images, the colours – every thing began to happen of its own accord.' On the theme of 'Inspiration', we can see that Pop artists are in no way inferior to early generations. What this theme implies, since Werther, is an idealised *Nature* to which one only needs to be faithful in order to be true. All you have to do is awaken or reveal it. In the words of musician and theorist John Cage, who inspired Rauschenberg and Jasper Johns: '. . . art should be an affirmation of life – not an attempt to bring order . . . but simply a way of *waking up* to the very life we are living, which is so excellent, once one gets one's mind and one's desires out of the way and lets it act of its own accord.' This affirmation of a revealed order – of an underlying *nature* shining through the universe of images and manufactured objects – leads to mystico-realist professions of faith: 'A flag was just a flag, a number was simply a number' (Jasper

Johns). Or again John Cage: 'We must set about discovering a means to let sounds be themselves'. All this presupposes an essence of the object, a level of absolute reality which never belongs to the everyday environment, but which plainly constitutes a surreality with respect to it. Wesselman thus speaks of the 'superrealism' of a common kitchen.

In brief, we are confronted with a bewildering sort of behaviourism produced by the juxtaposition of things as they appear (something resembling an impressionism of consumer society) coupled with a vaguely Zen or Buddhist mysticism stripping the Ego and Superego down to the 'Id' of the surrounding world, with a dash of Americanism thrown in for good measure!

But there is above all a grave equivocation and inconsistency. For, by manifesting the surrounding environment not as it is, which is to say first and foremost as an artificial field of manipulable signs, a total cultural artifact where neither sensation nor vision comes into play, but differential perception and the tactical game of significations; by manifesting it as a revealed nature and essence, Pop takes on a double connotation: on the one hand, the ideology of an integrated society (contemporary society = nature = an ideal society; but we have seen how this collusion forms part of its logic), and, on the other, the restoration of the whole *sacred process of art*, a process destroying its basic objective.

Pop claims to be an art of the commonplace (it is for this very reason that it is called Popular Art). But what is the commonplace if not a metaphysical category, a modern version of the category of the sublime? The object is only commonplace in its use, at the moment of its use (as with the 'working' radio in Wesselman's installations). But the object ceases to be commonplace once it begins to signify: as we have seen, the 'truth' of the contemporary object is to serve no purpose other than to signify, to be manipulated not as an instrument but as a sign. And the success of Pop in its better examples is that it demonstrates this to us.

Andy Warhol, whose approach is the most radical, is also the one who best epitomises the theoretical contradictions in this artistic practice, and the difficulties it encounters when it tries to envisage its real object. He says: 'The canvas is an absolutely everyday object, like this chair or that poster.' (Always this will to absorb and reabsorb art, where we find both American pragmatism – terrorism of the useful, blackmail of integration – and something like an echo of the mysticism of sacrifice.) He adds: 'Reality needs no intermediary, all you have to do is isolate it from the environment and put it on canvas'. But this is the whole problem: since the everydayness of this chair (or hamburger, tailfin, celebrity pin-up) is precisely its context, and specifically the serial context of all similar or slightly dissimilar chairs, etc. Everydayness is *difference in repetition*. By isolating a chair on canvas, I remove it from all everydayness, and at the same time I remove from the canvas all its character as an everyday object (which should, according to Warhol, make it absolutely resemble a chair). This is a familiar impasse: art can no more be absorbed by the everyday (the canvas = the chair) than it can capture the everyday as such (the chair isolated on canvas = the real chair). Immanence and transcendence are equally impossible: they are two sides of the same dream.

In brief, there is no essence of the everyday or the commonplace, and thus no art of the everyday: this is a mystical aporia. If Warhol (and the others) believe that, it is because they delude themselves about the very status of art and the artistic act, and this is not at all uncommon among artists. Furthermore, this mystical nostalgia can even be found in the productive act or gesture: 'I'd like to be a machine,' says Andy Warhol, who indeed paints with stencils and silkscreens, etc. There is no worse arrogance for art than the pretence of being machinic, and there is no worse conceit for someone who enjoys the status of creator, whether he wants it or not, than being dedicated to serial automatism. However, it is not possible to accuse Warhol and the other Pop artists of bad faith, since their rigorous logic runs up against the sociological and cultural status of art, about which they can do nothing. Their ideology reflects this powerlessness. When they try to desacralise their practice, society sacralises them all the more. And from this one can conclude that even their most radical attempt to securalise the themes and practice of their art ends up as an precedented exaltation and manifestation of the sacred in art. Quite simply, Pop artists fail to see that if a picture is to avoid being a sacred super-sign (a unique object, a signature, a noble and magical object of commerce), then content or the intentions of the author are not enough; it is the structures of cultural production that decide this. Ultimately, only the rationalisation of the market for paintings, as with any other manufacturing enterprise, could desacralise them and turn them into everyday objects.[4] Perhaps this is neither thinkable, nor possible, nor even desirable – who knows? In any case, it is the point of no return: either you stop painting, or else you continue at the cost of regressing to the traditional mythology of artistic creation. And this downhill slide leads to the recuperation of classical pictorial values: Oldenburg's 'Expressionist' treatment, Wesselmann's Fauvism à la Matisse, Lichtenstein's art nouveau and Japanese calligraphy, etc. What are we to make of these 'legendary' resonances? What are we to make of these techniques that seem to say: 'It's all painting just the same'? The logic of Pop is not to be found in an aesthetic of multiplication or in a metaphysic of the object – its logic is elsewhere.

Pop could be defined as a *game* of manipulating different levels of mental perception – a kind of mental Cubism which would seek to diffract objects not in terms of spatial analysis, but according to the modalities of perception elaborated across the centuries by an entire culture through its intellectual and technical apparatuses: objective reality, image as reflection, drawn figuration, technical figuration (the photo), abstract schematisation, discursive utterance, etc. On the other hand, the use of the phonetic alphabet and industrial techniques have imposed schemas of division, doubling, abstraction, and repetition (ethnographers have described the bewilderment experienced by 'primitives' upon being shown *absolutely* identical books: their whole view of the world is turned upside down). We can see in these various modes the countless figures of a *rhetoric of designation* and recognition. This is where Pop comes into its own: it works on the differences between these diverse levels or modes, and on the perception of these differences. Thus the silkscreen of a lynching is not an evocation, because it presupposes the transmutation of this lynching into a news item, into a journalistic sign by virtue of mass communications, a sign taken one step further by silkscreening. The repetition of the same photo presupposes the unique photo, and beyond that the real being of whom it is a reflection; furthermore, this real being could figure in the work without disrupting it – it would be only one more combination.

Just as there is no order of reality in Pop, but levels of signification, so is there no real space: the only space is that of the canvas, that of the juxtaposition of different sign elements and their relations. Nor is there any real time: the only time is that of reading, that of the differential perception of the object and its image, of a particular image and the same repeated, etc. It is the time necessary for a *mental correction*, for an *accommodation* to the image or artifact in its relation to the real object (it doesn't involve reminiscence, but the perception of an *immediate* and *logical* difference). Nor can this reading ever be a search for articulation or coherence, but always an extended scan, a verification of succession.

We can see that the activity Pop prescribes (once again in its ambition to be rigorous) has little to do with our 'aesthetic sensibility'. Pop is a 'cool' art: it demands neither aesthetic ecstasy nor affective or symbolic participation ('deep involvement'), but a kind of 'abstract involvement', an *instrumental curiosity* – one preserving something of childhood curiosity or the naive enchantment of discovery (and why not?, Pop can also be seen as popular illustration, or as a Book of Hours for consumers), but above all one triggering those intellectual reflexes of decoding, deciphering, etc., which we described before.

In a word, Pop is not popular art. For the ethos of popular culture (if it exists at all) is based precisely on unambiguous realism, on linear narration (and not repetition or the diffraction of levels), on allegory and the decorative (that is not Pop Art, since these two categories refer to something essentially 'other'), and on emotional participation associated with moral vicissitudes.[5] It is only on a quite rudimentary level that Pop can be mistaken for 'figurative' art, colourful imagery, a naive chronicle of consumer society, etc. It is true that Pop artists take pleasure in this pretence. Their candour is immense, as is their ambiguity. As for their humour, or the humour they are credited with, once again we are on tricky ground. In this regard, it would be instructive to observe public reactions. For many, the works provoke a laugh (at least the inclination to laugh) which is both moral and obscene (these canvases are obscene from the classical point of view). Then, a smile of derision, such that one cannot tell if they are judging the objects painted or the painting itself – a smile that turns willing accomplice, all more or less contorted in the shameful desolation of not knowing what angle to take on it: 'That can't really be serious, but we're not going to be scandalised by it, because perhaps deep down . . .' Even so, Pop is both full of humour and humourless. By all logic it has nothing to do with subversive or aggressive humour, with a surrealistic telescoping of objects. What is precisely involved is no longer the shortcircuiting of objects in their function, but the juxtaposition of them in order to analyse their relations. This approach is not terroristic,[6] but at best entails effects more like cultural estrangement. In fact, something entirely different is involved. Let us not forget, to return to the system being described, that a 'certain smile' belongs to the *obligatory signs* of consumption – a smile no longer comprised of humour, of critical distance, except as a reminder of that transcendence of critical value manifested today in a knowing wink. This false distance is present everywhere, in spy films, in Godard, in modern advertising which continually uses it as a cultural allusion, etc. At the very limit, one can no longer distinguish in this 'cool' smile between the smile of humour and that of commercial complicity. This is also what happens in Pop, whose smile sums up its whole ambiguity: it is not the smile of critical distance, but the smile of *collusion*.

The Orchestration of Messages

TV, radio, the press and advertising comprise a heterogeneous mass of signs and messages where all orders are equivalent. Here is a selection taken at random from radio:

- an ad for Remington razors,
- a summary of social unrest over the past fortnight,
- an ad for Dunlop SP-Sport tyres,
- a debate on the death penalty,
- an ad for Lip watches,
- a report on the war in Biafra,
- and an ad for new blue Crio laundry detergent.

In this litany alternating between the story of the world and portraits of objects (altogether forming a kind of poem in the style of Prévert, with alternate gloomy and rose-coloured passages – the latter of course being advertising), the accent apparently falls on information. But it also falls, paradoxically, on neutrality and impartiality: the discourse on the world tries to be detached. Its 'bland' tone directly clashes with the valedictory discourse on objects, with its shrill note of rapturous cheer – the whole pathos of real vicissitudes, of real persuasion, is transferred to the object and its discourse. In this careful blend of discourse on 'world affairs' and discourse on 'consumption' to the exclusive emotional advantage of the latter, advertising tends to function as backdrop, as a reassuring litany of interwoven signs, into which the vicissitudes of the world are inscribed as a diversion. These latter, neutralised by cutting, immediately fall victim to consumption themselves. The newscast is not the hodgepodge it seems: its systematic alternation dictates a single form of reception, that of consumption.

It is not just because the valedictory tone of advertising suggests that the story of the world is fundamentally unimportant, and that the only things worthy of consideration are consumer goods. This is secondary. Its real efficacy is more subtle: it prescribes through the systematic succession of messages an *equivalence* between story and news item, between event and spectacle, between news and advertising *at the level of the sign*. This is where the true effect of consumption lies, and not in the express discourse of advertising. It consists, thanks to the technical supports, the technical media of TV and radio, of cutting up events of the world into discontinuous, successive, and non-contradictory messages, into signs which can be juxtaposed and combined with other signs in the abstract realm of broadcasting. What we consume, then, is not a particular spectacle or image as such; it is the potential succession of all possible spectacles – and the certainty that this law of succession and division of programs will ensure that nothing will emerge from them which is not a spectacle or sign of one kind or another.

'The Medium is the Message'

Here we need to accept, in this sense at least, McLuhan's formula 'the medium is the message' as fundamental to the analysis of consumption. It indicates that the true message delivered by the media of radio and TV, one decoded and 'consumed' at a deep unconscious level, is not the manifest content of sounds and images, but a coercive system, linked to the very technical nature of these media, for disarticulating the real into successive and equivalent signs – the *normalised*, programmed, and miraculous transition from Vietnam to the variety show through their total mutual abstraction.

And there is something like a law of technological inertia which says that the closer you get to 'live' documentary reportage, and the more finely attuned to reality is the colour and resolution, the wider becomes the gulf between perfection in technical perfection and the real world; and the 'truer' becomes the assertion that, for TV and radio, the primary function of each message is to refer to another message, as Vietnam does to advertising, and advertising does to the newscast, etc. – their systematic juxtaposition being the discursive mode of the medium, its message, its meaning. But in thus uttering itself as the message, we can easily see how it imposes a whole divisible system of interpretation on the world.

This technological process of mass communication delivers a highly imperative sort of message: *the message of message consumption*, of fragmentation and spectacularisation, of misrecognition of the world and the valorisation of information as commodity, the exaltation of content as sign. In brief, its function is one of packaging (in the publicity sense of the word – in the sense that advertising is the 'mass' medium par excellence, one whose devices permeate all the others) and of misrecognition.

This is true of all the media, and even of the medium of books or 'literacy', which McLuhan made into a major demonstration of his theory. He maintains that the appearance of the printed book was a fundamental turning point for our civilisation – not so much through the content (ideological, informational, scientific, etc.) passed from one generation to the next, but through *the profound constraint of systematisation exerted by its technical nature*. He maintains that the book is first a *technical* model, and that the order of communication which governs it (the visible fragmentation into letters, words, pages, etc.) is ultimately a more fruitful and far-reaching model than any symbol, idea, or phantasm constituting its manifest discourse: 'The effects of technology do not occur at the level of opinions and concepts, but alter sense ratios or patterns of perception steadily and without any resistance.'

It is obvious that the content mostly conceals from us the real function of the medium. It presents itself as message, whereas its real message (compared to which the manifest discourse is perhaps only a connotation) is the profound structural change brought about in human relations in terms of scale, models, and habits. Put crudely, the 'message' of a railway is not the coal or passengers it transports, but a new vision of the world, a new state of conurbation, etc. The 'message' of TV is not the images it transmits, but the new modes of perception and relations imposed by it, the alteration of traditional family or group structures. Further still, in the case of TV and modern mass media, what is received, assimilated and 'consumed' is less a particular spectacle than potentially all spectacles.

So the truth of mass media is that they function to neutralise the unique character of actual world events by replacing them with a multiple universe of mutually reinforcing and self-referential media. At the very limit, they become each other's reciprocal content – and this constitutes *the totalitarian 'message' of the consumer society*.

What the medium of TV circulates through its technical organisation is the idea (or ideology) of a world visualisable and divisible at will, one that is readable as images. It circulates the ideology of *the total dominance of a system of reading over a world now become a system of signs*. The images on TV aspire to the metalanguage of an absent world. Just as the most minor technical object or gadget promises the universal assumption of technology, so are these image-signs the presumption of an imagination exhausting the world, and a total assumption of the mode of reality to images which would be something like its memory cell, that of universal reading. Behind the 'consumption of images' is outlined an imperialistic system of reading: what will increasingly tend to exist is only that which can be read (or *must* be read: the 'legendary'). And then the truth of the world and its history will no longer be in question, but simply the internal coherence of a system of reading. It is on this chaotic, conflictual, and contradictory world that each medium thus imposes its most abstract and coherent logic; or imposes itself, according to McLuhan's formula, as the message. And it is the substance of a world fragmented, filtered, and reinterpreted according to this technical but 'legendary' code that we 'consume'. All actual cultural or political value has vanished from the whole materiality of the world, from a whole culture industrially converted into finished products and the material of signs.

If we consider the sign as an articulation of signifier and signified, then it is possible to specify two types of confusion. For the child, or for the 'primitive', the signifier can disappear in favour of the signified (like the child who mistakes his own image for a living being, or those African television viewers who wonder what becomes of the man that disappears from the screen). Conversely, in the image centered on itself, or in the message centered on the code, the signifier becomes its own signified; there is a confused circularity of the two in favour of the signifier, an abolition of the signified and *a tautology of the signifier*. This is what defines consumption, or the systematic *effect of consumption*, at the level of mass media. Instead of arriving at the world via the mediation of the image, it is the image which turns round on itself via the detour of the world (it is the signifier which designates itself behind the alibi of the signified).

One passes from the message centered on the signified (the transitive message) to the message centered on the signifier – in the case of TV, for example, from the events signified by the image to the consumption of the image as such (which is to say as something precisely different from those events, or as Brecht would say, as a spectacular and 'culinary' substance, devouring itself in the very course of its absorption, and never referring beyond it). Also different in the sense that the image presents them neither to be perceived nor comprehended in their historical, social, or cultural specificity, but delivers all of them to indiscriminant reinterpretion according to the same code, whose structure is at once *technical* and *ideological* – in other words, in the case of TV, the ideological code of mass culture (the system of moral, social, or political values), and the mode of division and articulation of the medium itself, prescribe a certain type of discursivity which neutralises the multiple and fluctuating content of messages, for which it substitutes its own rigid constraints of meaning. This profound discursivity of the medium is, as opposed to the manifest discourse of images, decoded *unconsciously* by the spectator.

The Medium of Advertising

In this sense, advertising is perhaps the most remarkable mass medium of our epoch. Just as it potentially glorifies all objects when speaking of a particular one, and just as it actually refers, when speaking of a particular object or trademark, to a totality of objects and a universe entirely made up of objects and trademarks, so does it address all consumers through each of them, and each consumer through all of them, thus simulating a *totality of consumers*, and retribalising them in a McLuhanesque sense; in other words, through an immanent complicity or collusion at the direct level of the message, but above all at the level of the very code of the medium itself. Each advertising image prescribes a consensus among all those individuals potentially summoned to decipher it; which is to say, in decoding the message, to automatically conform to the code in which this image has been encoded.

Thus the function of advertising as mass communication is not related to its content, its modes of diffusion, its overtly economic or psychological objectives, or the actual size of its audience (even though all of this has its importance and serves as its support), but to its very logic as an autonomised medium: which is to say, a medium no longer referring to real objects, to a real reference in the world, but referring *one sign to another, one object to another, one consumer to another*. In a similar fashion, the book becomes a means of mass communication when it refers one of its readers to all the other readers (thus the substance of reading is no longer meaning, but quite simply the sign of cultural complicity), and when the book-object refers to others in the same collection, etc. One could analyse the way in which the symbolic system of language itself becomes a mass medium at the level of the trademark and the discourse of advertising.[7] Everywhere mass communication is defined by this systematisation at the level of the technical medium and its code, by this systematic production of messages – not about the world, but about the medium itself.[8]

The Pseudo-event and Neo-reality

Here we enter the world of the pseudo-event, of pseudo-history and of pseudo-culture described by Daniel Boorstin in *The Image*; in other words, a world of events, history, culture and ideas produced not from the fluctuating and contradictory nature of reality, but *produced as artifacts from the technical manipulation of the medium and its coded elements*. It is this, and nothing else, which defines all signification whatsoever as *consumable*. It is this generalised *substitution of the code for the reference* that defines mass media consumption.

The raw event is exchange, and not the material of exchange. It is not 'consumable' unless filtered, fragmented, and re-elaborated by a whole series of industrial procedures – by the mass media – into a finished product, into the material of finished and combined signs, analogous to the finished objects of industrial production. Makeup on the face undergoes the same operation: the systematic substitution of its real but imperfect features by a network of abstract and coherent messages made up of technical elements and a code of prescribed significations (the code of 'beauty').

We should be careful not to interpret this immense enterprise for producing artifacts, makeup, pseudo-objects and pseudo-events that invades our everyday existence as the denaturation or falsification of authentic 'content'. Given everything mentioned thus far, we can readily see that the misappropriation of meaning, depoliticisation of politics, deculturation of culture, and desexualisation of the body in mass media consumption is situated quite beyond the 'tendentious' reinterpretation of *content*. It is in *form* that everything has changed: everywhere there is, in lieu and in place of the real, its substitution by a 'neo-real' entirely produced from a combination of coded elements. An immense *process of simulation* has taken place throughout all of everday life, in the image of those 'simulation models' on which operational and computer sciences are based. One 'fabricates' a model by combining characteristics or elements of the real; and, by making them 'act out' a future event, structure or situation, tactical conclusions can be drawn and applied to reality. It can be used as an analytical tool under controlled scientific conditions. In mass communications, this procedure assumes *the force of reality*, abolishing and volatilising the latter in favour of that *neo-reality of a model* materialised by the medium itself.

But once again, let us be wary of language which automatically refers to the 'false', the 'pseudo' and the 'artifical'. And let us return with Boorstin to advertising in our attempt to grasp this new logic, which is also a new practice and a new 'mentality'.

Notes

1. Cf. Daniel Boorstin, *L'Image* [*The Image: A Guide to Pseudo-Events in America* (1961), New York, Atheneum, 1971].
2. Cubists still searched for the 'essence' of space, attempting to unveil its 'secret geometry', etc. With Dada, Duchamp and the Surrealists, objects were stripped of their (bourgeois) function and paraded in their subversive banality, as a reminder of lost essence and that order of authenticity evoked through the absurd. For Ponge, there was still an active poetic consciousness or perception in his attachment to naked and concrete objects. In brief, whether critical or poetic, all art, 'without which things would be no more than what they are', feeds (before Pop) on transcendence.
3. Cf. below, 'The Consumption of Consumption' [*La Société de consommation*, pp. 311–16].
4. In this sense, the truth of Pop would be the wage and the billboard, not the commission and the art gallery.

5. 'Popular' art is not attached to objects, but first and always to man and his exploits. It wouldn't depict a delicatessen or an American flag, but a-man-eating or a-man-saluting-the-American-flag.

6. In fact, we often read this 'terrorist' humour into it. But through critical nostalgia on our part.

7. It is easy to see how language [*langage*] can be 'consumed' in this sense. Language becomes an object of consumption or a fetish from the moment that, instead of being a vehicle for meaning, it takes on the connotations, vocabulary, and inflections of membership in a group, class, or caste (the intellectual jargon of the 'smart' set, or the political jargon of parties and cliques); from the moment that language, instead of being *the means of exchange*, becomes the *material of exchange* for the private use of a group or class (its real function being, behind the alibi of a message, one of collusion and recognition); and from the moment that, instead of bringing meaning into circulation, it circulates itself as a password or token of passage in a tautological group process (the group is what it speaks).

   It is no longer language [*langue*] employed as a system of distinct denotative signs, but consumed as a system of connotation, as a distinctive code.

8. The same process applies to the 'consumption of medicine'. We are witnessing an extraordinary inflation of the demand for health, directly linked to raised standards of living. There is no longer any distinction between the demand for 'basic' health care (but on what definition of minimum health and bio-psychosomatic equilibrium could it be based?) and the compulsion of consumers for medical, surgical and dental services. The practice of medicine has changed into *the use of doctors themselves*; and this extravagent and ostentatious use of the doctor-object, of medication as an object, links up with the dual residence and the automobile for displaying one's social standing. Here again, medication, and above all doctors for the well-heeled classes (Balint: 'The medication most frequently dispensed in general medicine is the doctor himself'), have become an end in themselves, after having been a means to health considered as the ultimate good. They are thus

consumed, according to the same systematic misappropriation of practical and objective functions for the purpose of mental manipulation, of a kind of fetishistic calculus of signs.

In all truth, we need to distinguish two levels of this 'consumption': the 'neurotic' need to receive medication and medical care for reducing anxiety. This demand is no less objective than the one relating to organic complaints, but it still involves an aspect of 'consumption' to the extent that the doctor no longer has a specific value: as someone who reduces anxiety, or as an agent of care, he is substitutable for any other mechanism of partial regression – alcohol, 'shopping', and col- lecting (the consumer 'collects' doctors and medicines). Here the doctor is consumed as one sign among others (in the same way that the washing machine is consumed as a sign of wealth and status – see above).

Thus, in a very real sense, what the 'consumption of medi- cine' institutes is, through this neurotic logic of individuals, a logic of social status that integrates the doctor – beyond all objective usefulness and on a par with any other *measure* of worth – into the general system as a sign. We can see that medical consumption is based on the abstraction (or reduc- tion) of the medical function. Everywhere we discover this form of systematic misappropriation as the very principle of consumption.

CHAPTER THREE

The Linguistic Imaginary

In 1976 Editions Gallimard published what has subsequently, in retrospect, been praised as one of Baudrillard's most significant works. Mike Gane, who wrote an introduction to the English edition, saw it as 'without doubt Jean Baudrillard's most important book'. *L'Echange Symbolique et Mort* was not published in full in English translation until 1993 by which time Baudrillard had been labelled, misleadingly, as a 'postmodernist' for at least a decade. The book, read as a whole, categorically gives the lie to such allegations. The extract here is from Sage's 1993 publication translated by Ian Hamilton Grant as *Symbolic Exchange and Death*. By the time of the French publication in the mid 1970s Baudrillard had also published two more books much influenced by debates around Marxism. *Pour Une Critique de l'Economie Politique du Signe* came out with Gallimard in 1970 and *Le Miroir de la Production* was published by Casterman in 1973. For many years in the English-speaking world it was the Marxist influenced books which tended to be discussed rather than the text which concentrated on developing the twin ideas of symbolic exchange and simulation, both so central to all of Baudrillard's work for the next thirty years. The book when first published in 1976 appeared in Gallimard's Bibliothèque des Sciences Humaines which included books by fellow French theorists like Claude Lévi-Strauss and Michel Foucault. Within a year Baudrillard had published *Oublier Foucault* ('Forget Foucault' in English) which caused a considerable personal rift with Foucault and to some extent increased Baudrillard's outsider stance in the French academy. It is Émile Durkheim and Marcel Mauss who are in the background in *Symbolic Exchange and Death* rather than Karl Marx. There is little in this mid-1970s text which linked the author to postmodernism, a movement in philosophy and the social sciences which was to receive a major boost in Jean-François Lyotard's report on the 'post-modern condition' first written in 1979.

'The Linguistic Imaginary', from *Symbolic Exchange and Death*, trans. Iain Hamilton Grant, London: Sage, 1993.

The Linguistic Imaginary

We must now leave Saussure and look at how the linguists dealt with the poetic and the questions it brought to bear on their 'science'. All things considered, the defence they put up in the face of this danger is the same as that mounted by the adherents of political economy (and its Marxist critics) in the face of the symbolic alternative in previous societies and in our own. All of them chose to differentiate and modulate their categories while not changing their principle of rationality in any way, that is, without changing the arbitrariness and the imaginary that made them hypostatise the order of discourse and the order of production as universals. As scientists, they have good reason to believe in this order, since they are agents of order.

Thus the linguists concede that the arbitrary character of the sign is a bit shaken by the poetic; but certainly not the signifier/signified distinction, nor therefore the law of equivalence and the function of representation. Indeed, in a certain way, the signifier in this instance represents the signified far better, since it 'expresses' it directly following a *necessary* correlation between each element of the substance of the signifier and what it is supposed to express, instead of referring to it arbitrarily, as in discourse. The signifier's autonomy is conceded:

> The conceptual messages transmitted through the intermediary of sound necessarily differ from the pre-conceptual contents in the sound sequences and rhythms themselves. They either happen to converge or diverge. (I. Fonagy, *Diogène*, 51)

However, this is basically so that the signifier better embodies, not merely by convention, but in its materiality and its flesh, what it has to say: 'In Swinburne's lines, we feel the breeze passing . . .'. Instead of it being, as in conceptual language, the unit of primary articulation, *the phoneme, the unit of secondary articulation, becomes representative*, while, however, the form of the representation has not itself changed. It is always a question of *referring*, no longer to the concept by means of the terms of the *langue* nor syntax, but by means of vowels and syllables, the atoms of language, and their combination in rhythm, to an elementary presence, to an original instance of things (the 'breeze' as primary process!). Between the substance of language and the substance of the world (wind, water, feelings, passions, the unconscious; everything 'pre-conceptual', which is in fact already conceptualised, without appearing to be, by a whole code of perception), there is always a positive correlation at play, a play of equivalence amongst *values*.

In this way, muted vowels would stand for the dark and obscure, etc., and there would no longer be an *arbitrary* conceptual equivalence in this case, but a *necessary* phonemic equivalence. Thus Rimbaud's vowel-sonnet, and Fonagy's entire exposition of the 'symbolism' of linguistic sounds (*Diogène*, 51, p. 78): everyone would agree to recognise that '*i*' is lighter, faster and thinner than '*u*'; that '*k*' and '*r*' are harder than '*l*', etc.

> The feeling of thinness associated with the vowel '*i*' may be the result of a subconscious kinaesthetic perception of the position of the tongue in the emission of this sound. The '*r*' appears masculine [!] by reason of the greater muscular effort required to emit it in comparison with the alveolar '*l*' or the labial '*m*'.

A real metaphysics of an original *langue*, a desperate attempt to rediscover a *natural deposit* of the poetic, an expressive genius of language, that would only have to be captured and transcribed.

In fact, all this is coded, and it is just as arbitrary to correlate the repetition of the phoneme '*f*' with the passing breeze as it is to correlate the word 'table' with the concept of table. There is nothing more in common between them than there is between a piece of music and what it 'evokes' (landscape or passion), other than cultural convention, or a *code*. That this code claims to be anthropological ('naturally' soft vowels) takes nothing away from its arbitrary character. Conversely moreover, we can clearly maintain, with Benveniste, that the very strong cultural convention that binds the word 'table' to the concept of 'table' imposes genuine *necessity*, and that at bottom the sign is never arbitrary. This is correct: the fundamental arbitrariness lies not in the internal organisation of the sign, but in the imposition of the sign as *value*, that is to say, in the presupposition of two instances and their equivalence in accordance with the law: the sign acting as a stand-in, as emanating from a reality that makes signs to you. Such is linguistics' metaphysics, and such is its imaginary. Its interpretation of the poetic is still haunted by this presupposition.

By contrast, when Harpo Marx waves a real sturgeon instead of pronouncing the password 'sturgeon', then indeed, by substituting the referent of the term and by abolishing their separation, he really explodes the arbitrariness at the same time as the system of representation, in a poetic act *par excellence*: putting the signifier 'sturgeon' to death by its own referent.

Whether conceptual or pre-conceptual, it is always the 'message' and the 'aim of the message as such', by which Jakobson defines the poetic function, which by autonomising the operation of the signifying material merely refers it to a *supplementary* effect of signification. Something other than the concept comes through, but it is still some *thing*; another is realised through the very play of the signifier, but it remains a *value*; the signifying material functions at another level, its own, but it continues to *function*: moreover, Jakobson makes the poetic function supplementary rather than alternative, just one linguistic function out of many – a surplus-value of signification due to which the signifier itself is taken into account as an autonomous value. The poetic gives you more!

The 'self-presence' [*présence à lui-même*] of the signifier is analysed in terms of redundancy, as an internal echo, as resonance, phonetic recurrence, etc. (Hopkins: 'The verse is a discourse that repeats, either wholly or partially, the same phonemic figure'). Or again:

It is acknowledged that poets worthy of the name possess a delicate and penetrating sensibility as regards the impressive *value* of the words and sounds with which they compose; to communicate this value to their readers, they are often moved to *represent*, around the principal word, the phonemes that characterise it, in such a way that, in short, this word becomes the generator of the entire line in which it appears. (M. Grammont, *Traité de phonétique* [Paris: Delagrave], 1933)

In all this, the 'labour' of the signifier always appears as a positive assemblage, concurrent with that of the signified, which sometimes coincide, and sometimes diverge, to cite Fonagy again, but in any case the outcome is merely *'a subjacent current of signification'* – no question of escaping the being of discourse. And it could not be otherwise from a perspective that conceives the poetic as the autonomisation of one of the functional categories of the order of discourse.

The other Jakobsonian formula maintains this illusion: the poetic function projects the principle of equivalence from the axis of selection to the axis of combination. Equivalence is promoted to the rank of the constitutive process of the sequence.

In poetry, one syllable is equalized with any other syllable of the same sequence; word stress is assumed to equal word stress, as unstress equals unstress, long is matched with long, short is matched with short . . . [Jakobson, 'Linguistics and Poetics' in *Language in Literature*, ed. K. Pomorska and S. Rudy, Cambridge, MA: Harvard, 1987, p. 71]

Of course, articulation is no longer that of customary syntax, it is always rather a question of a *constructive* architecture; that anything other than a scansion of equivalence could start to play a role in prosody is never envisaged. Jakobson is content to substitute the *ambiguity* of the signified for the *ambivalence* of the signifier.

Ambiguity is what characterises the poetic and distinguishes it from the discursive: 'Ambiguity is an intrinsic, inalienable character of any self-focussed message briefly, a corollary feature of poetry' (Jakobson, 'Linguistics and Poetics', p. 85). 'The machinations of ambiguity are among the very roots of poetry' (Empson, *Seven Types of Ambiguity* [London: Chatto & Windus, 1963]). Jakobson again:

> The supremacy of the poetic function over the referential function
> does not obliterate the reference but makes it ambiguous. The
> double-sensed message finds correspondence in a split addresser, a
> split addressee, as well as in a split reference. ['Linguistics and
> Poetics', p. 85]

In this way, all the categories of discursive communication 'work
loose' in the poetic (all, curiously, except the code, of which
Jakobson does not speak: what does the code become? Does it too
become ambiguous? But it would then be the end of *langue* and linguistics). Ambiguity is not dangerous in itself. It does not change the
principles of identity and equivalence in the slightest, nor does it
change the principle of meaning as value; it merely produces floating values, renders identities diffuse, and makes the rules of the referential game more complex, without abolishing anything. Thus, for
Jakobson, the ambiguous sender and addressee merely signifies the
uncoupling of the I/YOU relation, internal to the message, from the
author/reader relation: the positions of the respective subjects have
not been lost, in some sense they expand indefinitely − subjects
become unsettled *in their subject-positions*. Thus the message becomes unsettled, ambiguous, in its definition; all categories (sender,
addressee, message, referent) move, work loose in their respective
positions, but the structural grid of discourse remains the same.

'The machinations of ambiguity' do not therefore make a great
deal of difference to the form of discourse. Jakobson has this bold
formula:

> Poetry does not consist in adding rhetorical ornament to discourse:
> it involves a total revaluation of discourse and all its components,
> whatever they may be.

Bold and ambiguous, since the components (sender/addressee,
message/code, etc.) maintain their separate existences, they are
simply 'revalued'. The general economy remains the same − the
political economy of discourse. At no point does this thought
advance to the point of the *abolition* of separate functions: the
abolition of the subject of communication (and therefore the
sender/addressee distinction); the abolition of the message as such
(and therefore of all the code's structural autonomy). All this work,
in which the radical character of the poetic act consists, is

swamped by 'ambiguity' and by a certain hesitation as regards linguistic categories. A 'discourse within a discourse', a message centred on itself': all this merely defines a *rhetoric of ambiguity*. But the ambiguous discourse, squinting at itself (a strabismus of signs), remains the discourse of positivity, *the discourse of the sign as value*.

In the poetic, by contrast, language turns back on itself to be abolished. It is not 'centred' on itself, it *decentres* itself. It undoes the entire process of the constructive logic of the sign, resolving all the internal specularity that makes a sign a sign: something full, reflected, centred on itself, and, as such, effectively ambiguous. The poetic is the loss of the spectacular closure of the sign and the message.

At bottom, this is the same metaphysics that has governed the theory of artistic form since romanticism: the bourgeois metaphysics of totality. Art should properly evoke 'this quality of being a whole and of belonging to the larger, all-inclusive, whole which is the universe in which we live' (John Dewey, *Art as Experience*, pp. 194–5; quoted in Umberto Eco, *The Open Work* [tr. Anna Cancogni, London: Hutchinson Radius, 1989], p. 26). Eco appropriates this cosmology for himself, and retranscribes it in linguistic terms. The totalisation of meaning takes place by means of a 'chain reaction' and the infinite subdivision of signifieds:

> All this is attained by means of an identification between signifier and signified . . . the aesthetic sign . . . is not confined to a given denotatum, but rather expands every time the structure within which it is inevitably *embodied*, is duly appreciated – a sign whose signified, resounding relentlessly against its signifier, keeps acquiring new echoes. (ibid., p. 36)

This, then, is a schema of a first (denotative) phase of reference, followed by a second phase of 'harmonic' reference, where a 'theoretically unlimited' chain reaction is operative – hence the evocation of the cosmic.

This theory serves as the basic ideology of everything we have been able to say about the poetic (nor does psychoanalysis escape this) – ambiguity, polysemia, polyvalence, polyphony of meaning: it is always a matter of the *radiation of the signified*, of a simultaneity of significations.

> The linear character of discourse hides an harmonious concert of different messages. (Fonagy, *Diogène*, 51, p. 104)

The semantic density of language, the wealth of information, etc.: the poet 'liberates' all sorts of virtualities (with, as a corollary, a differential hermeneutics of the role played by the reader: every interpretation 'enriches' the text with that reader's personal harmonies). This whole myth plays on a 'savage' pre-conceptual anteriority and a 'virginity' of meaning:

> The poet rejects the usual and appropriate term for the concept, which is a skeletal reduction of all previous experiences, when he finds himself in front of an untamed, virginal, reality . . . The word must be recreated each time from an intense personal experience; the skeleton of the thing in itself must be attired in living flesh so as to give it the concrete reality the thing has for me. (ibid., p. 97)

We are no longer sure whether to undress the concept or dress it up in order to rediscover the virginity of the poetic! In any case, it is a question of uncovering 'the secret correspondences that might exist between things'.

This romantic theory, with its conception of 'genius', paradoxically turns out to be rewritten today in terms of information theory. This polyphonic 'wealth' can be put in terms of 'additional information'. At the level of the signified: Petrarch's poetry constitutes a 'large capital of information' on love (Eco, *The Open Work*, p. 54). At the level of the signifier a certain type of disorder, rupture and negation of the customary and predictable linguistic order increases the rate of information of the message. There would be a 'dialectical tension' between the elements of order and disorder that can serve as a base-rate within the poetic. Whereas the most probable use of the linguistic system would yield nothing, the unexpectedness of the poetic, its relative improbability, determines a minimum rate of information. Here again, the poetic gives you more.

Thus the semiological imaginary easily reconciles romantic polyphony and quantitative description:

> The structure of poetry can most rigorously be described and interpreted in terms of a chain of possibilities. . . . A superior accumulation at mid-range frequencies of a certain class of phonemes, or the contrasting assemblage of two opposed classes in the phonemic

texture of a line, a strophe, or a poem, plays the role of a *'subjacent current of signification'*. (Fonagy, *Diogène*, 51)

'In language, form has a manifestly granular structure, which is open to a quantitative description' (Jakobson). With this we can confront Kristeva:

> Words are not non-decomposable entities held together by their meaning, but assemblages of signifying, phonemic and scriptural atoms leaping from word to word, thus creating unsuspected and unconscious relations between the elements of the discourse: this putting into relation of signifying elements constitutes a *signifying infrastructure of the langue*. (Julia Kristeva, 'Poésie et négativité', in *Séméiotikè* [Paris: Seuil, 1969], p. 185)

All these formulas converge on the idea of a 'Brownian' stage of language, an emulsional stage of the signifier, homologous to the molecular stage of physical matter, that liberates 'harmonies' of meaning just as fission or fusion liberate new molecular affinities. The whole conceived as an 'infrastructure', a 'subjacent current', that is to say, as a logically prior, or structurally more elementary, stage of discourse, just like matter. This is a scientistic, 'materialist' view of discourse, where the atom and the molecule are properly assimilated to the secondary articulation of language, as the molecular stage – an original stage, prior to the differentiating organisation of meaning – is to the poetic, Besides, Kristeva is not afraid of her own metaphor: she says that modern science has broken the body down into simple elements in the same way as (poetic) linguistics has disarticulated signification into signifying atoms.

There, concurrently with the metaphysics of primary articulation (the metaphysics of signifieds, bound to the play of signifying units), what we might call the *metaphysics of secondary articulation* takes shape, in which the effect of infrastructural signification is bound up with the play of distinct units, the minimal entities of discourse, where they are once again taken as positive valencies (just as atoms and molecules have an elementary valency), as phonemic materiality whose assemblage takes place in terms of linkages and probabilities.

But the poetic is no more based on the autonomous articulation of the phonemic levy than on that of words or syntax. *It does not play secondary articulation off against the primary.*[1] It is the abolition of the analytic distinction of the articulations on which language's capacity for discourse and its operational autonomy rests, as the means of expression (and as the object of linguistics). In any case, why should the phonemic level be more 'materialist' than that of the lexical concept or the sentence? As soon as we turn the phonemic into minimal substances, the phoneme, like the atom, becomes an idealist reference. With the physics of the atom, science relentlessly entrenches its positivist rationality. It has not brought the phonemic any closer to another mode, which would presuppose the respective extermination of the object and subject of science. Perhaps today it is reaching its borders, at the same time as materialism is in total theoretical crisis, without meanwhile being able to step beyond its shadow: there is no 'dialectical' transition between science, even at the apogee of its crisis, and something perhaps beyond it and irremediably separated from it, since science is founded on the basis of the denegation (not dialectical negation, but *de*negation) of dialectics. The most rigorous materialism will never lead beyond the principle of the rationality of value.

Tel Quel have taken the deconstruction of the sign furthest, up to the total 'liberation' of the signifier. End of the mortgage of the signified and the message, there is no 'polysemia', it is the signifier that is plural. No more 'ambiguity' of the message, just the intertextuality of the signifier, which is linked with and is produced by its pure 'material' logic. The endless text of the paragram, *significance* is the real level of the productivity of language, a productivity beyond value, opposed to the signification of the sign-product.

Julia Kristeva, in 'Poésie et négativité' (pp. 185ff.) comes closest to acknowledging a poetic form, even if the superstition of a 'materialist production' of meaning leads her nevertheless, by returning the poetic to the semiotic order, to censoriously describe it as a radical alternative.

She posits the *ambivalence* of the poetic signified (and not its mere ambiguity): it is concrete and general at the same time, it includes both (logical) affirmation and negation, it announces the simultaneity of the possible and the impossible; far from postulating the 'concrete versus the general', it explodes this conceptual break: bivalent logic (0/1) is abolished by ambivalent logic. Hence the very particular negativity of the poetic. The bivalent logic of discourse rests on the negation internal to the judgement, it founds the concept and its self-equivalence (the signified is what it is). The negativity of the poetic is a radical negativity *bearing on the logic of judgement itself*. Something 'is' and is not what it is: a utopia (in the literal sense) of the signified. The thing's self-equivalence (and, of course, the subject's) is volatilised. Thus the poetic signified is the space where 'Non-Being intertwines with Being in a thoroughly disconcerting manner'. But there is a danger (which can be seen in outline in Kristeva's work) of taking this 'space' as a *topic* again, and taking the 'intertwining' as, once again, the dialectic. There is a danger of *filling* this space up with every figure of substitution: 'Metaphor, metonymy, and all the tropes are inscribed in space surrounded by this double semantic structure.' The danger of the metaphor, of an economy of metaphor that remains positive. In Kristeva's chosen example, Baudelaire's *meubles voluptueux* ('voluptuous furniture'), the poetic effect does not stem from an added erotic value, a play of additional phantasms nor from a metaphorical or metonymic 'value'. It stems from the short-circuit of the two, the furniture being no longer furniture and the voluptuous pleasure no longer being voluptuous pleasure – the furniture (*meubles*) becomes voluptuous, and the voluptuous pleasure becomes mobile – nothing remains of the two separated fields of value. Neither of the two terms is poetic in itself, no more than their synthesis is: they are poetic in that the one is volatilised in the other. There is no relation between (poetic) enjoyment and the voluptuous pleasure as such. In love, there is only voluptuous pleasure – but it becomes enjoyment when it is volatilised into furniture. And the furniture is cancelled by the voluptuous pleasure in the same way: the same reversal sweeps away the proper position of each term. It is in this sense that Rimbaud's formula stands: 'It is true literally, in every sense.'

Metaphor is simply the *transfer of value from one field to the other*, to the point of the 'absorption of a multiplicity of texts (meanings) in the message' (Kristeva, 'Poésie et négativité', p. 194). The poetic implies the *reversibility of one field onto the other*, and thus the annulment of their respective values. Whereas values are combined, implicated and intertextualised in the metaphor according to a play of 'harmonies' (the 'secret accord of language'), in poetic enjoyment they are annulled: radical ambivalence is non-valence.

Kristeva, then, reduces the radical theory of ambivalence to a theory of intertextuality and the 'plurality of codes'. The poetic can no longer be distinguished from discourse save by 'the infinite nature of its code'; it is a plural discourse, the other only being the limit case of a monological discourse, a discourse with only one code. There is therefore a place for both types of discourse in a *general semiotics*: 'The semiotic practice of speech [discourse] is only one possible semiotic practice' (ibid., p. 215). Semanalysis has a duty to take them all into account, without exclusion, that is to say, without neglecting the irreducibility of the poetic, but equally without reducing it to the logic of the sign. Semanalysis has a duty to constitute a 'non-reductive typology of the plurality of semiotic practices'. There is an increasing intricacy of the different logics of meaning:

> The functioning of speech [*la parole*] is impregnated with paragrammatism, just as the functioning of poetic language is circumscribed by the laws of speech. (ibid., p. 214)

Once again Starobinski's doubts about Saussure come to the surface: the latter's tolerance of both the poetic and the discursive in the name of universal rules of language (here in the name of a 'genuinely materialist' science called semiotics). In fact, this is a reductive and repressive position. For from the poetic to the discursive there is no difference in their respective articulation of meaning, there is a radical antagonism. Neither of them is an 'infrastructure of signification' (would the logical discourse on it be its 'superstructure'?). Further, discourse, logos, is not a particular case in the infinity of codes: it is *the* code that puts an end to infinity, it is the discourse of closure that puts an end to the poetic, to the para- and the ana-grammatic. Conversley, it is on the basis of its dismantling, its destruction, that language revives the possibility of 'infinity'. In fact, 'infinity of codes' is a bad term, since it permits the amalgam of the one and the 'infinite' in the 'mathematics' of the text, and their distribution along a single chain. It must be said, in terms of radical incompatabilty and antagonism, that it is on the basis of the destruction of the discourse of *value* that language revives the possibility of *ambivalence*: this is the poetic revolution in relation to discourse, where the one can only be the death of the other.

The semiotic project is only a more subtle way of neutralising the radicality of the poetic and saving the hegemony of linguistics (re-baptised 'semiotics'), no longer by pure and simple annexation, but under cover of the ideology of 'plurality'.

The subversion of linguistics by the poetic does not stop here: it leads one to wonder whether the rules of language even hold good for the field of language over which they prevail, that is to say, in the dominant sphere of communication (similarly, the failure of political economy to give an account of anterior societies leads one, as an after-effect, to wonder if these principles have any value for us). Now it is true that the immediate practice of language is somewhat resistant to the rational abstraction of linguistics. O. Mannoni puts this well in 'The ellipsis and the bar':

> Linguistics originates from the bar it has installed between the signifier and the signified, and their reunion spells its death – which brings us back to *conversation in everyday life*. ('L'ellipse et la barre', in *Clefs pour l'imaginaire*, p. 35)

The Saussurian bar has facilitated the renewal of linguistic theory from top to bottom. In the same way, Marxism, by means of the concept of a material infrastructure opposed to the 'superstructure', has established something like an 'objective' and revolutionary analysis of society. Science is based on rupture. In exactly the same way, a 'science', a rationalist practice (organisation), originates from the distinction between theory and practice. Every science and every rationality lasts as long as this rupture lasts. Dialectics makes endless formal adjustments to this rupture, it never resolves it. To dialecticise the infra- and the superstructure, theory and practice, or even signifier and signified, *langue* and *parole*, is merely a vain effort at totalisation. Science lives and dies with the rupture.

This is indeed why current non-scientific practice, both linguistic and social, is revolutionary in some way, *because it does not make these kinds of distinctions*. Just as it has *never made a*

distinction between mind and body, whereas every dominant religion and philosophy survives only on the basis of this distinction,
so our, everybody's, immediate and 'savage' social practices do not
make a distinction between theory and practice, infra- and superstructure: of itself and without debating the issue, it is transversal,
beyond rationality, whether bourgeois or Marxist. Theory, 'good'
Marxist theory, never analyses *real* social practice, it analyses the
object that it produces for itself through separating this practice
into an infra- and a superstructure, or, in other words, it analyses
the social field that it produces for itself through the dissociation
between theory and practice. Theory will never lead back to 'practice' since it only exists through having vivisected it: fortunately
this practice is beginning to return to and even overcome it. But
this brings with it the end of dialectical and historical materialism.

In the same way, the immediate, everyday linguistic practice
of speech and the 'speaking subject' pays no attention to the
distinction between the sign and the world (nor that between
signifier and signified, the arbitrary character of the sign, etc.).
Benveniste says and acknowledges this, but only as regards
memory, since this is precisely the stage that science overcomes it
and leaves it far behind: it interests only the linguistic subject,
the subject of the *langue*, which is at the same time the subject of
knowledge: Benveniste himself. Somewhere, however, the other
is right, speaking in advance [*en deçà*] of the distinction between
sign and world, in total 'superstition' – the other (along with ourselves and even Benveniste) knows more, it is true, about the
essentials than Benveniste the linguist. For the methodology of
the separation of signifier and signified holds no better than the
methodology of the separation of the mind and the body. The
same imaginary in both cases. In the one case, psychoanalysis[2]
came to say what this was, as, in the other, did poetics. But there
has basically never been any need for psychoanalysis nor for
poetics: no-one has ever believed in them apart from the scholars
and linguists themselves (just as, in the final analysis, no-one has
ever believed in economic determinism other than economic scientists and their Marxist critics).

Virtually, and literally, speaking, *there has never been a linguistic subject*; it is not even true of we who speak that we purely and

simply reflect the code of linguistics. Likewise, there has never been an *economic subject*, a *homo oeconomicus* – this fiction has never been inscribed anywhere other than in a code – there has never been *a subject of consciousness*, and there has never been *a subject of the unconscious*. In the simplest practice, there is always something that cuts across these simulation models, which are all rational models; there has always been a radicality absent from every code, every 'objective' rationalisation, that has basically only ever given rise to a single great subject: *the subject of knowledge*, whose form is shattered from today, from now, by undivided speech.[3] Basically we have all known this for much longer than Descartes, Saussure, Marx and Freud.

Notes

1. This is the illusion of being able to separate the two articulations, and eventually extract the one from the other. It is the illusion of being able to rediscover, by splitting the primary, 'significative' articulation, the equivalent to non-linguistic signs in language (gestures, sounds, colours). This illusion leads J.-F. Lyotard, in *Discours, figure* (Paris: Klincksieck, 1971) to grant the level of the visual or the cry an absolute privilege as spontaneous transgression, always already beyond the discursive and closer to the figural. This illusion remains trapped by the very concept of double articulation, whereby the linguistic order again finds a means to establish itself in the interpretation of what escapes it.

2. Careful here: this all holds for psychoanalysis itself, which also thrives on the rupture between primary and secondary processes, and will die at the end of this separation. And it is true that psychoanalysis is 'revolutionary' and 'scientific' when it explores the entire field of channels from the standpoint of this rupture (in the unconscious). But perhaps we will see one day that real, total and immediate practice does not obey this postulate, or that analytic simulation model; that *symbolic* practice is from the very first beyond the distinction between primary and secondary processes. To this day, the unconscious and the subject of the unconscious, psychoanalysis and the

subject of (psychoanalytic) knowledge, has lived – the analytic field will have disappeared as such into the separation that it instituted itself – for the benefit of the symbolic field. We can already see many signs that this has already taken place.

3. This speech has nothing to do with linguistic sense of the word '*parole*', since the latter is trapped with the *langue-parole* opposition and is subject to the *langue*. Undivided (symbolic) speech itself denies the theory-practice distinction. Only 'linguistic' *parole* says only what it says. But such speech has never existed, unless in the dialogue of the dead. Concrete, actual speech says what it says, *along with everything else at the same time*. It does not observe the law of the discrete sign and the separation of the agencies, it speaks at every level at the same time, or better, it undoes the level of the *langue*, and thus linguistics itself. The latter, by contrast, seeks to impose a *parole* which would be nothing but the execution of the *langue*, that is to say, the discourse of power.

CHAPTER FOUR

The Ecliptic of Sex

In 1979 Editions Galilée published *De La Seduction*, a book which was to outrage its select band of readers, especially feminists. In the reception of much of his work Baudrillard has been interpreted as explicitly anti-feminist and this work certainly added fuel to the fire. Macmillan published an English translation by Brian Singer in 1990 and the first chapter of this edition of *Seduction* provides the extract here. The English edition had a stunning Man Ray cover and was published in the CultureTexts series edited by Canadian 'performance theorists' Arthur and Marilouise Kroker. The series was self-consciously dedicated to representing the 'forward breaking-edge of postmodern theory and practice' and the Krokers, along with a small group of like-minded others around the cyber journal C-THEORY, promoted Baudrillard for many years as extreme postmodernist theorist extraordinaire, especially in the realm of bodies and sexualities. *Seduction*, on any reading, does not support such an interpretation and still remains a relatively little known, and little read, text in Baudrillard's oeuvre. It was undoubtedly a long while before English-speaking readers caught up with its concepts and approach and, as with the reception of *Symbolic Exchange and Death*, once *Seduction* was properly absorbed and analysed the trajectory of Baudrillard's work since the mid-1970s became much clearer. Advertised as 'Baudrillard's most provocative book' in the 1990s, *Seduction* challenged 'all modern theory, even, indeed, the rules of theoretical production itself' as *Liberation* noted at the time of its first publication in the late 1970s. Baudrillard used terms usually associated with theories of sexuality such as seduction, orgy, pornography, obscene, liberation and desire throughout his work but such concepts were rarely applied to sexuality per se. They were instead employed by

Baudrillard as part of his more general analysis of contemporary culture, opposing symbolic exchange (including seduction) to what he saw as the semiotic, or simulated, order.

'The Ecliptic of Sex', from *Seduction*, trans. Brian Singer, London: Macmillan, 1990.

Nothing is less certain today than sex, behind the liberation of its discourse. And nothing today is less certain than desire, behind the proliferation of its images.

In matters of sex, the proliferation is approaching total loss. Here lies the secret of the ever increasing production of sex and its signs, and the hyperrealism of sexual pleasure, particularly feminine pleasure. The principle of uncertainty has extended to sexual reason, as well as political and economic reason.

The state of sex's liberation is also that of its indetermination. No more want, no more prohibitions, and no more limits: it is the loss of every referential principle. Economic reason is sustained only by penury; it is put into question with the realization of its objective, the abolition of the spectre of penury. Desire too is sustained only by want. When desire is entirely on the side of demand, when it is operationalized without restrictions, it loses its imaginary and, therefore, its reality; it appears everywhere but in generalized simulation. It is the ghost of desire that haunts the defunct reality of sex. Sex is everywhere, except in sexuality (Barthes).

In sexual mythology, the transition towards the feminine is contemporaneous with the passage from determination to general indetermination. The feminine is not substituted for the masculine as one sex for another, according to some structural inversion. It is substituted as the end of the determinate representation of sex, as the flotation of the law that regulates the difference between the sexes. The ascent of the feminine corresponds to both the apogee of sexual pleasure and a catastrophe relative to sex's reality principle.

And so it is femininity that is gripping, in the present and fatal situation of sex's hyperreality – as it was yesterday, but in direct contrast, in irony and seduction.

*   *   *

Freud was right: there is but one sexuality, one libido – and it is masculine. Sexuality has a strong, discriminative structure centered on the phallus, castration, the Name-of-the Father, and repression. There is none other. There is no use dreaming of some non-phallic, unlocked, unmarked sexuality. There is no use seeking, from within this structure, to have the feminine pass through to the other side, or to cross terms. Either the structure remains the same, with the female being entirely absorbed by the male, or else it collapses, and there is no longer either female or male – the degree zero of the structure. This is very much what is happening today: erotic polyvalence, the infinite potentiality of desire, different connections, diffractions, libidinal intensities – all multiple variants of a liberatory alternative coming from the frontiers of a psychoanalysis free of Freud, or from the frontiers of desire free of psychoanalysis. Behind the effervescence of the paradigm of sex, everything is converging towards the non-differentiation of the structure and its potential neutralization.

The danger of the sexual revolution for the female is that she will be enclosed within a structure that condemns her to either discrimination when the structure is strong, or a derisory triumph within a weakened structure.

The feminine, however, is, and has always been, somewhere else. That is the secret of its strength. Just as it is said that something lasts because its existence is not adequate to its essence, it must be said that the feminine seduces because it is never where it thinks it is, or where it thinks itself. The feminine is not found in the history of suffering and oppression imputed to it – women's historical tribulations (though by guile it conceals itself therein). It suffers such servitude only when assigned to and repressed within this structure – to which the sexual revolution assigns and represses it all the more dramatically. But by what aberrant complicity (complicit with what? if not, precisely, the male) would one have us believe that this is the female's history? Repression is already here in full force, in the narrative of women's sexual and political misery, to the exclusion of every other type of strength and sovereignty.

There is an alternative to sex and to power, one that psycho-analysis cannot know because its axiomatics are sexual. And yes, this alternative is undoubtedly of the order of the feminine, understood outside the opposition masculine/feminine, that opposition being essentially masculine, sexual in intention, and incapable of being overturned without ceasing to exist.

This strength of the feminine is that of seduction.

*   *   *

One may catch a glimpse of another, parallel universe (the two never meet) with the decline of psychoanalysis and sexuality as strong structures, and their cleansing within a *psy* and molecular universe (that of their final liberation). A universe that can no longer be interpreted in terms of psychic or psychological rela-tions, nor those of repression and the unconscious, but must be interpreted in the terms of play, challenges, duels, the strategy of appearances – that is, the terms of seduction. A universe that can no longer be interpreted in terms of structures and diacritical oppositions, but implies a seductive reversibilty – a universe where the feminine is not what opposes the masculine, but what seduces the masculine.

In seduction the feminine is neither a marked nor an unmarked term. It does not mask the 'autonomy' of desire, pleasure or the body, or of a speech or writing that it has supposedly lost(?). Nor does it lay claim to some truth of its own. It seduces.

To be sure, one cails the sovereignty of seduction feminine by convention, the same convention that claims sexuality to be fun-damentally masculine. But the important point is that this form of sovereignty has always existed – delineating, from a distance, the feminine as something that is nothing, that is never 'pro-duced,' is never where it is produced (and certainly cannot, there-fore, be found in any 'feminist' demand). And this not from the perspective of a psychic or biological bi-sexuality, but that of the trans-sexuality of seduction which the entire organization of sex tends to reject – as does psychoanalysis in accordance with the axiom that there is no other structure than that of sexuality (which renders it incapable, by definition, of speaking about anything else).

*   *   *

What does the women's movement oppose to the phallocratic structure? Autonomy, difference, a specificity of desire and pleasure, a different relation to the female body, a speech, a writing – *but never seduction.* They are ashamed of seduction, as implying an artificial presentation of the body, or a life of vassalage and prostitution. They do not understand *that seduction represents mastery over the symbolic universe, while power represents only mastery of the real universe.* The sovereignty of seduction is incommensurable with the possession of political or sexual power.

There is a strange, fierce complicity between the feminist movement and the order of truth. For seduction is resisted and rejected as a misappropriation of women's true being, a truth that in the last instance is to be found inscribed in their bodies and desires. In one stroke the immense privilege of the feminine is effaced: the privilege of having never acceded to truth or meaning, and of having remained absolute master of the realm of appearances. The capacity immanent to seduction to deny things their truth and turn it into a game, the pure play of appearances, and thereby foil all systems of power and meaning with a mere turn of the hand. The ability to turn appearances in on themselves, to play on the body's appearances, rather than with the depths of desire. Now all appearances are reversible . . . only at the level of appearances are systems fragile and vulnerable . . . meaning is vulnerable only to enchantment. One must be incredibly blind to deny the sole force that is equal and superior to all others, since with a simple play of the *strategy of appearances*, it turns them upside down.

*   *   *

Anatomy is destiny, Freud said. One might be surprised that the feminist movement's rejection of this definition, phallic by definition, and sealed with the stamp of anatomy, opens onto an alternative that remains fundamentally biological and anatomical:

> Indeed, woman's pleasure does not have to choose between clitoral activity and vaginal passivity, for example. The pleasure of the vaginal caress does not have to be substituted for that of the clitoral caress. They each contribute, irreplaceably to woman's pleasure. Among other caresses . . . Fondling the breasts, touching the vulva, spreading the lips, stroking the posterior wall of the vagina, brushing against the mouth of the uterus, and so on. To evoke only a few of the most specifically female pleasures. (Luce Irigaray)

Parole de femme? But it is always an anatomical speech, always that of the body. What is specific to women lies in the diffraction of the erogenous zones, in a decentered eroticism, the diffuse polyvalence of sexual pleasure and the transfiguration of the entire body by desire: this is the theme song that runs through the entire female, sexual revolution, but also through our entire culture of the body, from the Anagrammes of Bellmer to Deleuze's mechanized connections. It is always a question of the body, if not the anatomical, then the organic, erogenous body, the functional body that, even in fragmented and metaphorical form, would have pleasure as its object and desire as its natural manifestation. But then either the body is here only a metaphor (and if this is the case, what is the sexual revolution, and our entire culture, having become a body culture, talking about?), or else, with this body speech, this woman speech, we have, very definitely, entered into an anatomical destiny, into anatomy as destiny. There is nothing here radically opposed to Freud's maxim.

Nowhere is it a question of seduction, the body worked by artifice (and not by desire), the body seduced, the body to be seduced, the body in its passion separated from its truth, from that ethical truth of desire which obsesses us – that serious, profoundly religious truth that the body today incarnates, and for which seduction is just as evil and deceitful as it once was for religion. Nowhere is it a question of the body delivered to appearances. Now, *seduction alone is radically opposed to anatomy as destiny*. Seduction alone breaks the distinctive sexualization of bodies and the inevitable phallic economy that results.

Any movement that believes it can subvert a system by its infrastructure is naive. Seduction is more intelligent, and seemingly spontaneously so. Immediately obvious – seduction need not be demonstrated, nor justified – it is there all at once, in the reversal of all the alleged depth of the real, of all psychology, anatomy, truth, or power. It knows (this is its secret) that *there is no anatomy*, nor psychology, that all signs are reversible. Nothing belongs to it, except appearances – all powers elude it, but it 'reversibilizes' all their signs. How can one oppose seduction? The only thing truly at stake is mastery of the strategy of appearances, against the force of being and reality. There is no need to play being against being, or truth against truth; why become stuck undermining foundations, when a *light* manipulation of appearances will do.

Now woman is but appearance. And it is the feminine as appearance that thwarts masculine depth. Instead of rising up against such 'insulting' counsel, women would do well to let themselves be seduced by its truth, for here lies the secret of their strength, which they are in the process of losing by erecting a contrary, feminine depth.

*   *   *

It is not quite the feminine as surface that is opposed to the masculine as depth, but the feminine as indistinctness of surface and depth. Or as indifference to the authentic and the artificial. Joan Rivière, in 'Feminité sans mascarade' (*La Psychoanalyse* no. 7), makes a fundamental claim – one that contains within it all seduction: 'Whether femininity be authentic or superficial, it is fundamentally the same thing.'

This can be said only of the feminine. The masculine, by contrast, possesses unfailing powers of discrimination and absolute criteria for pronouncing the truth. The masculine is certain, the feminine is insoluble.

Now, surprisingly, this proposition, that in the feminine the very distinction between authenticity and artifice is without foundation, also defines the space of simulation. Here too one cannot distinguish between reality and its models, there being no other reality than that secreted by the simulative models, just as there is no other femininity than that of appearances. Simulation too is insoluble.

This strange coincidence points to the ambiguity of the feminine: it simultaneously provides radical evidence of simulation, and the only possibility of its overcoming – in seduction, precisely.

CHAPTER FIVE

The Beaubourg Effect: Implosion and Deterrence

In 1981 Editions Galilée published what was to become Baudrillard's most famous book *Simulacres et Simulation*. Published by the University of Michigan Press in 1994 in English translation by Sheila Faria Glaser, *Simulacra and Simulation* is the book which appears in the film *The Matrix*, directed by the Wachowski brothers in the late 1990s. There were two sequels *The Matrix: Reloaded* and *The Matrix: Revolutions* in 2003 by which time Baudrillard had given interviews rejecting the film as misunderstanding his notion of simulation and the real. However, Baudrillard figured prominently in thinking around the film's production and consumption and the leading actors in *The Matrix* were provided with the white-cover English edition of *Simulacra and Simulation* to read. There is no doubt at all that association with the film gave Baudrillard the greatest global popular cultural boost in his life and career. The Sheila Faria Glaser translation into English is the extract here. *Simulacra and Simulation* is in fact made up of a series of short essays written and published at different times up to and including 1981. In one section, at page 1 in the English translation, Baudrillard begins with the infamous quote attributed to Ecclesiastes in the Bible, which ends with the words 'The simulacrum is true', which he later admitted was completely imaginary and made up. The extract here is a short piece entitled 'The Beaubourg Effect', first written and published in French between the publication of *Symbolic Exchange and Death* and *Seduction*. It consists of a rant against the high modernist (sometimes mistakenly referred to as 'postmodernist') Pompidou Centre in Paris famous for its architecture featuring its innards (pipes, ducts, etc.) on its outside in a public display of self-conscious modernist construction. While neo-Marxist theorists like Fredric Jameson were providing critiques of postmodernism in art and architecture as the 'cultural logic of late capitalism' Baudrillard was engaged in a quite different enterprise.

'The Beaubourg Effect: Implosion and Deterrence', from
***Simulacra and Simulation*, trans. Sheila Faria Glaser,**
Ann Arbour, MI: University of Michigan Press, 1994.

The Beaubourg effect, the Beaubourg machine, the Beaubourg *thing* – how to give it a name? Enigma of this carcass of flux and signs, of networks and circuits – the final impulse to translate a structure that no longer has a name, the structure of social relations given over to superficial ventilation (animation, self-management, information, media) and to an irreversibly deep implosion. Monument to the games of mass simulation, the Pompidou Center functions as an incinerator absorbing all the cultural energy and devouring it – a bit like the black monolith in *2001*: insane convection of all the contents that came there to be materialized, to be absorbed, and to be annihilated.

All around, the neighborhood is nothing but a protective zone – remodeling, disinfection, a snobbish and hygienic design – but above all in a figurative sense: it is a machine for making emptiness. It is a bit like the real danger nuclear power stations pose: not lack of security, pollution, explosion, but a system of maximum security that radiates around them, the protective zone of control and deterrence that extends, slowly but surely, over the territory – a technical, ecological, economic, geopolitical glacis. What does the nuclear matter? The station is a matrix in which an absolute model of security is elaborated, which will encompass the whole social field, and which is fundamentally a model of deterrence (it is the same one that controls us globally, under the sign of peaceful coexistence and of the simulation of atomic danger).

The same model, with the same proportions, is elaborated at the Center: cultural fission, political deterrence.

This said, the circulation of fluids is unequal. Ventilation, cooling, electrical networks – the 'traditional' fluids circulate there very well. Already the circulation of the human flux is less assured (the archaic solution of escalators in plastic sleeves, one ought to be aspirated, propelled, or something, but with a mobility that would be up to this baroque theatricality of fluids that is the source of the originality of the carcass). As for the material of the works, of objects, of books and the so-called polyvalent interior space, these no longer circulate at all. It is the opposite of Roissy, where from a futurist center of 'spatial' design radiating toward 'satellites,' etc., one ends up completely flat in front of . . . traditional airplanes. But the incoherence is the same. (What happened to money, this other fluid, what happened to its mode of circulation, of emulsion, of fallout at Beaubourg?)

Same contradiction even in the behavior of the personnel, assigned to the 'polyvalent' space and without a private work space. On their feet and mobile, the people affect a cool demeanor, more supple, very contemporary, adapted to the 'structure' of a 'modern' space. Seated in their corner, which is precisely not one, they exhaust themselves secreting an artificial solitude remaking their 'bubble.' Therein is also a great tactic of deterrence: one condemns them to using all their energy in this individual defense. Curiously, one thus finds the same contradiction that characterizes the Beaubourg thing: a mobile exterior, commuting, cool and modern – an interior shriveled by the same old values.

This space of deterrence, articulated on the ideology of visibility, of transparency, of polyvalency, of consensus and contact, and sanctioned by the blackmail to security, is today, virtually, that of all social relations. All of social discourse is there, and on this level as well as on that of the treatment of culture, Beaubourg flagrantly contradicts its explicit objectives, a nice monument to our modernity. It is nice to think that the idea did not come to some revolutionary spirit, but to the logicians of the established order, deprived of all critical intelligence, and thus closer to the truth, capable, in their obstinacy, of putting in place a machine that is fundamentally uncontrollable, that in its very success escapes them, and that is the most exact reflection, even in its contradictions, of the current state of things.

Certainly, all the cultural contents of Beaubourg are anachronistic, because only an empty interior could correspond to this architectural envelope. The general impression being that everything here has come out of a coma, that everything wants to be animation and is only reanimation, and that this is good because culture is dead, a condition that Beaubourg admirably retraces, but in a dishonest fashion, whereas one should have triumphantly accepted this death and erected a monument or an antimonument equivalent to the phallic inanity of the Eiffel Tower in its time. Monument to total disconnection, to hyperreality and to the implosion of culture – achieved today for us in the effect of transistorized circuits always threatened by a gigantic short circuit.

Beaubourg is already an imperial compression – figure of a culture already crushed by its own weight – like moving automobiles suddenly frozen in a geometric solid. Like the cars of Caesar, survivors of an ideal accident, no longer external, but internal to the metallic and mechanical structure, and which would have produced tons of cubic scrap iron, where the chaos of tubes, levers, frames, of metal and human flesh inside is tailored to the geometric size of the smallest possible space – thus the culture of Beaubourg is ground, twisted, cut up, and pressed into its smallest simple elements – a bundle of defunct transmissions and metabolisms, frozen like a science-fiction mecanoid.

But instead of breaking and compressing all culture here in this carcass that in any case has the appearance of a compression, instead of that, one *exhibits* Caesar there. One exhibits Dubuffet and the counterculture, whose inverse simulation acts as a referential for the defunct culture. In this carcass that could have served as a mausoleum to the useless operationality of signs, one reexhibits Tinguely's ephemeral and autodestructive machines under the sign of the eternity of culture. Thus one neutralizes everything together: Tinguely is embalmed in the museal institution, Beaubourg falls back on its supposed artistic contents.

Fortunately, this whole simulacrum of cultural values is annihilated in advance by the external architecture.[1] Because this architecture, with its networks of tubes and the look it has of being an expo or world's fair building, with its (calculated?)

fragility deterring any traditional mentality or monumentality, overtly proclaims that our time will never again be that of duration, that our only temporality is that of the accelerated cycle and of recycling, that of the circuit and of the transit of fluids. Our only culture in the end is that of hydrocarbons, that of refining, cracking, breaking cultural molecules and of their recombination into synthesized products. This, the Beaubourg Museum wishes to conceal, but the Beaubourg cadaver proclaims. And this is what underlies the beauty of the cadaver and the failure of the interior spaces. In any case, the very ideology of 'cultural production' is antithetical to all culture, as is that of visibility and of the polyvalent space: culture is a site of the secret, of seduction, of initiation, of a restrained and highly ritualized symbolic exchange. Nothing can be done about it. Too bad for the masses, too bad for Beaubourg.

What should, then, have been placed in Beaubourg?

Nothing. The void that would have signified the disappearance of any culture of meaning and aesthetic sentiment. But this is still too romantic and destructive, this void would still have had value as a masterpiece of anticulture.

Perhaps revolving strobe lights and gyroscopic lights, striating the space, for which the crowd would have provided the moving base element?

In fact, Beaubourg illustrates very well that an order of simulacra only establishes itself on the alibi of the previous order. Here, a cadaver all in flux and surface connections gives itself as content a traditional culture of depth. An order of prior simulacra (that of meaning) furnishes the empty substance of a subsequent order, which, itself, no longer even knows the distinction between signifier and signified, nor between form and content.

The question: 'What should have been placed in Beaubourg?' is thus absurd. It cannot be answered because the topical distinction between interior and exterior should no longer be posed. There lies our truth, the truth of Möbius – doubtless an unrealizable utopia, but which Beaubourg still points to as right, to the degree to which any of its contents is a *countermeaning* and annihilated in advance by the form.

Yet – yet . . . if you had to have something in Beaubourg – it should have been a labyrinth, a combinatory, infinite library, an aleatory redistribution of destinies through games or lotteries – in short, the universe of Borges – or even the circular Ruins: the slowed-down enchainment of individuals dreamed up by each other (not a dreamworld Disneyland, a laboratory of practical fiction). An experimentation with all the different processes of representation: defraction, implosion, slow motion, aleatory linkage and decoupling – a bit like at the Exploratorium in San Francisco or in the novels of Philip K. Dick – in short a culture of simulation and of fascination, and not always one of production and meaning: this is what might be proposed that would not be a miserable anticulture. Is it possible? Not here, evidently. But this culture takes place elsewhere, everywhere, nowhere. From today, the only real cultural practice, that of the masses, ours (there is no longer a difference), is a manipulative, aleatory practice, a labyrinthine practice of signs, and one that no longer has any meaning.

In another way, however, it is not true that there is no coherence between form and content at Beaubourg. It is true if one gives any credence to the official cultural project. But exactly the opposite occurs there. Beaubourg is nothing but a huge effort to transmute this famous traditional culture of meaning into the aleatory order of signs, into an order of simulacra (the third) that is completely homogeneous with the flux and pipes of the facade. And it is in order to prepare the masses for this new semiurgic order that one brings them together here – with the opposite pretext of acculturating them to meaning and depth.

One must thus start with this axiom: Beaubourg is a *monument of cultural deterrence*. Within a museal scenario that only serves to keep up the humanist fiction of culture, it is a veritable fashioning of the death of culture that takes place, and it is a veritable *cultural mourning* for which the masses are joyously gathered.

And they throw themselves at it. There lies the supreme irony of Beaubourg: the masses throw themselves at it not because they salivate for that culture which they have been denied for centuries, but because they have for the first time the opportunity to massively participate in this great mourning of a culture that, in the end, they have always detested.

The misunderstanding is therefore complete when one de-nounces Beaubourg as a cultural mystification of the masses. The masses, themselves, rush there to enjoy this execution, this dis-memberment, this operational prostitution of a culture finally truly liquidated, including all counterculture that is nothing but its apotheosis. The masses rush toward Beaubourg as they rush toward disaster sites, with the same irresistible élan. Better: they *are* the disaster of Beaubourg. Their number, their stampede, their fascination, their itch to see everything is objectively a deadly and catastrophic behavior for the whole undertaking. Not only does their weight put the building in danger, but their adhe-sion, their curiosity annihilates the very contents of this culture of animation. This rush can no longer be measured against what was proposed as the cultural objective, it is its radical negation, in both its excess and success. It is thus the masses who assume the role of catastrophic agent in this structure of catastrophe, it is *the masses themselves who put an end to mass culture.*

Circulating in the space of transparency, the masses are cer-tainly converted into flux, but at the same time, through their opacity and inertia, they put an end to this 'polyvalent' space. One invites the masses to participate, to simulate, to play with the models – they go one better: they participate and manipulate so well that they efface all the meaning one wants to give to the operation and put the very infrastructure of the edifice in danger. Thus, always a sort of parody, a hypersimulation in response to cultural simulation, transforms the masses, who should only be the livestock of culture, into the agents of the exe-cution of this culture, of which Beaubourg was only the shame-ful incarnation.

One must applaud this success of cultural deterrence. All the antiartists, leftists, and those who hold culture in contempt have never even gotten close to approaching the dissuassive efficacy of this monumental black hole that is Beaubourg. It is a truly revo-lutionary operation, precisely because it is involuntary, *insane* and uncontrolled, whereas any operation meant to put an end to culture only serves, as one knows, to resurrect it.

To tell the truth, the only content of Beaubourg is the masses themselves, whom the building treats like a converter, like a black box, or, in terms of input-output, just like a refinery handles petroleum products or a flood of unprocessed material.

It has never been so clear that the content – here, culture, elsewhere, information or commodities – is nothing but the phantom support for the operation of the medium itself, whose function is always to induce mass, to produce a homogeneous human and mental flux. An immense to-and-fro movement similar to that of suburban commuters, absorbed and ejected at fixed times by their workplace. And it is precisely work that is at issue here – a work of testing, polling, and directed interrogation: the people come here to select objects-responses to all the questions they might ask themselves, or rather *they come themselves in response to* the functional and directed question that the objects constitute. More than a chain of work it is thus a question of a programmatic discipline whose constraints have been effaced behind a veneer of tolerance. Well beyond traditional institutions of capital, the hypermarket, or the Beaubourg 'hypermarket of culture,' is already the model of all future forms of controlled socialization: retotalization in a homogeneous space-time of all the dispersed functions of the body and of social life (work, leisure, media culture), retranscription of all the contradictory currents in terms of integrated circuits. Space-time of a whole operational simulation of social life.

For that, the mass of consumers must be equivalent or homologous to the mass of products. It is the confrontation and the fusion of these two masses that occurs in the hypermarket as it does at Beaubourg, and that makes of them something very different from the traditional sites of culture (monuments, museums, galleries, libraries, community arts centers, etc.). Here a critical mass beyond which the commodity becomes hypercommodity, and culture hyperculture, is elaborated – that is to say no longer linked to distinct exchanges or determined needs, but to a kind of total descriptive universe, or integrated circuit that implosion traverses through and through – incessant circulation of choices, readings, references, marks, decoding. Here cultural objects, as elsewhere the objects of consumption, have no other end than to maintain you in a state of mass integration, of transistorized flux, of a magnetized molecule. It is what one comes to learn in a hypermarket: hyperreality of the commodity – it is what one comes to learn at Beaubourg: the hyperreality of culture.

Already with the traditional museum this cutting up, this regrouping, this interference of all cultures, this unconditional aestheticization that constitutes the hyperreality of culture begins, but the museum is still a memory. Never, as it did here, has culture lost its memory in the service of stockpiling and functional redistribution. And this translates a more general fact: that throughout the 'civilized' world the construction of stockpiles of objects has brought with it the complementary process of stockpiles of people – the line, waiting, traffic jams, concentration, the camp. That is 'mass production,' not in the sense of a massive production or for use by the masses, but the production of *the masses*. The masses as the final product of all sociality, and, at the same time, as putting an end to sociality, because these masses that one wants us to believe *are* the social, are on the contrary the site of the implosion of the social. *The masses are the increasingly dense sphere in which the whole social comes to be imploded, and to be devoured in an uninterrupted process of simulation.*

Whence this concave mirror: it is from seeing the masses in the interior that the masses will be tempted to rush in. Typical marketing method: the whole ideology of transparency here takes on its meaning. Or again: it is in staging a reduced ideal model that one hopes for an accelerated gravitation, an automatic agglutination of culture as an automatic agglomeration of the masses. Same process: nuclear operation of a chain reaction, or specular operation of white magic.

Thus for the first time, Beaubourg is at the level of culture what the hypermarket is at the level of the commodity: *the perfect circulatory operator*, the demonstration of anything (commodity, culture, crowd, compressed air) *through its own accelerated circulation*.

But if the supply of objects brings along with it the stockpiling of men, the latent violence in the supply of objects brings with it the inverse violence of men.

Every stock is violent, and there is a specific violence in any mass of men also, because of the fact that it implodes – a violence proper to its gravitation, to its densification around its own locus of inertia. The masses are a locus of inertia and through that a locus of a completely new, inexplicable violence different from explosive violence.

Critical mass, implosive mass. Beyond thirty thousand it poses the risk of 'bending' the structure of Beaubourg. If the masses magnetized by the structure become a destructive variable of the structure itself – if those who conceived of the project wanted this (but how to hope for this?), if they thus programmed the chance of putting an end with one blow to both architecture and culture – then Beaubourg constitutes the most audacious object and the most successful happening of the century!

Make Beaubourg bend! New motto of a revolutionary order. Useless to set fire to it, useless to contest it. Do it! It is the best way of destroying it. The success of Beaubourg is no longer a mystery: the people go there *for that*, they throw themselves on this building, whose fragility already breathes catastrophe, with the single goal of making it bend.

Certainly they obey the imperative of deterrence: one gives them an object to consume, a culture to devour, an edifice to manipulate. But at the same time they expressly aim, and without knowing it, at this annihilation. The onslaught is the only act the masses can produce as such – a projectile mass that challenges the edifice of mass culture, that witty replies with its *weight* (that is to say with the characteristic most deprived of meaning, the stupidest, the least cultural one they possess) to the challenge of culturality thrown at it by Beaubourg. To the challenge of mass acculturation to a sterilized culture, the masses respond with a destructive irruption, which is prolonged in a brutal manipulation. To mental deterrence the masses respond with a direct physical deterrence. It is their own challenge. Their ruse, which is to respond in the very terms by which they are solicited, but beyond that, to respond to the simulation in which one imprisions them with an enthusiastic social process that surpasses the objectives of the former and acts as a destructive hypersimulation.[2]

People have the desire to take everything, to pillage everything, to swallow everything, to manipulate everything. Seeing, deciphering, learning does not touch them. The only massive affect is that of manipulation. The organizers (and the artists and intellectuals) are frightened by this uncontrollable watchfulness, because they never count on anything but the apprenticeship of the masses to the *spectacle* of culture. They never count on this active, destructive fascination, a brutal and original response to the gift of an incomprehensible culture, an attraction that has all the characteristics of breaking and entering and of the violation of a sanctuary.

Beaubourg could have or should have disappeared the day after the inauguration, dismantled and kidnapped by the crowd, which would have been the only possible response to the absurd challenge of the transparency and democracy of culture – each person taking away a fetishized bolt of this culture itself fetishized.

The people come to *touch*, they look as if they were touching, their gaze is only an aspect of tactile manipulation. It is certainly a question of a tactile universe, no longer a visual or discursive one, and the people are directly implicated in a process: to manipulate/to be manipulated, to ventilate/to be ventilated, to circulate/to make circulate, which is no longer of the order of representation, nor of distance, nor of reflection. It is something that is part of panic, and of a world in panic.

Panic in slow motion, no external variable. It is the violence internal to a saturated ensemble. *Implosion*.

Beaubourg cannot even burn, everything is foreseen. Fire, explosion, destruction are no longer the imaginary alternative to this type of building. It is implosion that is the form of abolishing the 'quaternary' world, both cybernetic and combinatory.

Subversion, violent destruction is what corresponds to a mode of production. To a universe of networks, of combinatory theory, and of flow correspond reversal and implosion.

The same for institutions, the state, power, etc. The dream of seeing all that explode by dint of contradictions is precisely nothing but a dream. What is produced in reality is that the institutions implode of themselves, by dint of ramifications, feedback, overdeveloped control circuits. *Power implodes*, this is its current mode of disappearance.

Such is the case for the city. Fires, war, plague, revolutions, criminal marginality, catastrophes: the whole problematic of the anticity, of the negativity internal or external to the city, has some archaic relation to its true mode of annihilation.

Even the scenario of the underground city – the Chinese version of the burial of structures – is naive. The city does not repeat itself any longer according to a schema of *reproduction* still dependent on the general schema of production, or according to a schema of resemblance still dependent on a schema of representation. (That is how one still restored after the Second World War.) The city no longer revives, even deep down – it is remade starting from a sort of genetic code that makes it possible to repeat it indefinitely starting with an accumulated cybernetic memory. Gone even the Borgesian utopia, of the map coextensive with the territory and doubling it in its entirety: today the simulacrum no longer goes by way of the double and of duplication, but by way of genetic miniaturization. End of representation and implosion, there also, of the whole space in an infinitesimal memory, which forgets nothing, and which belongs to no one. Simulation of an immanent, increasingly dense, irreversible order, one that is potentially saturated and that will never again witness the liberating explosion.

We *were* a culture of liberating violence (rationality). Whether it be that of capital, of the liberation of productive forces, of the irreversible extension of the field of reason and of the field of value, of the conquered and colonized space including the universal – whether it be that of the revolution, which anticipates the future forms of the social and of the energy of the social – the schema is the same: that of an expanding sphere, whether through slow or violent phases, that of a liberated energy – the imaginary of radiation.

The violence that accompanies it is that of a wider world: it is that of production. This violence is dialectical, energetic, cathartic. It is the one we have learned to analyze and that is familiar to us: that which traces the paths of the social and which leads to the saturation of the whole field of the social. It is a violence that is *determined*, analytical, liberating.

A whole other violence appears today, which we no longer know how to analyze, because it escapes the traditional schema of explosive violence: *implosive* violence that no longer results from the extension of a system, but from its saturation and its retraction, as is the case for physical stellar systems. A violence that follows an inordinate densification of the social, the state of an overregulated system, a network (of knowledge, information, power) that is overencumbered, and of a hypertrophic control investing all the interstitial pathways.

This violence is unintelligible to us because our whole imaginary has as its axis the logic of expanding systems. It is indecipherable because undetermined. Perhaps it no longer even comes from the schema of indeterminacy. Because the aleatory models that have taken over from classical models of determination and causality are not fundamentally different. They translate the passage of defined systems of expansion to systems of production and expansion on all levels – in a star or in a rhizome, it doesn't matter – all the philosophies of the release of energy, of the irradiation of intensities and of the molecularization of desire go in the same direction, that of a saturation as far as the interstitial and the infinity of networks. The difference from the molar to the molecular is only a modulation, the last perhaps, in the fundamental energetic process of expanding systems.

Something else if we move from a millennial phase of the liberation and disconnection of energies to a phase of implosion, after a kind of maximum radiation (see Bataille's concepts of loss and expenditure in this sense, and the solar myth of an inexhaustible radiation, on which he founds his sumptuary anthropology: it is the last explosive and radiating myth of our philosophy, the last fire of artifice of a fundamentally general economy, but this no longer has any meaning for us), to a phase of the *reversion of the social* – gigantic reversion of a field once the point of saturation is reached. The stellar systems also do not cease to exist once their radiating energy is dissipated: they implode according to a process that is at first slow, and then progressively accelerates – they contract at a fabulous speed, and become involutive systems, which absorb all the surrounding energies, so that they become black holes where the world as we know it, as radiation and indefinite energy potential, is abolished.

Perhaps the great metropolises – certainly these if this hypothesis has any meaning – have become sites of implosion in this sense, sites of the absorption and reabsorption of the social itself whose golden age, contemporaneous with the double concept of capital and revolution, is doubtless past. The social involutes slowly or brutally, in a field of inertia, which already envelops the political. (The opposite energy?) One must stop oneself from taking implosion for a negative process – inert, regressive – like the one language imposes on us by exalting the opposite terms of evolution, of revolution. Implosion is a process specific to incalculable consequences. May 1968 was without a doubt the first implosive episode, that is to say contrary to its rewriting in terms of revolutionary prosopopeia, a first violent reaction to the saturation of the social, a retraction, a challenge to the hegemony of the social, in contradiction, moreover, to the ideology of the participants themselves, who thought they were going further into the social – such is the imaginary that still dominates us – and moreover a good part of the events of 1968 were still able to come from that revolutionary dynamic and explosive violence, but something else began at the same time there: the violent involution of the social, determined on that score, and the consecutive and sudden implosion of power, in a brief moment of time, but that never stopped afterward – fundamentally it is that which continues, the implosion, of the social, of institutions, of power – and not at all an unlocatable revolutionary dynamic. On the contrary, revolution itself, the idea of revolution also implodes, and this implosion carries weightier consequences than the revolution itself.

Certainly, since 1968, and thanks to 1968, the social, like the desert, grows – participation, management, generalized self-management, etc. – but at the same time it comes close in multiple places, more numerous than in 1968, to its disaffection and to its total reversion. Slow seism, intelligible to historical reason.

Notes

1. Still something else annihilates the cultural project of Beaubourg: the masses themselves also flood in to take pleasure in it (we will return to this later).
2. In relation to this critical mass, and to its radical understanding of Beaubourg, how derisory seems the demonstration of the students from Vincennes the evening of its inauguration!

CHAPTER SIX

Please Follow Me

In 1983 a book of photographs and text by Sophie Calle and Jean Baudrillard entitled *Suite Venitienne* was published by Editions de l'Etoile and Cahiers du Cinema in Paris. The genesis of the book is a strange story. In 1979 the French photographer Sophie Calle had invited twenty-eight friends, neighbours and strangers to sleep in her bed one after the other for a week while she photographed them and wrote notes. Subsequently Calle followed strangers around on the streets of Paris without their knowledge, photographing them for some months. In February 1980 she went to Venice to follow one of these strangers who was going to the city. She again kept notes in a diary and photographed the stranger and the streets of the city. The book consists of the Calle diary and her black and white photographs in the first part and Baudrillard's essay in part two, entitled *Please Follow Me*. The English translation of Baudrillard by Dany Barash and Danny Hatfield published by the small Seattle-based independent outfit, Bay Press, is the extract published here. Baudrillard's interest in photography was consistent from at least the early 1960s and he frequently wrote about photography in his books, but his own production of photography can be dated from the mid 1980s until the time of his death. He began producing photography in earnest shortly after his collaboration with Sophie Calle was published. Frequently his own photographs concentrated on rooms and streets and were not unlike the Calle photographs in the book extracted here. His work has been compared to the understated photography of fellow countryman Henri Cartier-Bresson. Photography seemed to be the one art form he regarded differently from the others and his critical poetics of the modern object are in many ways best exemplified in his photographic output. In his production and eventually public exhibition of his own photographs,

Baudrillard became in the eyes of critics and contemporary cultural commentatators no longer a 'sociologist' or a 'philosopher' but an 'artist'.

'Please Follow Me', from *Please Follow Me*, in *Suite Venitienne*, by Sophie Calle, trans. Dany Barash and Danny Hatfield, Seattle, WA: Bay Press, 1988.

A strange arrogance compels us not only to possess the other, but also to penetrate his secret, not only to be desired by him, but to be fatal to him, too. The sensuality of behind-the-scenes power: the art of making the other disappear. That requires an entire ritual.

First, following people at random on the street for one hour, two hours, in brief, unordered sequences – the idea that people's lives are haphazard paths that have no meaning and lead nowhere and which, for that very reason, are 'curious' (fascinating, but undoubtedly curious of you as well).

The other's tracks are used in such a way as to distance you from yourself. You exist only in the trace of the other, but without his being aware of it; in fact, you follow your own tracks almost without knowing it yourself. Therefore, it is not to discover something about the other or where he's heading – nor is it 'drifting' in search of the random path: All of this, which corresponds to various contemporary ideologies, is not particularly seductive. And yet this experience is entirely a process of seduction.

You seduce yourself by being absent, by being no more than a mirror for the other who is unaware – as with Kierkegaard's mirror, hanging on the opposite wall: The young girl doesn't think of it, but the mirror does. You seduce yourself into the other's destiny, the double of his path, which, for him, has meaning, but when repeated, does not. *It's as if someone behind him knew that he was going nowhere* – it is in some way robbing him of his objective: seducing him. The cunning demon of seduction slips between him and himself, between you and him. This is so powerful that people can often sense they are being followed, through some sort of intuition that something has penetrated their space, altering its curvature – a feeling of being reflected without knowing it.

One day Sophie decides to add another dimension to this 'experience.' She learns that someone she barely knows is traveling to Venice. She decides to follow him throughout his trip. Arriving in Venice, she telephones a hundred hotels and ends up locating the one where he is staying. She convinces the owner of the house across the street to let her use a window, so she can watch this man's comings and goings (he is there on vacation). She has a camera, and at every opportunity, she photographs him, the places he has been, and the places he has photographed. She expects nothing of him; she does not want to know him. She does not consider him to be particularly attractive.

    It is carnival time in Venice. As he might recognize her, she dons a blond wig to cover her dark hair. She puts on make-up; she disguises herself. But carnival pleasures do not interest her; following him is her only concern. At great effort she spends fourteen days on his trail. She learns his plans by questioning people in shops he has visited. She even discovers the departure time of his train back to Paris so that, having taken a different train, she's able to wait for him and take a last picture of him as he disembarks.

Did she secretly desire that he kill her or, finding this pursuit intolerable (especially, since she wasn't consciously expecting anything, least of all a sexual adventure), that he throw himself upon her to do her violence – or that, turning toward her as Orpheus bringing Eurydice back from Hell, he make her suddenly disappear? Did she simply wish to assume his destiny, or that he assume hers? This game, as any other game, had its basic rule: Nothing was to happen, not one event that might establish any contact or relationship between them. This is the price of seduction. The secret must not be broken, at the risk of the story's falling into banality.

Certainly there is something murderous in the situation for the one who is followed. He can feel resentful and victimized. But that is not Sophie's object (even if that notion had taken shape over the course of hours and days – she is also taking a risk: the other might turn the situation to his own advantage and, having sensed the strategem, drag her into the destiny of his choice – he is not a victim; he has, after all, as much power as she does). No, murder is more subtle: It consists of following someone step by step, of *erasing his traces* along the way, and no one can live without traces. If you leave no traces, or if someone takes it upon himself to wipe them out, you are as good as dead. That's what makes anyone turn around after awhile when being followed. Even without warning or clues, he will have some presentiment of this black magic of erased traces, the sorcery that surrounds him. The powerful blond figure behind the scenes leaves no traces as she follows him: She has lost herself in the other's traces. But she steals his traces. She photographs him. She photographs him continuously. Here the photography does not have the voyeur's or archivist's perverse function. It simply says: Here, at that time, at that place, in that light, there was someone. And it also says, at the same time: There was no reason to be there, at that place, at that moment – indeed, there was no one there – I who followed him, I can assure you that no one was there. These are not souvenir snapshots of a presence, but rather shots of an absence, the absence of the followed, that of the follower, that of their reciprocal absence.

'Follow me, then,' she was told, 'I am more interesting to follow than the housewife on the corner.' But that is a misconception and confuses primary interest with the aesthetic intensity of seduction. It does no good to discover, while shadowing someone, that he has, for instance, a double life, save to heighten curiosity – what's important is that *it is the shadowing in itself that is the other's double life*. To shadow another is to give him, in fact, a double life, a parallel existence. Any commonplace existence can be transfigured (without one's knowledge), any exceptional existence can be made commonplace. It is this effect of doubling that makes the object surreal in its banality and weaves around it the strange (eventually dangerous?) web of seduction.

'The Big Sleep'[1] is of the same inspiration: to draw the other (or the others) into an arbitrary, inexplicable game that does not even have – above all does not have – the excuse of sex (for which the bed is the spontaneous invitation). To follow someone, but not to approach him, to make people sleep in one's bed, but without sleeping with them: still the same displacement, the same slight *clinamen* (what a wonderful word for the bed, precisely!), which is the characteristic of seduction and which, for this very reason, few people can resist. The most extraordinary aspect of 'The Big Sleep' was the ease with which people allowed themselves to be convinced, consenting to this enigmatic project that normally would have provoked immediate resistance. And not only aesthetes accustomed to the delights of stylish little 'happenings,' no, but also the apprentice baker on the corner, the baby-sitter, etc. Either people are truly gullible (fascinating hypothesis, but not too appealing), or else one must think that it is by soliciting them in the strangest, the most preposterous way, that they are seduced most easily. Indeed they want to be seduced, that is to say not solicited within their raison d'être, but *drawn outside of their raison d'être*, and the same people who most obstinately resist justifiable, reasonable, explicit requests (requests for help, requests for opinion, affective and psychological requests) are prepared to play the arbitrary and absurd game of seduction. We are, in the end, secretly flattered that something is asked or even demanded of us for no reason, or contrary to reason: It spares us the commonplace and honors us in a more profound complicity. It is on this level that the seduction is played out, and rightfully so: There are few people in whom this basic reflex, this spontaneous response to the challenge of irrationality, has been destroyed by the habits of reason.

It is to the unknown that one yields most impulsively; it is toward the unknown that one feels the most total, the most instinctive obligation. That is one of the rules of the game and part of its arbitrary nature, which alone inflames the passions. The unknown man who is followed or the unknown woman who invites you to sleep over is like a sentence that surprises you, like the illogical act that makes you laugh – one of those things that Canetti described as 'effective because they are unexpected.' We have no reservations about them, we encourage them, we rush toward them with a momentum equal to that with which in other circumstances we would oppose them.

The secret of this enigmatic solicitation, in both 'The Big Sleep,' and 'The Shadowing,' during which Sophie *never* encounters refusals or indifference – everyone helps her in her improbable project, without even asking why – is that of a double, symbolic obligation.

A challenge involves the overwhelming necessity of meeting it. One cannot opt not to respond to a challenge, but one can very well not respond to a request. And yet, if you ask someone to come and lie down in your bed, *to sleep there*, or if you candidly reveal that you have traveled very far to this foreign city in search of a friend whose address you don't know, you have taken a gamble: Either the other person challenges your folly (at the risk of seeming niggardly and cowardly), or he enters into the game according to the same rules, that is, for no reason. Therefore, it is necessary that Sophie, herself, have *no* reason; that her overture make no sense, in order to have a chance of success in this sphere of strangeness, absurd complicity, fatal consent. We are tired of solidarity, contracts, and exchange. We are very willing to consent to anything, provided it be absurd – we are very willing to submit ourselves to anything, as long as the request is irrational. It is because Sophie, herself, submits to an absurd task, because she prostitutes herself, as it were, to a senseless enterprise that requires more patience, servitude, boredom, and energy than any amorous passion, that she effortlessly obtains from others this irrational complicity that no consideration for her well-being could ever have inspired. It is to the challenge that the people respond; it is the absurd that they obey.

The other source of passion, which is in a way the opposite of challenge, is the secret wish to submit oneself blindly to the other's desire. When Sophie invites people to sleep eight hours at her home, she removes herself from her own life and installs others in it. That also secretly means, 'I have no motive, nothing compels me, I will get nothing from it, and you will not profit by it, but for eight hours, I will take charge of your life.' For eight hours you are released from your life and from the *responsibility of sleeping* (one can hardly imagine what burden the least of our actions, including that of relaxing, becomes for each of us as soon as we have to assume it, be answerable for it before ourselves: an incredible servitude, not willful, but a *servitude of the will*). Blessed, beneficent is anything that takes us to the unwilled, into dreamlike disengagement, Rimbaud would say, from our own life. In taking charge of others' lives, even for a stipulated and limited time, Sophie finds herself, as well, released from her own – a marvelous benefit on both sides, and by marvelous I mean a strange benefit, a reflection of another world where we do not have to attend to our own desire, our own sleep, our own will, but to that or those of others – with another attending to yours, etc., in a perfectly unalienated succession since we would no longer be busy stealing each other's time, sleep, freedom, life.

And so it happens that, in the staging of sleep by proxy (vicarious sleep), people's dreams, their boredom, their eventual uneasiness, their sexual fantasies belong to her, to Sophie, in a sense, but in a slight and seductive sense. They do not belong to her on her own terms, but rather because of the game and by the rules of the game. Convention saves all, the artificial pact on something as natural as sleep, the pact that is perfectly ritual and ceremonial, not perverse, spares us the obscenity (psychological or aesthetic) of manipulating and appropriating someone else's desire. It is never necessary to claim someone else's desire, to win him or to deceive him. One need only know how to be his shadow.

The scenario is the same in 'The Shadowing.' To follow the other is to take charge of his itinerary; it is to watch over his life without him knowing it. It is to play the mythical role of the shadow, which, traditionally, follows you and protects you from the sun – the man without a shadow is exposed to the violence of a life without mediation – it is to relieve him of that existential burden, the responsibility for his own life. Simultaneously, she who follows is herself relieved of responsibility for her own life as she follows blindly in the footsteps of the other. Again, a wonderful reciprocity exists in the cancellation of each existence, in the cancellation of each subject's tenuous position as a subject. Following the other, one replaces him, exchanges lives, passions, wills, transforms oneself in the other's stead. It is perhaps the only way man can finally fulfill himself. An ironic way but all the more certain.

In comparison with our ideas of liberation, of individual autonomy, which exhaust themselves running after their own shadow (is there genuine desire for all of this?), how much more subtle, more amazing, more discreet and arrogant all at once is the idea still alive in the practical philosophy of the Far East, that someone else looks after your life. Someone else anticipates it, accomplishes it, fulfills it, according to a pact whereby you renounce responsibility for something that does not 'belong' to you anyway, which is really more easy to enjoy without constant direction from the will.

Besides, nothing prevents you from taking charge of someone else's life – something people are often more gifted at than taking care of their own – and then from one to the other, each one relieved from the servitude of living, truly free and exposed, not to his own delirium anymore, but only to the ritual or amorous intercession of the other. In the end it is no more than a service, and it is certainly no more absurd to envision things this way than to rely on the decisions of a State, of a lottery . . . or of one's own will.

It is true that Venice serves as an unconscious magnet for this kind of problem. The city is built like a trap, a maze, a labyrinth that inevitably, however fortuitously, brings back people to the same points, over the same bridges, onto the same plazas, along the same quays. By the nature of things, everyone is followed in Venice; everyone runs into each other, everyone recognizes each other (hence the quite reasonable hope of finding someone there without any directions). Venice is an immense palace in which corridors and mirrors direct a ritual traffic. Perfectly opposed to the extensive, unlimited city, Venice has no equal in the inverse extreme except New York (and sometimes, curiously, in this inverse extreme their charms bear a certain resemblance).

Better yet, the only way not to meet someone in Venice is to follow him from a distance and not lose sight of him. This is why the violent moments of the narrative, the dramatic moments, are those where the followed person, seized by a sudden inspiration, as they say, turns around, making an about-face like a cornered beast. The system reverses itself immediately, and the follower becomes the followed, for there are no side exits in Venice, and it is impossible to meet without recognizing each other. Who could hope to get out of this enclosed, insular, immersed, dead-ended city, even by following someone to the end. Never will he lead you to the outside, like the Pied Piper of Hamelin; he will always take you back to the center, by prodigious circumvolutions. And the only dramatic event in this circular maze is the unexpected about-face (a distant reminder of Orpheus and Eurydice), which risks shattering the fantastic illusion of a double life.

But, of course, shadowing implies this surprise. The possibility of reversal is necessary to it. One must follow in order to be followed, photograph in order to be photographed, wear a mask to be unmasked, appear in order to disappear, guess one's intentions in order to have your own guessed – all of that is Venice, but it is also the most profound, symbolic requirement. One has to be discovered. All of Sophie's anguish and desire during those days in Venice turn on this violent illumination; at the same time she attempts to avoid it. When you are unmasked, everything is there. And indeed the game stops there, on the Campo di S.S. Giovanni e Paolo, when he recognizes her. 'I cannot follow him anymore. He must be worried, wondering if I am there, behind him – now he thinks of me – but I will be on his trail. Differently.'

Consider one of life's original situations: that of a 'hide'n seek' game. What a thrill to be hidden while someone's looking for you, what a delightful fright to be found, but what a panic when, because you are too well hidden, the others give up looking for you after a while and leave. If you hide too well, the others forget you. You are forced to come out on your own when they don't want you anymore. That is hard to take. It's like turning too fine a phrase, so subtle that you are reduced to explaining it. Nothing is sadder than having to beg for existence and returning naked among the others. *Therefore, it's better not to know how to play too well*; it's better to know how to let others unmask you and to endure the rule of the game. Not too fast, not too late.

One shouldn't say, 'God exists, I met him,' but rather 'God exists, I followed him.' The encounter is always too true, too excessive, indiscreet. Note how people who meet acknowledge each other endlessly; note how people in love keep saying how much they love each other. Are they so sure of themselves? Is it because the meeting is a proof of existence? Quite different is the secret (and following someone is equivalent to the secret in the space of a city, as allusion is equivalent to the secret in speech, or the déjà-vu, the déjà-vecu is equivalent to the secret in time), which is a blind passion: She follows the other with eyes closed and doesn't want him to recognize her. Without having really chosen her subject, she exercises the fatal right of following him. Without ever having approached him, she knows him better than anyone. She can abandon him, certain to find him again the next day according to a kind of astral conjunction (there is a fine moment at the end of the day when, weary of the battle, she abandons her shadowing; and yet she knows that she will pick it up again the next day, one way or another, because the city is curved, because time is curved, but above all because the partner cannot escape the game – besides, chance led him very close to Sophie's starting point and takes him back to it every night).

There is a mystery in the tactile closeness of the people circulating between the walls of the narrow streets of Venice. The mixture of promiscuity and discretion is greater there than anywhere else (it is multiplied in the masks and mirrors game at carnival time). And there is a parallel mystery in the tactile distance kept between she who follows and he who is followed. Minimal distance at times, a dual relationship in space, a relationship of initiation that yields to all of the subject's whims (that is what we love in detective stories), a blind loyalty, but from a distance, and with no possible resolution. And yet, if one takes the time to think about it, all the secrecy of a life gathers itself in this metaphor of closed eyes, all our power is in what we can follow, in what we can attain with eyes closed. The mask, the disguise, the detection preserve that power – and at times the streets of a city such as Venice. How many pathways would you recognize with your eyes closed? How many faces or bodies would you recognize in caressing them with your eyes closed? And from whom would you accept anything with your eyes closed? And you, have you already closed your eyes on your own image, behaved blindly, lost your way blindly, loved blindly, and sensed in the darkness the tactile detour of the streets, the tactile detour of ideas?

Everything is there; one must never come into contact, one must follow, one must never love, one must be closer to the other than his own shadow. And one must vanish into the background before the other turns around.

Everything is at the vanishing point. Everything happens as the result of an unwarranted predestination: Why him, why Venice, why follow him? The very blindness with which this plan is carried out (which is the equivalent of an order received from elsewhere: You shall follow me for fourteen days – but this order was not given by anyone) already corresponds to that blinding effect and disappearance of will characteristic of the vanishing point. And starting there, everything converges into the same effect: The shadowing, Venice, the photography, all this is being played out beyond the vanishing point. The shadowing makes the other vanish into the consciousness of the one who follows him, into the traces that he unknowingly leaves behind – Venice is a vanished city, where all history has already disappeared and where one enters alive into the disappearance – and photography is itself an art of disappearance, which captures the other vanished in front of the lens, which preserves him vanished on film, which, unlike a gaze, saves nothing of the other but his vanished presence (according to Barthes, it's not so much the death that one reads there, but rather the vanishing. Death is the source of moral fright, vanishing is alone the source of a 'seductive' aesthetic of disappearance).

It is not by chance, either, that 'The Big Sleep' gathers together sleep – in itself a vanishing of consciousness – photography, and a succession of people who sleep and cross paths in the apartment: at once appearing then disappearing, one into another. One must add to this the vanishing of defenses, of resistance, that sort of hypnosis under which the people acquiesce to the plan for its very improbability.

Imagine a swooning woman: Nothing is more beautiful, since swooning is at once the experience of overwhelming pleasure and the escape from pleasure, a seduction and an escape from seduction.

Please follow me.

Note

1. In April 1979, Sophie Calle invited twenty-eight people (friends, neighbors, strangers) to sleep in her bed, each for eight hours, one after another, over the period of one week. She studied her sleeping guests, photographing them every hour and taking copious notes. The photographic record of this project, which Baudrillard calls 'The Big Sleep,' has been exhibited in Paris, Geneva, and New York City under the title 'The Sleepers.'

CHAPTER SEVEN

The Evil Demon of Images

In July 1984 Baudrillard gave the inaugural Maria Kuttna Memorial Lecture at the University of Sydney in Australia, a lecture series which was designed to present film-makers and theorists of cinema to the Australian public. Baudrillard had an enduring love of film and was a long-time fan of regularly going to the cinema. Kuttna had been a film critic and Baudrillard cites films such as *The China Syndrome* and *The Last Picture Show* in his lecture but it was his theorising of the moving image which was most in demand. Baudrillard's influence in Australia, and especially on the discipline of Australian Cultural Studies, in the 1980s was quite considerable. Journals such as *Art and Text* and *On the Beach* featured his writing translated from the French and in the same month as his film lecture the international conference 'Futur*Fall: Excursions into Postmodernity' took place in Sydney catapulting his ideas around the world and solidifying Baudrillard's growing international reputation for being the pre-eminent theorist of 'the postmodern' and the major global commentator on postmodernism's supposed pervasive relationship to the mass media and contemporary culture of the era. The extract here is the full text of the lecture, translated from the French by Paul Patton and Paul Foss. The Power Institute of Fine Arts in Sydney published both the proceedings of the 'Futur*Fall' conference and (in 1987) this translation of the text of the Memorial Lecture, together with an introduction by Alan Cholodenko and a revealing interview by Cholodenko and his colleagues with Baudrillard about the subject matter of 'The Evil Demon of Images' which was the English translation of the title of the talk. In the interview Baudrillard admitted as usual to the influence of Nietzsche but unusually also to 'the Manichean element in my work', a revealing insight into the source of much of Baudrillard's philosophy of the real and the illusory, which is so often mistakenly aligned with the quite different tradition of the relativism of postmodernism.

'The Evil Demon of Images', from *The Evil Demon of Images*, trans. Paul Patton and Paul Foss, Sydney: Power Institute of Fine Arts, 1987.

A propos the cinema and images in general (media images, technological images), I would like to conjure up the perversity of the relation between the image and its referent, the supposed real; the virtual and irreversible confusion of the sphere of images and the sphere of a reality whose nature we are less and less able to grasp. There are many modalities of this absorption, this confusion, this diabolical seduction of images. Above all, it is the reference principle of images which must be doubted, this strategy by means of which they always appear to refer to a real world, to real objects, and to reproduce something which is logically and chronlogically anterior to themselves. None of this is true. As simulacra, images precede the real to the extent that they invert the causal and logical order of the real and its reproduction. Benjamin, in his essay 'The Work of Art in the Age of Mechanical Reproduction', already pointed out strongly this modern revolution in the order of production (of reality, of meaning) by the precession, the anticipation of its reproduction.

It is precisely when it appears most truthful, most faithful and most in conformity to reality that the image is most diabolical — and our technical images, whether they be from photography, cinema or television, are in the overwhelming majority much more 'figurative', 'realist', than all the images from past cultures. It is in its resemblance, not only analogical but technological, that the image is most immoral and most perverse.

The appearance of the mirror already introduced into the world of perception an ironical effect of *trompe-l'oeil*, and we know what malefice was attached to the appearance of doubles. But this is also true of all the images which surround us: in general, they are analysed according to their value as representations, as media of presence and meaning. The immense majority of present day photographic, cinematic and television images are thought to bear witness to the world with a naive resemblance and a touching fidelity. We have spontaneous confidence in their realism. We are wrong. They only seem to resemble things, to resemble reality, events, faces. Or rather, they really do conform, but their conformity itself is diabolical.

We can find a sociological, historical and political equivalent to this diabolical conformity, to this evil demon of conformity, in the modern behaviour of the masses who are also very good at complying with the models offered to them, who are very good at reflecting the objectives imposed on them, thereby absorbing and annihilating them. There is in this conformity a force of seduction in the literal sense of the word, a force of diversion, distortion, capture and ironic fascination. There is a kind of fatal strategy of conformity.

A recent example may be found in Woody Allen's film, *Zelig*: in trying to be oneself, to cultivate difference and originality, one ends up resembling everyone and no longer seducing anyone. This is the logic of present-day psychological conformity. Zelig, on the other hand, is launched on an adventure of total seduction, in an involuntary strategy of global seduction: he begins to resemble everything which approaches him, everything which surrounds him. Nor is this the mimetic violence of defiance or parody, it is the mimetic non-violence of seduction. To begin to resemble the other, to take on their appearance, is to seduce them, since it is to make them enter the realm of metamorphosis despite themselves.

This seductive force, this fatal strategy, is a kind of animal genie or talent — not simply that of the chameleon, which is only its anecdotal form. It is not the conformism of animals which delights us; on the contrary, animals are never conformist, they are seductive, they always appear to result from a metamorphosis. Precisely because they are not individuals, they pose the enigma of their resemblance. If an animal knows how to conform, it is not to its own being, its own individuality (banal strategy), but to appearances in the world. This is what Zelig does too with his animal genie — he is polymorphous (but not perverse); he is incapable of functional adaptation to contexts, which is true conformism, our conformism, but able to seduce by the *play* of resemblance. Savages do no less when they put on the successive masks of their gods, when they 'become' their successive divinities – this is also to seduce them. It is of course against this strategy of seduction that psychiatry struggles, and it is what gives rise to the magical infatuation of the crowds for Zelig (in German, *Selig* means 'blessed').

The remarkable thing about this film is that it leads astray all possible interpretations. There is thus also a seduction of interpretation, with the complicity of certain intellectuals, as well as a polymorphous montage technique which allows it to ironically adapt to all possibilities.

More generally, the image is interesting not only in its role as reflection, mirror, representation of, or counterpart to, the real, but also when it begins to contaminate reality and to model it, when it only conforms to reality the better to distort it, or better still: when it appropriates reality for its own ends, when it anticipates it to the point that the real no longer has time to be produced as such.

It is not only daily life which has become cinematographic and televisual, but war as well. It has been said that war is the continuation of politics by other means; we can also say that images, media images, are the continuation of war by other means. Take *Apocalypse Now*. Coppola made his film the same way the Americans conducted the war – in this sense, it is the best possible testimony – with the same exaggeration, the same excessive means, the same monstrous candour . . . and the same success. War as a trip, a technological and psychedelic fantasy; war as a succession of special effects, the war become film well before it was shot; war replaced by technological testing. For the Americans, it was above all the latter: a test site, an enormous field on which to test their weapons, their methods, their power.

Coppola does the same thing: he tests the power of intervention of cinema, tests the impact of cinema become a vast machine of special effects. In this sense his film is very much the prolongation of war by other means, the completion of that incomplete war, its apotheosis. War becomes film, film becomes war, the two united by their mutual overflow of technology.

The real war was conducted by Coppola in the manner of Westmoreland. Leaving aside the clever irony of napalming Philippino forests and villages to recreate the hell of South Vietnam, everything is replayed, begun again through cinema: the Molochian joy of the shoot, the sacrificial joy of so many millions spent, of such a holocaust of means, of so many difficulties, and the dazzling paranoia in the mind of the creator who, from the beginning, conceived this film as a *world* historical event for which the Vietnam war would have been no more than a pretext, would ultimately not have existed – and we cannot deny it: 'in itself' the Vietnam war never happened, perhaps it was only a dream, a baroque dream of napalm and the tropics, a psychotropic dream in which the issue was not politics or victory but the sacrificial, excessive deployment of a power already filming itself as it unfolds, perhaps expecting nothing more than consecration by a superfilm, which perfects the war's function as a mass spectacle.

No real distance, no critical direction, no desire for any 'raised consciousness' in relation to the war: in a sense this is the brutal quality of the film, not to be undermined by any anti-war moral psychology. Coppola may very well dress up his helicopter captain in a cavalry hat and have him wipe out a Vietnamese village to the sound of Wagner – these are not critical, distant signs; they are immersed in the machinery, part of the special effect. Coppola makes films in the same manner, with the same nostalgic megalomania, with the same non-signifying fury, the same magnified Punch and Judy effect. One can ask, how is such a horror possible (not the war, properly speaking, but that of the film)? But there is no response, no possible judgement. The Vietnam war and the film are cut from the same cloth, nothing separates them: this film is part of the war. If the Americans (apparently) lost the other, they have certainly won this one. *Apocalypse Now* is a global victory. It has a cinematographic power equal and superior to that of the military and industrial complexes, of the Pentagon and governments. Nothing is understood in relation to war or cinema (at least the latter) unless one has grasped this indistinguishability – which is not the ideological or moral indistinguishability of good and evil, but that of the reversibility of destruction and production, of the immanence of something in its very revolution, of the organic metabolism of every technology, from carpet bombing to film stock . . .

As for the anticipation of reality by images, the precession of images and media in relation to events, such that the connection between cause and effect becomes scrambled and it becomes impossible to tell which is the effect of the other – what better example than the nuclear accident at Harrisburg, a 'real' incident which happened just after the release of *The China Syndrome*? This film is a fine example of the supremacy of the televised event over the nuclear event which itself remains improbable and in some sense imaginary.

Moreover, the film unintentionally shows this: it is the intrusion of TV into the reactor which as it were triggers the nuclear incident – because it is the anticipation and model of it in the day-to-day world: telefission of the real and of the real world – because TV and information in general are a kind of catastrophe in René Thom's formal, topological sense: a radical, qualitative change in an entire system. Or rather, TV and nuclear power are of the same kind: behind the 'hot' and negentropic concepts of energy and information, they have the same dissuasive force as cold systems. TV is also a nuclear, chain-reactive process, but implosive: it cools and neutralises the meaning and energy of events. Thus, behind the presumed risk of explosion, that is, of hot catastrophe, the nuclear conceals a long, cold catastrophe – the universalisation of a system of dissuasion, of deterrence.

The homology between nuclear power and television can be read directly in the images. Nothing resembles the command and control centre of the reactor more than the TV studios, and the nuclear consoles share the same imaginary as the recording and broadcasting studios. Everything happens between these two poles: the other core, that of the reactor, in principal the real core of the affair, remains concealed from us, like the real; buried and indecipherable, ultimately of no importance. The drama is acted out on the screens and nowhere else.

Harrisburg, Watergate and *Network* form the trilogy of *The China Syndrome* – an inextricable trilogy in which we cannot tell which is the effect or the symptom of the others: is the ideological argument (the Watergate effect) only the symptom of the nuclear (the Harrisburg effect) or the informational model (the *Network* effect)? – is the real (Harrisburg) only the symptom of the imaginary (*Network, The China Syndrome*) or vice versa? Marvellous indistinguishability, ideal constellation of simulation.

The conjunction of *The China Syndrome* and Harrisburg haunts us. But is it so involuntary? Without examining any magical links between simulacrum and reality, it is clear that *The China Syndrome* is not unrelated to the 'real' accident at Harrisburg, not by a causal logic but by those relations of contagion and unspoken analogy which link the real, models and simulacra: the induction of the nuclear incident at Harrisburg by the film corresponds, with disquieting obviousness, to the induction of the incident by TV in the film. A strange precession of a film before the real, the most astonishing we have seen: reality corresponding point by point to the simulacra, even down to the suspensive, incomplete character of the catastrophe, which is essential from the point of view of dissuasion: the real so arranged itself, in the image of the film, as to produce a *simulation* of catastrophe.

It is only a further step, which we should briskly take, to reverse our logical order and see *The China Syndrome* as the real event and Harrisburg its simulacrum. For it is by the same logic that the nuclear reality in the film follows from the television effect and Harrisburg in 'reality' follows from the cinema effect of *The China Syndrome*.

But the latter is not the original prototype of Harrisburg; one is not the simulacrum and the other the reality: there are only simulacra, and Harrisburg is a kind of simulation in the second degree. There is indeed a chain reaction: but *it is not the nuclear chain reaction but that of the simulacra* and of the simulation in which all the energy of the real is effectively engulfed, not in a spectacular nuclear explosion but in a secret and continuous implosion, which is perhaps taking a more deadly turn than all the explosions which presently lull us.

For an explosion is always a promise, it *is* our hope: see how much, in the film as well as at Harrisburg, everyone expects it to go up, that destruction speak its name and deliver us from this unnameable panic, from this invisible nuclear panic of dissuasion. Let the 'core' of the reactor expose at last its glowing power of destruction, let it reassure us as to the admittedly catastrophic presence of energy and gratify us with its spectacle. For the problem is that there is no nuclear spectacle, no spectacle of nuclear energy in itself (Hiroshima is past): it is for this reason that it is rejected – it would be perfectly accepted if it lent itself to spectacle like earlier forms of energy. Parousia of catastrophe: substantial boost to our messianic libido.

But that will never recur. What will happen will never be explosion but implosion. Never again will we see energy in its spectacular and pathetic form – all the romanticism of explosion which had so much charm, since it was also that of revolution – but only the cold energy of simulacra and its distillation in homeopathic doses into the cold systems of information.

What else does the media dream of if not raising up events by its very presence? Everyone deplores it, but everyone is secretly fascinated by this eventuality. Such is the logic of simulacra: no longer divine predestination, but the precession of models, which is no less inexorable. And it is for this reason that events no longer have any meaning: not because they are insignificant in themselves, but because they have been preceded by models with which their own process can only coincide.

For some time now, in the dialectical relation between reality and images (that is, the relation that we wish to believe dialectical, readable from the real to the image and vice versa), the image has taken over and imposed its own immanent ephemeral logic; an immoral logic without depth, beyond good and evil, beyond truth and falsity; a logic of the extermination of its own referent, a logic of the implosion of meaning in which the message disappears on the horizon of the medium. In this regard, we all remain incredibly naive: we always look for a good usage of the image, that is to say a moral, meaningful, pedagogic or informational usage, without seeing that the image in a sense revolts against this good usage, that it is the conductor neither of meaning nor good intentions, but on the contrary of an implosion, a denegation of meaning (of events, history, memory, etc.). I am reminded of *Holocaust*, the television series on the concentration camps . . .

Forgetting the extermination is part of the extermination itself. That forgetting, however, is still too dangerous and must be replaced by an artificial memory (everywhere, today, it is artificial memories which obliterate people's memories, which obliterate people from memory). This artificial memory replays the extermination – but too late for it to profoundly unsettle anything, and above all it does so via a medium which is itself cold, radiating oblivion, dissuasion and extermination in an even more systematic manner, if this is possible, than the camps themselves. TV, the veritable final solution to the historicity of every event. The Jews are recycled not through the crematory ovens or the gas chambers but through the sound track and images, through the cathode tube and the micro-chip. Forgetting, annihilation thereby achieves at last an aesthetic dimension – nostalgia gives them their final finish.

Henceforth, 'everyone knows', everyone has trembled before the extermination – a sure sign that 'it' will never happen again. But in effect what is thus exorcised so cheaply, at the cost of a few tears, will never recur because it is presently happening in the very form through which it is denounced, through the very medium of this supposed exorcism: television. The same process of forgetting, of liquidation, of extermination, the same annihilation of memories and of history, the same inverse, implosive radiation, the same absorption without trace, the same black hole as Auschwitz. They want us to believe that TV will remove the mortgage of Auschwitz by raising collective consciousness, whereas it is the perpetuation of it in a different guise, under the auspices not of a *site* of annihilation but a *medium* of dissuasion.

What everyone fails to understand is that *Holocaust* is above all (and exclusively) a *televised* event or rather object (McLuhan's fundamental rule which must not be forgotten). That is to say, it is an attempt to reheat a *cold* historical event – tragic but cold, the first great event of cold systems, those cooling systems of dissuasion and extermination which were subsequently deployed in other forms (including the Cold War, etc.) and in relation to the cold masses (the Jews no longer even concerned by their own death, eventually self-managing it, no longer even masses in revolt: dissuaded unto death, dissuaded even of their own death). To reheat this cold event via a cold medium, television, for masses who are themselves cold, who will only find in it the occasion for a tactile chill and a posthumous emotion, a dissuasive shiver, which sends them into oblivion with a kind of aesthetic good faith.

The cold light of television is inoffensive to the imagination (even that of children) since it no longer carries any imaginary, for the simple reason that *it is no longer an image.*

In this sense the TV image has to be placed in opposition to the cinema, which still carries an intense imaginary. Although it is contaminated more and more by TV, the cinema is still an image – that means not only a screen and a visual form but a myth, something that belongs to the sphere of the double, the phantasm, the mirror, the dream, etc. . . . Nothing of that in the TV image, which doesn't suggest anything and has a magnetic effect. The TV image is only a screen. More than that: a miniaturized terminal located in your head and *you* are the screen and the TV looks at you, goes through you like a magnetic tape – a tape, not an image.

Thus, properly speaking it is *Holocaust* the television film which constitutes the definitive holocaust event. Likewise, with *The Day After* it is not the atomic conflict depicted in the film but the film itself which is the catastrophic event.

This film should inspire a salutary terror, it should dissuade by the spectacle of terror. However, I don't see anything as a result of this film. The slides at the New York Museum of Natural History move me much more profoundly: you can shiver at the ice age and feel the charm of the prehistoric, but here I feel neither the shiver nor the charm of nuclear power, nor even suspense nor the final blinding flash.

Is it a bad film? Certainly. But isn't it rather that all this is unimaginable? Isn't it rather that, in our imaginary, nuclear conflict is a total event, without appeal and with no tomorrow, whereas here it simply brings about a regression of the human race according to the worst naive stereotypes of savagery? But we already know that state, indeed we have barely left it. Our desire is rather for something which no longer takes place on a human scale, for some anterior or ulterior mystery: what will the earth be like when we are no longer on it? In a word, we dream of our disappearance, and of seeing the world in its inhuman purity (which is precisely not the state of nature).

But these limits, these extremes that we imagine, this catastrophe – can it be metaphorised in images? It is not certain that its mythical evocation is possible, any more than that of our biomolecular destiny or that of the genetic code, which is the other dimension, the corollary of the nuclear. We can no longer be affected by it – proof that we have already been irradiated! Already to our minds the catastrophe is no more than a comic strip. Its filmic projection is only a diversion from the real nuclearisation of our lives. The real nuclear catastrophe has already happened, it happens every day, and this film is part of it. It is *it* which *is* our catastrophe. It does not represent it, it does not evoke it, on the contrary it shows that it has already happened, that it is already here, since it is impossible to imagine.

For all these reasons I do not believe in a pedagogy of images, nor of cinema, nor *a fortiori* in one of television. I do not believe in a dialectic between image and reality, nor therefore, in respect of images, in a pedagogy of message and meaning. The secret of the image (we are still speaking of contemporary, technical images) must not be sought in its differentiation from reality, and hence in its representative value (aesthetic, critical or dialectical), but on the contrary in its 'telescoping' into reality, its short-circuit with reality, and finally, in the implosion of image and reality. For us there is an increasingly definitive lack of differentiation between image and reality which no longer leaves room for representation as such.

This collusion between images and life, between the screen and daily life, can be experienced everyday in the most ordinary manner. Especially in America, not the least charm of which is that even outside the cinemas the whole country is cinematographic. You cross the desert as if in a western; the metropolis is a continual screen of signs and formulae. Life is a travelling shot, a kinetic, cinematic, cinematographic sweep. There is as much pleasure in this as in those Dutch or Italian towns where, upon leaving the museum, you rediscover a town in the very image of the paintings, as if it had stepped out of them. It is a kind of miracle which, even in a banal American way, gives rise to a sort of aesthetic form, to an ideal confusion which transfigures life, as in a dream. Here, cinema does not take on the exceptional form of a work of art, even a brilliant one, but invests the whole of life with a mythical ambience. Here it becomes truly exciting. This is why the idolatry of stars, the cult of Hollywood idols, is not a media pathology but a glorious form of the cinema, its mythical transfiguration, perhaps the last great myth of our modernity. Precisely to the extent that the idol no longer represents anything but reveals itself as a pure, impassioned, contagious image which effaces the difference between the real being and its assumption into the imaginary.

All these considerations are a bit wild, but that is because they correspond to the unrestrained film buff that I am and have always wished to remain – that is in a sense uncultured and fascinated. There is a kind of primal pleasure, of anthropological joy in images, a kind of brute fascination unencumbered by aesthetic, moral, social or political judgements. It is because of this that I suggest they are immoral, and that their fundamental power lies in this immorality.

This brute fascination for images, above and beyond all moral or social determination, is also not that of dreaming or the imaginary, understood in the traditional sense. Other images, such as those in painting, drawing, theatre or architecture, have been better able to make us dream or imagine; other modes of expression as well (undoubtedly language makes us dream better than the image). So there is something more than that which is peculiar to our modern media images: if they fascinate us so much it is not because they are sites of the production of meaning and representation – this would not be new – it is on the contrary because they are sites of the *disappearance* of meaning and representation, sites in which we are caught quite apart from any judgement of reality, thus sites of a fatal strategy of denegation of the real and of the reality principle.

We have arrived at a paradox regarding the image, our images, those which unfurl upon and invade our daily life – images whose proliferation, it should be noted, is potentially infinite, whereas the extension of meaning is always limited precisely by its end, by its finality: from the fact that images ultimately have no finality and proceed by total contiguity, infinitely multiplying themselves according to an irresistible epidemic process which no one today can control, our world has become truly infinite, or rather exponential by means of images. It is caught up in a mad pursuit of images, in an ever greater fascination which is only accentuated by video and digital images. We have thus come to the paradox that these images describe the equal impossibility of the real and of the imaginary.

For us the medium, the image medium, has imposed itself between the real and the imaginary, upsetting the balance between the two, with a kind of fatality which has its own logic. I call this a fatal process in the sense that there is a definitive immanence of the image, without any possible transcendent meaning, without any possible dialectic of history – fatal also in the sense not merely of an exponential, linear unfolding of images and messages but of an exponential enfolding of the medium around itself. The fatality lies in this endless enwrapping of images (literally: without end, without destination) which leaves images no other destiny than images. The same thing happens everywhere today, when production has no destiny apart from production – overdetermination of production by itself – when sex has no destiny other than sex – sexual overdetermination of sexuality. This process may be found everywhere today, for better and for worse. In the absence of rules of the game, things become caught up in their own game: images become more real than the real; cinema itself becomes more cinema than cinema, in a kind of vertigo in which (to return to our initial problem, that of resemblance) it does no more than resemble itself and escape in its own logic, in the very perfection of its own model.

I am thinking of those exact, scrupulous set-pieces such as *Chinatown, The Day of the Condor, Barry Lyndon, 1900, All the President's Men*, the very perfection of which is disturbing. It is as if we were dealing with perfect remakes, with extraordinary montages which belong more to a combinatory process (or mosaic in the McLuhanesque sense), with large photo, kino or historio-synthetic machines, rather than with real films. Let us be clear: their quality is not in question. The problem is rather that they leave us somehow totally indifferent.

Take *The Last Picture Show*. You need only be sufficiently distracted, as I was, to see it as a 1950s original production: a good film of manners and the ambience of small-town America, etc. A slight suspicion: it was a little too good, better adjusted, better than the others, without the sentimental, moral and psychological tics of the films of that period. Astonishment at the discovery that it is a 1970s film, perfectly nostalgic, brand new, retouched, a hyperrealist restitution of a 50s film. There is talk of remaking silent films, doubtless better than those of the period. A whole generation of films is appearing which will be to those we have known what the android is to man: marvellous, flawless artifacts, dazzling simulacra which lack only an imaginary and that particular hallucination which makes cinema what it is. Most of those that we see today (the best) are already of this order. *Barry Lyndon* is the best example: no better has been made, no better will be made, but *what* exactly? Evocation? No, not even evocation but *simulation*. All the toxic radiation has been filtered out, all the ingredients are present in precise doses, not a single mistake.

Cool, cold pleasure which is not even aesthetic properly speaking: functional pleasure, equational pleasure, pleasure of machination. We need only think of Visconti (*The Leopard, Senso*, etc., which recall *Barry Lyndon* in certain respects) in order to grasp the difference, not only in style but in the cinematographic act. With Visconti, there is meaning, history, a sensual rhetoric, dead moments, a passionate game, not only in the historical content but in the direction. None of that with Kubrick, who controls his film like a chessboard, and makes history an operational scenario. Nor does this refer back to the old opposition between finesse and geometry: there meaning was still in play, meaning was at stake. Whereas we are entering into an era of films which no longer have meaning properly speaking, large synthetic machines with variable geometry.

Is there already something of this in Sergio Leone's westerns? Perhaps. All registers tend in this direction. *Chinatown* is the detective story redesigned by laser. It is not really a question of perfection. Technical perfection can *belong* to the meaning, and in this case it is neither nostalgic nor hyperrealist; it is an effect of art. Here, it is an effect of model: it is one of the tactical reference values. In the absence of any real syntax of meaning there are only *tactical* values in a complex whole in which, for example, the CIA as an all-purpose mythological machine, Robert Redford as a polyvalent star, social relations as necessary references to history, and *technical virtuosity as a necessary reference to cinema* are all admirably combined.

Cinema and its trajectory: from the most fantastic or mythical to the realistic and hyperrealistic.

In its present endeavours cinema increasingly approaches, with ever increasing perfection, absolute reality: in its banality, in its veracity, in its starkness, in its tedium, and at the same time in its pretentiousness, in its pretention to be the real, the immediate, the unsignified, which is the maddest of enterprises (in the same way that the pretention of functionalist design to designate, as the highest degree of the object, the form in which it coincides with its function, its use-value, is properly an insane enterprise). No culture has ever had this naive and paranoiac, this puritanical and terrorist vision of signs. Terrorism is always of the real. Simultaneous with this attempt at absolute coincidence with the real, cinema also approaches an absolute coincidence with itself. This is not contradictory: it is the very definition of the hyperreal. Hypotyposis and specularity. Cinema plagiarises and copies itself, remakes its classics, retroactivates its original myths, remakes silent films more perfect than the originals, etc. All this is logical. *Cinema is fascinated by itself as a lost object just as it (and we) are fascinated by the real as a referential in perdition.* Previously there was a living, dialectical, full and dramatic relationship between cinema and the imaginary (that is, novelistic, mythical unreality, even down to the delirious use of its own technique). Today, there is an inverse negative relation between the cinema and reality: it results from the loss of specificity which both have suffered. Cold collage, cool promiscuity, asexual engagement of two cold media which evolve in asymptotic line towards one another: cinema attempting to abolish itself in the absolute of reality, the real already long absorbed in cinematographic (or televised) hyperreality.

CHAPTER EIGHT

The Gulf War: Is It Really Taking Place?

In 1991 the 'first' Gulf War took place. Or did it? In three separate articles, published in part by *Liberation* between January and March of 1991, subsequently put together in extended book form collectively as *La Guerre du Golfe n'a pas eu Lieu* by Editions Galilée in May 1991, Baudrillard seemingly demolished this proposition. There was a storm of protest at Baudrillard's supposed nihilism, relativism, postmodernism, naivety and amorality which had barely died down by the mid 1990s. For instance, Christopher Norris saw Baudrillard as a postmodernist intellectual whose work, especially on the Gulf War, should be shunned and pilloried as part of a growing body of 'uncritical theory'. Many others barely gave it the time of day or merely laughed it out of court. Baudrillard, who had a wicked prankster-like sense of humour, always resented the fact that his work was not taken more seriously. In 1995 the English translation of the book was duly published by Power Publications in Sydney, with no let up in the global vitriolic criticism and howls of derision. The translation was by Paul Patton, veteran follower and translator of Foucault and Baudrillard from the Department of Philosophy at the University of Sydney, who also supplied a fascinating and rigorous introduction to the English edition, essentially defending Baudrillard and placing the three articles in an overall context. They were published in the book as three separate chapters: 'The Gulf War Will Not Take Place', 'The Gulf War: Is It Really Taking Place?' and 'The Gulf War Did Not Take Place'. The overall title of the book in English was *The Gulf War Did Not Take Place*. The extract here is the whole of the second article, originally written in February 1991. Jean Baudrillard's writing in the three articles on the Gulf War is not at all an instance of collapsing the real into the image as was alleged at the time by much banal media culture analysis. Nor is it an example of the once ultra-leftist Baudrillard in later life shifting to the right and supporting the military-industrial complex.

'The Gulf War: Is It Really Taking Place?', from *The Gulf War Did Not Take Place*, trans. Paul Patton, Sydney: Power Institute of Fine Arts, 1995.

PS To demonstrate the impossibility of war just at the moment when it must take place, when the signs of its occurrence are accumulating, is a stupid gamble. But it would have been even more stupid not to seize the opportunity.

The Gulf War: is it really taking place?

We may well ask. On the available evidence (absence of images, and profusion of commentary), we could suppose an immense promotional exercise like that one which once advertised a brand-name (GARAP) whose product never became known. Pure promotion which enjoyed an immense success because it belonged to pure speculation.

The war is also pure and speculative, to the extent that we do not see the real event that it could be or that it would signify. It reminds us of that recent suspense advertisement: today I take off the top, tomorrow I take off the bottom; today I unleash virtual war, tomorrow I unleash real war. In the background, a third advertisement in which an avaricious and lubricious banker says: your money appeals to me. This sadly celebrated advertisement is reincarnated by Saddam Hussein saying to the West: your power appeals to me (as they rushed to palm off a good share of it to him); then to the Arabs, with the same hypocrisy: your religious war appeals to me (as they rushed to put all their money on him).

In this manner, the war makes its way by promotion and speculation, including the use of hostages transformed into marketing ploys, and in the absence of any clarification of plans, balance sheets, losses or operations. No enterprise would survive such uncertainty, except precisely speculative risk management, otherwise known as the strategy of turning a profit from the worst, in other words, war (= Highly Profitable Senseless Project or HPSP). War itself has taken this speculative turn: it is highly profitable but uncertain. It can collapse from one day to the next.

Nevertheless, from this point onwards the promotional advantages are fabulous. Defeated or not, Saddam is assured of an unforgettable and charismatic label. Victorious or not, American armaments will have acquired an unequalled technological label. And the sumptuary expenditure in materiel is already equivalent to that of a real war, even if it has not taken place.

We have still not left the virtual war, in other words a sophisticated although often laughable build-up against the backdrop of a global indeterminacy of will to make war, even in Saddam's case. Hence the absence of images – which is neither accidental nor due to censorship but to the impossibility of illustrating this indeterminacy of the war.

Promotional, speculative, virtual: this war no longer corresponds to Clausewitz's formula of politics pursued by other means, it rather amounts to *the absence of politics pursued by other means*. Non-war is a terrible test of the status and the uncertainty of politics, just as a stock market crash (the speculative universe) is a crucial test of the economy and of the uncertainty of economic aims, just as any event whatever is a terrible test of the uncertainty and the aims of information. Thus 'real time' information loses itself in a completely unreal space, finally furnishing the images of pure, useless, instantaneous television where its primordial function irrupts, namely that of filling a vacuum, blocking up the screen hole through which escapes the substance of events.

Nor is promotion the pursuit of the economy by other means. On the contrary, it is the pure product of uncertainty with regard to the rational aims of production. This is why it has become a relentless function, the emptiness of which fills our screens to the extent of the absence of any economic finality or rationality. This is why it competes victoriously with the war on our screens, both alternating in the same virtual credit of the image.

The media promote the war, the war promotes the media, and advertising competes with the war. Promotion is the most thick-skinned parasite in our culture. It would undoubtedly survive a nuclear conflict. It is our Last Judgement. But it is also like a bio-logical function: it devours our substance, but it also allows us to metabolise what we absorb, like a parasitic plant or intestinal flora, it allows us to turn the world and the violence of the world into a consumable substance. So, war or promotion?

The war, along with the fake and presumptive warriors, gen-erals, experts and television presenters we see speculating about it all through the day, watches itself in a mirror: am I pretty enough, am I operational enough, am I spectacular enough, am I sophisticated enough to make an entry onto the historical stage? Of course, this anxious interrogation increases the uncertainty with respect to its possible irruption. And this uncertainty invades our screens like a real oil slick, in the image of that blind sea bird stranded on a beach in the Gulf, which will remain the symbol-image of what we all are in front of our screens, in front of that sticky and unintelligible event.

Unlike earlier wars, in which there were political aims either of conquest or domination, what is at stake in this one is war itself: its status, its meaning, its future. It is beholden not to have an objective but to prove its very existence (this crisis of identity affects the existence of us all). In effect, it has lost much of its credibility. Who, apart from the Arab masses, is still capable of believing in it and becoming inflamed by it? Nevertheless, the spectacular drive of war remains intact. In the absence of the (greatly diminished) will to power, and the (problematic) will to knowledge, there remains today the widespread will to spectacle, and with it the obstinate desire to preserve its spectre or fiction (this is the fate of religions: they are no longer believed, but the disincarnate practice remains). Can war still be saved?

Certainly, Iran and Iraq did as much as they could to save the fiction of murderous, fratricidal, sacrificial and interminable (1914 style) war. But they were savages and that war from another period proved nothing with regard to the status and the possibility of a modern war. WW III did not take place and yet we are already beyond it, as though in the utopian space of a post-war-which-did-not-take-place, and it is in the suspense created by this non-place that the present confrontations unfold and the question is posed: can a war still take place?

This one is perhaps only a test, a desperate attempt to see whether war is still possible.

Empty war: it brings to mind those games in World Cup football which often had to be decided by penalties (sorry spectacle), because of the impossibility of forcing a decision. As though the players punished themselves by means of 'penalties' for not having been able to play and take the match in full battle. We might as well have begun with the penalties and dispensed with the game and its sterile stand-off. So with the war: it could have begun at the end and spared us the forced spectacle of this unreal war where nothing is extreme and which, whatever the outcome, will leave behind the smell of undigested programming, and the entire world irritated as though after an unsuccessful copulation.

It is a war of excesses (of means, of materiel, etc.), a war of shedding or purging stocks, of experimental deployment, of liquidation and firesale, along with the display of future ranges of weaponry. A war between excessive, superabundant and over-equipped societies (Iraq included), committed both to waste (including human waste) and the necessity of getting rid of it. Just as the waste of time nourishes the hell of leisure, so technological wastes nourish the hell of war. Wastes which incarnate the secret violence of this society, uncoerced and non-degradable defecation. The renowned American stocks of WW II surplus, which appeared to us as luxury, have become a suffocating global burden, and war functions well within its possibilities in this role of purgative and expenditure.

If the critical intellectual is in the process of disappearing, it seems by contrast that his phobia of the real and of action has been distilled throughout the sanguineous and cerebral network of our institutions. In this sense, the entire world including the military is caught up in a process of intellectualisation.

See them become confused in explanations, outdo themselves in justifications and lose themselves in technical details (war drifts slowly into technological mannerism) or in the deontology of a pure electronic war without hitches: these are aesthetes speaking, postponing settlement dates into the interminable and decisions into the undecidable. Their war-processors, their radars, their lasers and their screens render the passage to war as futile and impossible as the use of a word-processor renders futile and impossible the passage to the act of writing, because it removes from it in advance any dramatic uncertainty.

The generals also exhaust their artificial intelligence in correcting their scenario, polishing their war script so much that they sometimes make errors of manipulation and lose the plot. The famous philosophical épochè has become universal, on the screens as much as on the field of battle.

Should we applaud the fact that all these techniques of war-processing culminate in the elision of the duration and the violence of war? Only eventually, for the indefinite delay of the war is itself heavy with deadly consequences in all domains.

By virtue of having been anticipated in all its details and exhausted by all the scenarios, this war ends up resembling the hero of *Italien des Roses* (Richard Bohringer in the film by Charles Matton), who hesitates to dive from the top of a building for an hour and a half, before a crowd at first hanging on his movements, then disappointed and overcome by the suspense, exactly as we are today by the media blackmail and the illusion of war. It is as though it had taken place ten times already: why would we want it to take place again? It is the same in *Italien des Roses*: we know that his imaginary credit is exhausted and that he will not jump, and in the end nobody gives a damn whether he jumps or not because the real event is already left behind.

This is the problem with anticipation. Is there still a chance that something which has been meticulously programmed will occur? Does a truth which has been meticulously demonstrated still have a chance of being true? When too many things point in the same direction, when the objective reasons pile up, the effect is reversed. Thus everything which points to war is ambiguous: the build-up of force, the play of tension, the concentration of weapons, even the green light from the UN. Far from reinforcing the probability of the conflict, these function as a preventative accumulation, as a substitution for and diversion from the transition to war.

Virtual for five months, the war will shortly enter its terminal phase, according to the rule which says that what never began ends without having taken place. The profound indeterminacy of this war stems from the fact of its being both terminated in advance and interminable. The virtual succeeds itself – accidents aside, which could only be the irruption of the other in the field. But no-one wants to hear talk of the other. Ultimately, the undecidability of the war is grounded in the disappearance of alterity, of primitive hostility, and of the enemy. War has become a celibate machine.

Thanks to this war, the extraordinary confusion in the Arab world is in the process of infecting the West – just revenge. In return, we try desperately to unify and stabilise them in order to exercise better control. It is an historic arm-wrestle: who will stabilise the other before being destabilised themselves? Confronted by the virulent and ungraspable instability of the Arabs and of Islam, whose defence is that of the hysteric in all his versatility, the West is in the process of demonstrating that its values can no longer lay claim to any universality than that (extremely fragile) of the UN.

Faced with the Western logic of under-compensation (the West tends towards the euphemisation and even the inhibition of its power), the Oriental logic of Saddam responds with over-compensation. Although far from having proved himself against Iran, he attacks the West. He operates beyond the reach of his own forces, there where only God can help him. He undertakes an act of magical provocation and it is left to God, or some other predestined connection, to do the rest (this was in principle the role allotted to the Arab masses).

By contrast, through a kind of egocentric generosity or stupidity, the Americans can only imagine and combat an enemy in their own image. They are at once both missionaries and converts of their own way of life, which they triumphally project onto the world. They cannot imagine the Other, nor therefore personally make war upon it. What they make war upon is the alterity of the other, and what they want is to reduce that alterity, to convert it or failing that to annihilate it if it proves irreducible (the Indians). They cannot imagine that conversion and repentance, borne by their own good will, should have no echo in the other, and they are literally disturbed when they see Saddam playing with them and refusing to accede to their reasons. This is perhaps why they have decided to annihilate him, not out of hatred or calculation, but for the crime of felony, treachery, malevolent will and trickery (exactly as with the Indians).

For their part, the Israelis have no such tenderness. They see the Other in all its bare adversity without illusions or scruples. The Other, the Arab, is unconvertible, his alterity is without appeal; it must not be changed, it must be beaten down and subjugated. In doing so, however, while they may not understand they at least recognise it. The Americans, for their part, understand nothing and do not even recognise this fact.

It is not an important match which is being played out in the Gulf, between Western hegemony and the challenge from the rest of the world. It is the West in conflict with itself, by means of an interposed mercenary, after having been in conflict with Islam (Iran), also by means of an interposed Saddam. Saddam remains the fake enemy. At first the champion of the West against Islam, then the champion of Islam against the West. In both cases he is a traitor to his own cause since, even more than the few thousand incidental Westerners, it is the Arab masses that he holds hostage, captures for his own profit and immobilises in their suicidal enthusiasm. It is moreover towards Christmas, at the very moment when he frees the hostages (thereby skilfully stroking the Westerners with the same demagogy that he strokes the children in front of the TV), that he launches his call to the Arab people on the holy war.

It is thus a mistake to think that he would contribute to the unification of the Arab world and to honour him for that. In fact, he only did it to hoodwink them, to make them work for him, to deceive them once again and to render them powerless. People like him are necessary from time to time in order to channel irruptive forces. They serve as a poultice or an artifical purgative. It is a form of deterrence, certainly a Western strategy, but one of which Saddam, in his pride and his stupidity, is a perfect executant. He who loves decoys so much is himself no more than a decoy and his elimination can only demystify this war by putting an end to that objective complicity which itself is no decoy.

But, for this very reason, is the West determined to eliminate him?

The exhibition of American prisoners on Iraqi TV. Once more the politics of blackmail, of hostages, the humiliation of the USA by the spectacle of those 'repentants' forced to avow symbolically American dishonour. Our own as well, we whom the screens submit to the same violence, that of the battered, manipulated and powerless prisoner, that of forced voyeurism in response to the forced exhibitionism of the images. Along with the spectacle of these prisoners or these hostages, the screens offer us the spectacle of our powerlessness. In a case such as this, information exactly fulfils its role which is to convince us of our own abjection by the obscenity of what is seen. The forced perversion of the look amounts to the avowal of our own dishonour, and makes repentants of us as well.

That the Americans should have allowed themselves to be ridiculed without departing from their own programme and war indicates a weakness in their symbolic detonator. Humiliation remains the worst kind of test, arrogance (Saddam's) the worst kind of conduct, blackmail the worst kind of relationship and the acceptance of blackmail the worst kind of dishonour. The fact that this symbolic violence, worse than any sexual violence, should finally have been withstood without flinching testifies to the depth or the unconscious character of Western masochism. This is the rule of the American way of life: *nothing personal*: And they make war in the same manner: pragmatically and not symbolically. They thereby expose themselves to deadly situations which they are unable to confront. But perhaps they accept this in expiation of their power, in an equivalence which is after all symbolic?

Two intense images, two or perhaps three scenes which all concern disfigured forms or costumes which correspond to the masquerade of this war: the CNN journalists with their gas masks in the Jerusalem studios; the drugged and beaten prisoners repenting on the screen of Iraqi TV; and perhaps that sea-bird covered in oil and pointing its blind eyes towards the Gulf sky. It is a masquerade of information: branded faces delivered over to the prostitution of the image, the image of an unintelligible distress. No images of the field of battle, but images of masks, of blind or defeated faces, images of falsification. It is not war taking place over there but the disfiguration of the world.

There is a profound scorn in the kind of 'clean' war which renders the other powerless without destroying its flesh, which makes it a point of honour to disarm and neutralise but not to kill. In a sense, it is worse than the other kind of war because it spares life. It is like humiliation: by taking less than life it is worse than taking life. There is undoubtedly a political error here, in so far as it is acceptable to be defeated but not to be put out of action. In this manner, the Americans inflict a particular insult by not making war on the other but simply eliminating him, the same as one would by not bargaining over the price of an object and thereby refusing any personal relationship with the vendor. The one whose price you accept without discussion despises you. The one whom you disarm without seeing is insulted and must be avenged. There is perhaps something of this in the presentation of those humiliated captives on television. It is in a sense to say to America: you who do not wish to see us, we will show you what you are like.

Just as the psychical or the screen of the psyche transforms every illness into a symptom (there is no organic illness which does not find its meaning elsewhere, in an interpretation of the ailment on another level: all the symptoms pass through a sort of black box in which the psychic images are jumbled and inverted, the illness becomes reversible, ungraspable, escaping any form of realistic medicine), so war, when it has been turned into information, ceases to be a realistic war and becomes a virtual war, in some way symptomatic. And just as everything psychical becomes the object of interminable speculation, so everything which is turned into information becomes the object of endless speculation, the site of total uncertainty. We are left with the symptomatic reading on our screens of the effects of the war, or the effects of discourse about the war, or completely speculative strategic evaluations which are analogous to those evaluations of opinion provided by polls. In this manner, we have gone in a week from 20% to 50% and then to 30% destruction of Iraqi military potential. The figure fluctuates exactly like the fortunes of the stock market. 'The land offensive is anticipated today, tomorrow, in a few hours, in any case sometime this week . . . the climatic conditions are ideal for a confrontation, etc.' Whom to believe? There is nothing to believe. We must learn to read symptoms as symptoms, and television as the hysterical symptom of a war which has nothing to do with its critical mass. Moreover, it does not seem to have to reach its critical mass but remains in its inertial phase, while the implosion of the apparatus of information along with the accompanying tendency of the rate of information to fall seems to reinforce the implosion of war itself, with its accompanying tendency of the rate of confrontation to fall.

Information is like an unintelligent missile which never finds its target (nor, unfortunately, its anti-missile!), and therefore crashes anywhere or gets lost in space on an unpredictable orbit in which it eternally revolves as junk.

Information is only ever an erratic missile with a fuzzy destination which seeks its target but is drawn to every decoy – it is itself a decoy, in fact it scatters all over the environs and the result is mostly nil. The utopia of a targetted promotion or targetted information is the same as that of the targetted missile: it knows not where it lands and perhaps its mission is not to land but, like the missile, essentially to have been launched (as its name indicates). In fact, the only impressive images of missiles, rockets or satellites are those of the launch. It is the same with promotions or five year plans: the campaign launch is what counts, the impact or the end results are so uncertain that one frequently hears no more about them. The entire effect is in the programming, the success is that of the virtual model. Consider the Scuds: their strategic effectiveness is nil and their only (psychological) effect lies in the fact that Saddam succeeded in launching them.

The fact that the production of decoys has become an important branch of the war industry, just as the production of placebos has become an important branch of the medical industry and forgery a flourishing branch of the art industry – not to mention the fact that information has become a privileged branch of industry as such – all of this is a sign that we have entered a deceptive world in which an entire culture labours assiduously at its counterfeit. This also means that it no longer harbours any illusion about itself.

It all began with the leitmotif of precision, of surgical, mathematical and punctual efficacy, which is another way of not recognising the enemy as such, just as lobotomy is a way of not recognising madness as such. And then all that technical virtuosity finished up in the most ridiculous uncertainty. The isolation of the enemy by all kinds of electronic interference creates a sort of barricade behind which he becomes invisible. He also becomes 'stealthy,' and his capacity for resistance becomes indeterminable. In annihilating him at a distance and as it were by transparency, it becomes impossible to discern whether or not he is dead.

The idea of a clean war, like that of a clean bomb or an intelligent missile, this whole war conceived as a technological extrapolation of the brain is a sure sign of madness. It is like those characters in Hieronymus Bosch with a glass bell or a soap bubble around their head as a sign of their mental debility. A war enclosed in a glass coffin, like Snow White, purged of any carnal contamination or warrior's passion. A clean war which ends up in an oil slick.

The French supplied the planes and the nuclear power stations, the Russians the tanks, the English the underground bunkers and runways, the Germans the gas, the Dutch the gas masks, while the Italians supplied the decoy equivalents of everything – tanks, bunkers, inflatable bombers, missiles with artificial thermal emissions, etc. Before so many marvels, one is drawn to compete in diabolical imagination: why not false gas masks for the Palestinians? Why not put the hostages at decoy strategic sites, a fake chemical factory for example?

Has a French plane been downed? The question becomes burning, it is our honour which is at stake. That would constitute a proof of our involvement, and the Iraqis appear to take a malicious pleasure in denying it (perhaps they have a more accurate idea of our involvement?). Whatever the situation, it will be necessary here too to set up decoys, simulated losses and *trompe l'oeil* victims (as with the fake destruction of civic buildings in Timisoara or Baghdad).

A war of high technological concentration but poor definition. Perhaps it has gone beyond its critical mass by too strong a concentration?

Fine illustration of the communication schema in which emitter and receiver on opposite sides of the screen, never connect with each other. Instead of messages, it is missiles and bombs which fly from one side to the other, but any dual or personal relation is altogether absent. Thus an aerial attack on Iraq may be read in terms of coding, decoding and feedback (in this case, very bad, we cannot even know what we have destroyed). This explains the tolerance of the Israelis: they have only been hit by abstract projectiles, namely missiles. The least live bombing attack on Israel would have provoked immediate retaliation.

Communication is also a clean relation: in principle, it excludes any violent or personal affect. It is strange to see this disaffection, this profound indifference to one another, played out at the very heart of violence and war.

The fact that the undetectable Stealth bombers should have begun the war by aiming at decoys and undoubtedly destroying fake objectives, that the Secret Services (also 'furtive') should have been so mistaken in so many ways about the realities of Iraqi weaponry, and the strategists so wrong about the effects of the intensive electronic war, all testifies to the illusionism of force once it is no longer measured against an adversary but against its abstract operation alone. All the generals, admirals and other meretricious experts should be sent to an inflatable strategic site, to see whether these decoys wouldn't in fact attract a real bomb on their heads.

Conversely, the Americans' innocence in admitting their mistake (declaring five months later that the Iraqi forces are almost intact while they themselves are not ready to attack) and all that counter-propaganda which adds to the confusion would be moving if it did not testify to the same strategic idiocy as the triumphal declarations at the outset, and did not further take us for complicit witnesses of this suspicious sincerity of the kind which says: you see, we tell you everything. We can always give credit to the Americans for knowing how to exploit their failures by means of a sort of *trompe l'oeil* candour.

A UN bedtime story: the UN awoke (or was awakened) from its glass coffin (the building in New York). As the coffin fell and was shattered (at the same time as the Eastern Bloc), she spat out the apple and revived, as fresh as a rose, only to find at once the waiting Prince Charming: the Gulf War, also fresh from the arms of the cold war after a long period of mourning. No doubt together they will give birth to a New World Order, or else end up like two ghosts locked in vampiric embrace.

Seeing how Saddam uses his cameras on the hostages, the caressed children, the (fake) strategic targets, on his own smiling face, on the ruins of the milk factory, one cannot help thinking that in the West we still have a hypocritical vision of television and infor-mation, to the extent that, despite all the evidence, we hope for their proper use. Saddam, for his part, knows what the media and information are: he makes a radical, unconditional, perfectly cynical and therefore perfectly instrumental use of them. The Romanians too were able to make a perfectly immoral and mystificatory use of them (from our point of view). We may regret this, but given the principle of simulation which governs all information, even the most pious and objective, and given the structural unreality of images and their proud indifference to the truth, these cynics alone are right about information when they employ it as an unconditional simulacrum. We believe that they immorally pervert images. Not so. They alone are conscious of the profound immorality of images, just as the Bokassas and Amin Dadas reveal, through the parodic and Ubuesque use they make of them, the obscene truth of the Western political and democratic structures they borrowed. The secret of the underdeveloped is to parody their model and render it ridiculous by exaggeration. We alone retain the illusion of information and of a right to information. They are not so naive.

Never any acting out, or passage to action, but simply acting: roll cameras! But there is too much film, or none at all, or it was desensitised by remaining too long in the humidity of the cold war. In short, there is quite simply nothing to see. Later, there will be something to see for the viewers of archival cassettes and the generations of video-zombies who will never cease reconstituting the event, never having had the intuition of the non-event of this war.

The archive also belongs to virtual time; it is the complement of the event 'in real time,' of that instantaneity of the event and its diffusion. Moreover, rather than the 'revolution' of real time of which Virilio speaks, we should speak of an involution in real time; of an involution of the event in the instantaneity of everything at once, and of its vanishing in information itself. If we take note of the speed of light and the temporal short-circuit of pure war (the nanosecond), we see that this involution precipitates us precisely into the virtuality of war and not into its reality, it precipitates us into the absence of war. Must we denounce the speed of light?

Utopia of real time which renders the event simultaneous at all points on the globe. In fact, what we live in real time is not the event, but rather in larger than life (in other words, in the virtual size of the image) the spectacle of the degradation of the event and its spectral evocation (the 'spiritualism of information': event, are you there? Gulf War, are you there?) in the commentary, gloss, and verbose *mise en scène* of talking heads which only underlines the impossibility of the image and the correlative unreality of the war. It is the same aporia as that of *cinéma vérité* which seeks to short-circuit the unreality of the image in order to present us the truth of the object. In this manner, CNN seeks to be a stethoscope attached to the hypothetical heart of the war, and to present us with its hypothetical pulse. But this auscultation only provides a confused ultrasound, undecidable symptoms, and an assortment of vague and contradictory diagnoses. All that we can hope for is to see them die live (metaphorically of course), in other words that some event or other should overwhelm the information instead of the information inventing the event and commenting artificially upon it. The only real information revolution would be this one, but it is not likely to occur in the near future: it would presuppose a reversal of the idea we have of information. In the meantime, we will continue with the involution and encrustation of the event in and by information, and the closer we approach the live and real time, the further we will go in this direction.

The same illusion of progress occurred with the appearance of speech and then colour on screen: at each stage of this progress we moved further away from the imaginary intensity of the image. The closer we supposedly approach the real or the truth, the further we draw away from them both, since neither one nor the other exists. The closer we approach the real time of the event, the more we fall into the illusion of the virtual. God save us from the illusion of war.

At a certain speed, the speed of light, you lose even your shadow. At a certain speed, the speed of information, things lose their sense. There is a great risk of announcing (or denouncing) the Apocalypse of real time, when it is precisely at this point that the event volatilises and becomes a black hole from which light no longer escapes. War implodes in real time, history implodes in real time, all communication and all signification implode in real

time. The Apocalypse itself, understood as the arrival of catastrophe, is unlikely. It falls prey to the prophetic illusion. The
world is not sufficiently coherent to lead to the Apocalypse.

Nevertheless, in confronting our opinions on the war with the
diametrically opposed opinions of Paul Virilio, one of us betting
on apocalyptic escalation and the other on deterrence and the
indefinite virtuality of war, we concluded that this decidedly
strange war went in both directions at once. The war's programmed escalation is relentless and its non-occurrence no less
inevitable: the war proceeds at once towards the two extremes of
intensification and deterrence. The war and the non-war take
place at the same time, with the same period of deployment and
suspense and the same possibilities of de-escalation or maximal
increase.

What is most extraordinary is that the two hypotheses, the
apocalypse of real time and pure war along with the triumph of
the virtual over the real, are realised at the same time, in the same
space-time, each in implacable pursuit of the other. It is a sign
that the space of the event has become a hyperspace with multiple refractivity, and that *the space of war has become definitively
non-Euclidean*. And that there will undoubtedly be no resolution
of this situation: we will remain in the undecidability of war,
which is the undecidability created by the unleashing of the two
opposed principles.

Soft war and pure war go boating.

There is a degree of popular good will in the micro-panic distilled
by the airwaves. The public ultimately consents to be frightened,
and to be gently terrorised by the bacteriological scenarios, on
the basis of a kind of affective patriotism, even while it preserves
a fairly profound indifference to the war. But it censors this indifference, on the grounds that we must not cut ourselves off from
the world scene, that we must be mobilised at least as extras in
order to rescue war: we have no other passion with which to
replace it. It is the same with political participation under normal
circumstances: this is largely second hand, taking place against a
backdrop of spontaneous indifference. It is the same with God:
even when we no longer believe, we continue to believe that we

believe. In this hysterical replacement function, we identify at once those who are superfluous and they are many. By contrast, the few who advance the hypothesis of this profound indifference will be received as traitors.

By the force of the media, this war liberates an exponential mass of stupidity, not the particular stupidity of war, which is considerable, but the professional and functional stupidity of those who pontificate in perpetual commentary on the event: all the Bouvards and Pécuchets for hire, the would-be raiders of the lost image, the CNN types and all the master singers of strategy and information who make us experience the emptiness of television as never before. This war, it must be said, constitutes a merciless test. Fortunately, no one will hold this expert or general or that intellectual for hire to account for the idiocies or absurdities proffered the day before, since these will be erased by those of the following day. In this manner, everyone is amnestied by the ultra-rapid succession of phony events and phony discourses. The laundering of stupidity by the escalation of stupidity which reconstitutes a sort of total innocence, namely the innocence of washed and bleached brains, stupefied not by the violence but by the sinister insignificance of the images.

Chevènement in the desert: *Morituri te salutant*! Ridiculous. France with its old Jaguars and its presidential slippers.

Capillon on television: the benefit of this war will have been to recycle our military leaders on television. One shudders at the thought that in another time, in a real war, they were operational on the battlefield.

Imbroglio: that pacifist demonstration in Paris, thus indirectly for Saddam Hussein, who does want war, and against the French Government which does not want it, and which from the outset gives all the signs of refusing to take part, or of doing so reluctantly.

Deserted shops, suspended vacations, the slowdown of activity, the city turned over to the absent masses: it may well be that, behind the alibi of panic, this war should be the dreamed-for opportunity to soft-pedal, the opportunity to slow down, to ease off the pace. The crazed particles calm down, the war erases the guerrilla warfare of everyday life. Catharsis? No: renovation. Or perhaps, with everyone glued at home, TV plays out fully its role of social control by collective stupefaction: turning uselessly upon itself like a dervish, it affixes populations all the better for deceiving them, as with a bad detective novel which we cannot believe could be so pointless.

Iraq is being rebuilt even before it has been destroyed. After-sales service. Such anticipation reduces even further the credibility of the war, which did not need this to discourage those who wanted to believe in it.

Sometimes a glimmer of black humour: the twelve thousand coffins sent along with the arms and ammunition. Here too, the Americans demonstrate their presumption: their projections and their losses are without common measure. But Saddam challenged them with being incapable of sacrificing ten thousand men in a war: they replied by sending twelve thousand coffins.

The overestimation of losses is part of the same megalomaniac light show as the publicised deployment of 'Desert Shield' and the orgy of bombardment. The pilots no longer even have any targets. The Iraqis no longer even have enough decoys to cater for the incessant raids. The same target must be bombed five times. Mockery.

The British artillery unleashed for twenty-four hours. Long since there was nothing left to destroy. Why then? In order 'to cover the noise of the armoured columns advancing towards the front by the noise of the bombardment.' Of course, the effect of surprise must be maintained (it is February 21). The best part is that there was no longer anyone there, the Iraqis had already left. Absurdity.

Saddam is a mercenary, the Americans are missionaries. But once the mercenary is beaten, the missionaries become *de facto* the mercenaries of the entire world. But the price for becoming a perfect mercenary is to be stripped of all political intelligence and all will. The Americans cannot escape it: if they want to be the police of the world and the New World Order, they must lose all political authority in favour of their operational capacity alone. They will become pure executants and everyone else pure extras in the consensual and policed New World Order.

Whoever the dictator to be destroyed, any punitive force sure of itself is even more frightening. Having assumed the Israeli style, the Americans will henceforth export it everywhere and, just as the Israelis did, lock themselves into the spiral of unconditional repression.

For the Americans, the enemy does not exist as such. *Nothing personal*. Your war is of no interest to me, your resistance is of no interest to me. I will destroy you when I am ready. Refusal to bargain, whereas Saddam Hussein, for his part, bargains his war by overbidding in order to fall back, attempting to force the hand by pressure and blackmail, like a hustler trying to sell his goods. The Americans understand nothing in this whole psychodrama of bargaining, they are had every time until, with the wounded pride of the Westerner, they stiffen and impose their conditions. They understand nothing of this floating duel, this passage of arms in which, for a brief moment, the honour and dishonour of each is in play. They know only their virtue, and they are proud of their virtue. If the other wants to play, to trick and to challenge, they will virtuously employ their force. They will oppose the other's traps with their character armour and their armoured tanks. For them, the time of exchange does not exist. But the other, even if he knows that he will concede, cannot do so without another form of procedure. He must be recognised as interlocutor: this is the goal of the exchange. He must be recognised as an enemy: this is the whole aim of the war. For the Americans, bargaining is cheap whereas for the others it is a matter of honour (mutual) personal recognition, linguistic strategy (language exists, it must be honoured) and respect for time (altercation demands a rhythm, it is the price of there being an Other). The Americans take no account of these primitive subtleties. They have much to learn about symbolic exchange.

By contrast, they are winners from an economic point of view. No time lost in discussion, no psychological risk in any duel with the other: it is a way of proving that time does not exist, that the other does not exist, and that all that matters is the model and mastery of the model.

From a military point of view, to allow this war to endure in the way they have (instead of applying an Israeli solution and immediately exploiting the imbalance of force while short-circuiting all retaliatory effects), is a clumsy solution lacking in glory and full of perverse effects (Saddam's aura among the Arab masses). Nevertheless, in doing this, they impose a suspense, a temporal vacuum in which they present to themselves and to the entire world the spectacle of their virtual power. They will have allowed the war to endure as long as it takes, not to win but to persuade the whole world of the infallibility of their machine.

The victory of the model is more important than victory on the ground. Military success consecrates the triumph of arms, but the programming success consecrates the defeat of time. War-processing, the transparency of the model in the unfolding of the war, the strategy of relentless execution of a programme, the electrocution of all reaction and any live initiative, including their own: these are more important from the point of view of general deterrence (of friends and foes alike) than the final result on the ground. Clean war, white war, programmed war: more lethal than the war which sacrifices human lives.

We are a long way from annihilation, holocaust and atomic apocalypse, the total war which functions as the archaic imaginary of media hysteria. On the contrary, this kind of preventative, deterrent and punitive war is a warning to everyone not to take extreme measures and inflict upon themselves what they inflict on others (the missionary complex): the rule of the game that says everyone must remain within the limits of their power and not make war by any means whatever. Power must remain virtual and exemplary, in other words, virtuous. The decisive test is the planetary apprenticeship in this regulation. Just as wealth is no longer measured by the ostentation of wealth but by the secret circulation of speculative capital, so war is not measured by being waged but by its speculative unfolding in an abstract, electronic and informational space, the same space in which capital moves.

While this conjuncture does not exclude all accident (disorder in the virtual), it is nevertheless true that the probability of the irruption of those extreme measures and mutual violence which we call war is increasingly low.

Saddam the hysteric. Interminable shit kicker. The hysteric cannot be crushed: he is reborn from his symptoms as though from his ashes. Confronted by a hysteric, the other becomes paranoid, he deploys a massive apparatus of protection and mistrust. He suspects the hysteric of bad faith, of ruse and dissimulation. He wants to constrain him to the truth and to transparency. The hysteric is irreducible. His means are decoys and the overturning of alliances. Confronted with this lubricity, this duplicity, the paranoid can only become more rigid, more obsessional. The most violent reproach addressed to Saddam Hussein by Bush is that of being a liar, a traitor, a bad player, a trickster. *Lying son of a bitch!* Saddam, like a good hysteric, has never given birth to his own war: for him, it is only a phantom pregnancy. By contrast, he has until now succeeded in preventing Bush from giving birth to his. And, with the complicity of Gorbachev, he almost succeeded in fucking him up the ass. But the hysteric is not suicidal, this is the advantageous other side to Saddam. He is neither mad nor suicidal, perhaps he should be treated by hypnosis?

The Iraqis and the Americans have at least one thing in common, a heinous crime which they (and with them the West) share. Many things about this war are explained by this anterior crime from which both sides sought to profit with impunity. The secret expiation of this crime feeds the Gulf War in its confusion and its allure of the settling of accounts. Such is the shared agreement to forget it that little is spoken about this prior episode (even by the Iranians), namely the war against Iran. Saddam must avenge his failure to win, even though he was the aggressor and sure of his impunity. He must avenge himself against the West which trained him for it, while the Americans, for their part, must suppress him as the embarrassing accomplice in that criminal act.

For any government official or despot, power over his own people takes precedence over everything else. In the case of the

Gulf War, this provides the only chance of a solution or a de-escalation. Saddam will prefer to concede rather than destroy his internal hegemony or sacrifice his army, etc. In this sense, sheltering his planes in Iran is a good sign: rather than an offensive sign, it is the ploy of a burglar who stashes his haul in order to retrieve it when he comes out of prison, thus an argument against any heroic or suicidal intention.

While one fraction of the intellectuals and politicians, specialists in the reserve army of mental labour, are whole-heartedly in favour of the war, and another fraction are against it from the bottom of their hearts, but for reasons no less disturbing, all are agreed on one point: this war exists, we have seen it. There is no interrogation into the event itself or its reality; or into the fraudulence of this war, the programmed and always delayed illusion of battle; or into the machination of this war and its amplification by information, not to mention the improbable orgy of materiel, the systematic manipulation of data, the artificial dramatisation . . . If we do not have practical intelligence about the war (and none among us has), at least let us have a sceptical intelligence towards it, without renouncing the pathetic feeling of its absurdity.

But there is more than one kind of absurdity: that of the massacre and that of being caught up in the illusion of massacre. It is just as in La Fontaine's fable: the day there is a real war you will not even be able to tell the difference. The real victory of the simulators of war is to have drawn everyone into this rotten simulation.

CHAPTER NINE

Pataphysics of the Year 2000

The 1990s was a decade which Baudrillard had already advised us, in the 1980s, we should miss out while we went straight to the end of the century. In some respects Baudrillard's work during the 1990s started to seem more and more millenarian as references to the threshold year of 2000 increased. The first one which appeared in French, translated into English, is the extract here. Looking back on the end of the century it is hard to overestimate how far this 'end-of-the-millennium' spirit had percolated into media forms, especially popular culture. Baudrillard's writing chimed perfectly with the times. In 1992 Editions Galilee published *L'Illusion de la Fin* which in a number of its short essays drew attention to the coming end of the millennium in eight years' time. It evocatively questioned what later became the 'Y2K' apocalyptic historical watershed in its title. In 1994 Polity Press published an English translation by Chris Turner under the overall title *The Illusion of the End*. The suggestion was that many imaginary end-points had come and gone in history and this was merely another 'illusory' one. Pataphysics being the 'science of imaginary solutions', the title of the essay extracted here seems most appropriate. In another chapter in the book Baudrillard wrote of 'the reversal of history', 'the end of linearity' and the rewinding of modernity. In the extract here, which in fact begins the book, Baudrillard predicted provocatively that 'the year 2000 will not take place' just as he had written previously that 'the Gulf War will not take place'. It is a trait of Baudrillard's work that linear history is to be constantly questioned and *The Illusion of the End* is a particularly good example of a book in which he pushes this idea way beyond its limit. Baudrillard plays with the idea of an acceleration of modernity and a slowing down of history, before questioning teleology in general. In the same year that neo-conservativism's erstwhile pin-up boy Francis

Fukuyama published *The End of History*, Baudrillard was arguing that the idea of the 'end of history' was illusory.

'Pataphysics of the Year 2000', from *The Illusion of the End*, trans. Chris Turner, Cambridge: Polity, 1994.

A tormenting thought: as of a certain point, history was no longer *real*. Without noticing it, all mankind suddenly left reality; everything happening since then was supposedly not true; but we supposedly didn't notice. Our task would now be to find that point, and as long as we didn't have it, we would be forced to abide in our present destruction.

Elias Canetti

Various plausible hypotheses may be advanced to explain this vanishing of history. Canetti's expression 'all mankind suddenly left reality' irresistibly evokes the idea of that escape velocity a body requires to free itself from the gravitational field of a star or planet. Staying with this image, one might suppose that the acceleration of modernity, of technology, events and media, of all exchanges – economic, political and sexual – has propelled us to 'escape velocity', with the result that we have flown free of the referential sphere of the real and of history. We are 'liberated' in every sense of the term, so liberated that we have taken leave of a certain space-time, passed beyond a certain horizon in which the real is possible because gravitation is still strong enough for things to be reflected and thus in some way to endure and have some consequence.

A degree of slowness (that is, a certain speed, but not too much), a degree of distance, but not too much, and a degree of liberation (an energy for rupture and change), but not too much, are needed to bring about the kind of condensation or significant crystallization of events we call history, the kind of coherent unfolding of causes and effects we call reality [*le réel*].

Once beyond this gravitational effect, which keeps bodies in orbit, all the atoms of meaning get lost in space. Each atom pursues its own trajectory to infinity and is lost in space. This is precisely what we are seeing in our present-day societies, intent as they are on accelerating all bodies, messages and processes in all directions and which, with modern media, have created for every event, story and image a simulation of an infinite trajectory. Every political, historical and cultural fact possesses a kinetic energy which wrenches it from its own space and propels it into a hyperspace where, since it will never return, it loses all meaning. No need for science fiction here: already, here and now – in the shape of our computers, circuits and networks – we have the particle accelerator which has smashed the referential orbit of things once and for all.

So far as history is concerned, its telling has become impossible because that telling (*re-citatum*) is, by definition, the possible recurrence of a sequence of meanings. Now, through the impulse for total dissemination and circulation, every event is granted its own liberation; every fact becomes atomic, nuclear, and pursues its trajectory into the void. In order to be disseminated to infinity, it has to be fragmented like a particle. This is how it is able to achieve a velocity of no-return which carries it out of history once and for all. Every set of phenomena, whether cultural totality or sequence of events, has to be fragmented, disjointed, so that it can be sent down the circuits; every kind of language has to be resolved into a binary formulation so that it can circulate not, any longer, in our memories, but in the luminous, electronic memory of the computers. No human language can withstand the speed of light. No event can withstand being beamed across the whole planet. No meaning can withstand acceleration. No history can withstand the centrifugation of facts or their being short-circuited in real time (to pursue the same train of thought: no sexuality can withstand being liberated, no culture can withstand being hyped, no truth can withstand being verified, etc.).

Nor is theory in a position to 'reflect (on)' anything. It can only tear concepts from their critical zone of reference and force them beyond a point of no-return (it too is moving into the hyperspace of simulation), a process whereby it loses all 'objective' validity but gains substantially in real affinity with the present system.

The second hypothesis regarding the vanishing of history is the opposite of the first. It has to do not with processes speeding up but slowing down. It too comes directly from physics.

Matter slows the passing of time. To put it more precisely, time at the surface of a very dense body seems to be going in slow motion. The phenomenon intensifies as the density increases. The effect of this slowing down will be to increase the length of the light-wave emitted by this body as received by the observer. Beyond a certain limit, time stops and the wavelength becomes infinite. The wave no longer exists. The light goes out.

There is a clear analogy here with the slowing down of history when it rubs up against the astral body of the 'silent majorities'. Our societies are dominated by this mass process, not just in the demographic and sociological sense, but in the sense of a 'critical mass', of passing beyond a point of no-return. This is the most significant event within these societies: the emergence, in the very course of their mobilization and revolutionary process (they are all revolutionary by the standards of past centuries), of an equivalent force of inertia, of an immense indifference and the silent potency of that indifference. This inert matter of the social is not produced by a lack of exchanges, information or communication, but by the multiplication and saturation of exchanges. It is the product of the hyperdensity of cities, commodities, messages and circuits. It is the cold star of the social and, around that mass, history is also cooling. Events follow one upon another, cancelling each other out in a state of indifference. The masses, neutralized, mithridatized by information, in turn neutralize history and act as an *écran d'absorption*.[1] They themselves have no history, meaning, consciousness or desire. They are the potential residue of all history, meaning and desire. As they have unfurled in our modernity, all these fine things have stirred up a mysterious counter-phenomenon, and all today's political and social strategies are thrown out of gear by the failure to understand it.

This time we have the opposite situation: history, meaning and progress are no longer able to reach their escape velocity. They are no longer able to pull away from this overdense body which slows their trajectory, which slows time to the point where, right now, the perception and imagination of the future are beyond us. All social, historical and temporal transcendence is absorbed by that mass in its silent immanence. Political events already lack sufficient energy of their own to move us: so they run on like a silent film for which we bear collective irresponsibility. History comes to an end here, not for want of actors, nor for want of violence (there will always be more violence), nor for want of events (there will always be more events, thanks be to the media and the news networks!), but by deceleration, indifference and stupefaction. It is no longer able to transcend itself, to envisage its own finality, to dream of its own end; it is being buried beneath its own immediate effect, worn out in special effects, imploding into current events.

Deep down, one cannot even speak of the end of history here, since history will not have time to catch up with its own end. Its effects are accelerating, but its meaning is slowing inexorably. It will eventually come to a stop and be extinguished like light and time in the vicinity of an infinitely dense mass . . .

Humanity too had its big bang: a certain critical density, a certain concentration of people and exchanges presides over this explosion we call history, which is merely the dispersal of the dense and hieratic nuclei of previous civilizations. Today we have the reversive effect: crossing the threshold of the critical mass where populations, events and information are concerned triggers the opposite process of historical and political inertia. In the cosmic order, we do not know whether we have reached the escape velocity which would mean we are now in a definitive state of expansion (this will doubtless remain eternally uncertain). In the human order, where the perspectives are more limited, it may be that the very escape velocity of the species (the acceleration of births, technologies and exchanges over the centuries) creates an excess of mass and resistance which defeats the initial energy and takes us down an inexorable path of contraction and inertia.

Whether the universe is expanding to infinity or retracting towards an infinitely dense, infinitely small nucleus depends on its critical mass (and speculation on this is itself infinite by virtue of the possible invention of new particles). By analogy, whether our human history is evolutive or involutive perhaps depends on humanity's critical mass. Has the history, the movement, of the species reached the escape velocity required to triumph over the inertia of the mass? Are we set, like the galaxies, on a definitive course distancing us from one another at prodigious speed, or is this dispersal to infinity destined to come to an end and the human molecules to come back together by an opposite process of gravitation? Can the human mass, which increases every day, exert control over a pulsation of this kind?

There is a third hypothesis, a third analogy. We are still speaking of a point of disappearance, a vanishing point, but this time in music. I shall call this the stereophonic effect. We are all obsessed with high fidelity, with the quality of musical 'reproduction'. At the consoles of our stereos, armed with our tuners, amplifiers and speakers, we mix, adjust settings, multiply tracks in pursuit of a flawless sound. Is this still music? Where is the high fidelity threshold beyond which music disappears as such? It does not disappear for lack of music, but because it has passed this limit point; it disappears into the perfection of its materiality, into its own special effect. Beyond this point, there is neither judgement nor aesthetic pleasure. It is the ecstasy of musicality, and its end.

The disappearance of history is of the same order: here again, we have passed that limit where, by dint of the sophistication of events and information, history ceases to exist as such. Immediate high-powered broadcasting, special effects, secondary effects, fading and that famous feedback effect which is produced in acoustics by a source and a receiver being too close together and in history by an event and its dissemination being too close together and thus interfering disastrously – a short-circuit between cause and effect like that between the object and the experimenting subject in microphysics (and in the human sciences!). These are all things which cast a radical doubt on the event, just as excessive high fidelity cass radical doubt on music. Elias Canetti puts it well: beyond this point, nothing is true. It is for this reason that the *petite musique* of history also eludes our grasp today, that it vanishes into the microscopics or the stereophonics of news.

Right at the very heart of news, history threatens to disappear. At the heart of hi-fi, music threatens to disappear. At the heart of experimentation, the object of science threatens to disappear. At the heart of pornography, sexuality threatens to disappear. Everywhere we find the same stereophonic effect, the same effect of absolute proximity to the real, the same effect of simulation.

By definition, this vanishing point, this point short of which history *existed* and music *existed*, cannot be pinned down. Where must stereo perfection end? The boundaries are constantly being pushed back because it is technical obsession which redraws them. Where must news reporting end? One can only counter this fascination with 'real time' — the equivalent of high fidelity — with a moral objection, and there is not much point in that.

The passing of this point is thus an irreversible act, contrary to what Canetti seems to hope. We shall never get back to pre-stereo music (except by an additional technical simulation effect); we shall never get back to pre-news and pre-media history. The original essence of music, the original concept of history have disappeared because we shall never again be able to isolate them from their model of perfection which is at the same time their model of simulation, the model of their enforced assumption into a hyper-reality which cancels them out. We shall never again know what the social or music were before being exacerbated into their present useless perfection. We shall never again know what history was before its exacerbation into the technical perfection of news: we shall never again know what anything was before disappearing into the fulfilment of its model.

So, with this, the situation becomes novel once again. The fact that we are leaving history to move into the realm of simulation is merely a consequence of the fact that history itself has always, deep down, been an immense simulation model. Not in the sense that it could be said only to have existed in the narrative made of it or the interpretation given, but with regard to the time in which it unfolds – that linear time which is at once the time of an ending and of the unlimited suspending of the end. The only kind of time in which a history can take place, if, by history, we understand a succession of non-meaningless facts, each engendering the other by cause and effect, but doing so without any absolute necessity and all standing open to the future, unevenly poised. So different from time in ritual societies where the end of everything is in its beginning and ceremony retraces the perfection of that original event. In contrast to this *fulfilled* order of time, the liberation of the 'real' time of history, the production of a linear, deferred time may seem a purely artificial process. Where does this suspense come from? Where do we get the idea that what must be accomplished (Last Judgement, salvation or catastrophe) must come at the end of time and match up with some incalculable appointed term or other? This model of linearity must have seemed entirely fictitious, wholly absurd and abstract to cultures which had no sense of a deferred day of reckoning, a successive concatenation of events and a final goal. And it was, indeed, a scenario which had some difficulty establishing itself. There was fierce resistance in the early years of Christianity to the postponement of the coming of God's Kingdom. The acceptance of this 'historical' perspective of salvation, that is, of its remaining unaccomplished in the immediate present, was not achieved without violence, and all the heresies would later take up this leitmotif of the immediate fulfilment of the promise in what was akin to a defiance of time. Entire communities even resorted to suicide to hasten the coming of the Kingdom. Since this latter was promised at the end of time, it seemed to them that they had only to put an end to time right away.

The whole of history has had a millennial (millenarian) challenge to its temporality running through it. In opposition to the historical perspective, which continually shifts the stakes on to a hypothetical end, there has always been a fatal exigency, a fatal strategy of time which wants to shoot straight ahead to a point beyond the end. It cannot be said that either of these tendencies has really won out, and the question 'to wait or not to wait?' has remained, throughout history, a burning issue. Since the messianic convulsion of the earliest Christians, reaching back beyond the heresies and revolts, there has always been this desire to anticipate the end, possibly by death, by a kind of seductive suicide aiming to turn God from history and make him face up to his responsibilities, those which lie beyond the end, those of the final fulfilment. And what, indeed, is terrorism, if not this effort to conjure up, in its own way, the end of history? It attempts to entrap the powers that be by an immediate, total act. Without awaiting the final term of the process, it sets itself at the ecstatic end-point, hoping to bring about the conditions for the Last Judgement. An illusory challenge, of course, but one which always fascinates, since, deep down, neither time nor history has ever been accepted. Everyone remains aware of the arbitrariness, the artificial character of time and history. And we are never fooled by those who call on us to hope.

And, terrorism apart, is there not also a hint of this parousic exigency in the global fantasy of catastrophe that hovers over today's world? A demand for a violent resolution of reality, when this latter eludes our grasp in an endless hyper-reality? For hyper-reality rules out the very occurrence of the Last Judgement or the Apocalypse or the Revolution. All the ends we have envisaged elude our grasp and history has no chance of bringing them about, since it will, in the interim, have come to an end (it's always the story of Kafka's Messiah: he arrives too late, a day too late, and the time-lag is unbearable). So one might as well short-circuit the Messiah, bring forward the end. This has always been the demonic temptation: to falsify ends and the calculation of ends, to falsify time and the occurrence of things, to hurry them along, impatient to see them accomplished, or secretly sensing that the promise of accomplishment is itself also false and diabolical.

Even our obsession with 'real time', with the instantaneity of news, has a secret millenarianism about it: cancelling the flow of time, cancelling delay, suppressing the sense that the event is happening elsewhere, anticipating its end by freeing ourselves from linear time, laying hold of things almost before they have taken place. In this sense, 'real time' is something even more arti-ficial than a recording, and is, at the same time, its denial – if we want immediate enjoyment of the event, if we want to experience it at the instant of its occurrence, as if we were there, this is because we no longer have any confidence in the meaning or purpose of the event. The same denial is found in apparently opposite behaviour – recording, filing and memorizing every-thing of our own past and the past of all cultures. Is this not a symptom of a collective presentiment of the end, a sign that events and the living time of history have had their day and that we have to arm ourselves with the whole battery of artificial memory, all the signs of the past, to face up to the absence of a future and the glacial times which await us? Are not mental and intellectual structures currently going underground, burying themselves in memories, in archives, in search of an improbable resurrection? All thoughts are going underground in cautious anticipation of the year 2000. They can already scent the terror of the year 2000. They are instinctively adopting the solution of those cryogenized individuals plunged into liquid nitrogen until the means can be found to enable them to survive.

These societies, these generations which no longer expect anything from some future 'coming', and have less and less confidence in history, which dig in behind their futuristic technologies, behind their stores of information and inside the beehive networks of communication where time is at last wiped out by pure circulation, will perhaps never reawaken. But they do not know that. The year 2000 will not perhaps take place. But they do not know that.

Note

1. The French is retained here, since to translate this by the English term 'dark trace screen' would be to forfeit the connection Baudrillard wishes to maintain with the idea of absorption.

CHAPTER TEN

Impossible Exchange

By the end of the century Baudrillard had started to produce a familiar aphoristic, poetic writing style across the board, not just in his *Cool Memories* diaries. He had after all started in the field of literature in the 1950s and 1960s and published a book of poems called *L'Ange de Stuc* ('Stucco Angel' in English) in 1978. In 1999 Editions Galilée published *L'Echange Impossible* which comprised discourses on his own novel terms like 'radicality of thought', 'radical uncertainty' and 'impossible exchange' but which had no footnotes or referencing system at all. It is theory, but not as we know it. For the remainder of his life Baudrillard wrote everything in this 'theory-fiction' style. In 2001 Verso published *Impossible Exchange* with an English translation and added footnotes by Chris Turner. The extract here is from the beginning of the book and is a development of the implications of Baudrillard's term 'impossible exchange'. The influence of Georges Bataille (the idea of the accursed share and general economy) and Marcel Mauss (the notion of gift-exchange) was always already present throughout most of Baudrillard's writing and it is evident here, too. Baudrillard's anthropology opens itself up to criticisms of him as nostalgic for a long gone primitive society. Yet among Baudrillard's influences in the 1960s were the likes of the semiotician Roland Barthes, not conservative, traditional anthropologists. In fact Baudrillard always wanted to go beyond classical, Marxist or structuralist anthropology to produce a new, radical anthropology of modernity. His idea of the three orders of simulacra which he developed in his work from the 1970s onwards suggested the West had passed through several stages since the eighteenth century, including industrial society and consumer society. The fourth order of simulacra, or information society, which began to be prominent in his later writing featured the notion of 'impossible exchange' in 'radical uncertainty' and absorbed much of Baudrillard's attention from the late 1990s until he died.

'Impossible Exchange', from *Impossible Exchange*, trans. Chris Turner, London: Verso, 2001.

Everything starts from impossible exchange. The uncertainty of the world lies in the fact that it has no equivalent anywhere; it cannot be exchanged for anything. The uncertainty of thought lies in the fact that it cannot be exchanged either for truth or for reality. Is it thought which tips the world over into uncertainty, or the other way round? This in itself is part of the uncertainty.

There is no equivalent of the world. That might even be said to be its definition – or lack of it. No equivalent, no double, no representation, no mirror. Any mirror whatsoever would still be part of the world. There is not enough room both for the world and for its double. So there can be no verifying of the world. This is, indeed, why 'reality' is an imposture. Being without possible verification, the world is a fundamental illusion. Whatever can be verified locally, the uncertainty of the world, taken overall, is not open to debate. There is no integral calculus of the universe. A differential calculus, perhaps? 'The Universe, made up of multiple sets, is not itself a set' (Denis Guedj).

This is how it is with any system. The economic sphere, the sphere of all exchange, taken overall, cannot be exchanged for anything. There is no meta-economic equivalent of the economy anywhere, nothing to exchange it for as such, nothing with which to redeem it in another world. It is, in a sense, insolvent, and in any event insoluble to a global intelligence. And so it, too, is of the order of a fundamental uncertainty.

This it tries to ignore. But the indeterminacy induces a fluctuation of equations and postulates at the very heart of the economic sphere and leads, in the end, to that sphere lurching off into speculation, its criteria and elements all interacting madly.

The other spheres – politics, law and aesthetics – are character-ized by this same non-equivalence, and hence the same eccen-tricity. Literally, they have no meaning outside themselves and cannot be exchanged for anything. Politics is laden with signs and meanings, but seen from the outside it has none. It has nothing to justify it at a universal level (all attempts to ground politics at a metaphysical or philosophical level have failed). It absorbs everything which comes into its ambit and converts it into its own substance, but it is not able to convert itself into – or be reflected in – a higher reality which would give it a meaning.

Here again, this impossible equivalence finds expression in the increasing undecidability of its categories, discourses, strategies and issues. The political – together with its *mise-en-scène* and its discourse – proliferates in scale with its fundamental illusoriness.

There is great uncertainty, even in the sphere of living matter and biology. Schemes for genetic experimentation and investiga-tion are becoming infinitely ramified, and the more ramified they become, the more the crucial question is left unanswered: who rules over life, who rules over death? Complex as it may be, the phenomenon of life cannot be exchanged for any ultimate purpose. One cannot conceive life and the ultimate purpose of life at one and the same time. And this uncertainty haunts the field of biology, rendering it also increasingly speculative, as each further discovery is made – not through some temporary incap-acity on the part of science, but because it is approaching the definitive uncertainty which is its absolute horizon.

The transcription and 'objective' assessment of an overall system have, ultimately, no more meaning than the assessment of the weight of the earth in millions of billions of tons – a figure which has no meaning outside of a calculation internal to the ter-restrial system.

Metaphysically, it is the same: the values, purposes and causes we delineate are valid only for a form of thought which is human, all too human. They are irrelevant to any other reality whatever (perhaps even to 'reality' *tout court*).

The sphere of the real is itself no longer exchangeable for the sphere of the sign. As with floating currencies, the relationship between the two is growing undecidable, and the rate at which they exchange increasingly random. Both are becoming speculative, each in its own space. Reality is growing increasingly technical and efficient; everything that can be done is being done, though without any longer meaning anything. And the metalanguages of reality (the human and social sciences, technical and operational languages) are also developing eccentrically, after the fashion of their objects. As for the sign, it is passing into the pure speculation and simulation of the virtual world, the world of the total screen, where the same uncertainty hovers over the real and 'virtual reality' once they go their separate ways. The real no longer has any force as sign, and signs no longer have any force of meaning.

Any system invents for itself a principle of equilibrium, exchange and value, causality and purpose, which plays on fixed oppositions: good and evil, true and false, sign and referent, subject and object. This is the whole space of difference and regulation by difference which, as long as it functions, ensures the stability and dialectical movement of the whole. Up to this point, all is well. It is when this bipolar relationship breaks down, when the system short-circuits itself, that it generates its own critical mass, and veers off exponentially. When there is no longer any internal reference system within which exchange can take place (between production and social wealth, for example, or between news coverage and real events), you get into an exponential phase, a phase of speculative disorder.

The illusion of the economic sphere lies in its having aspired to ground a principle of reality and rationality on the forgetting of this ultimate reality of impossible exchange. Now, that principle is valid only within an artificially bounded sphere. Outside that sphere lies radical uncertainty. And it is this exiled, foreclosed uncertainty which haunts systems and generates the illusion of the economic, the political, and so on. It is the failure to understand this which leads systems into incoherence, hypertrophy and, in some sense, leads them to destroy themselves. For it is from the inside, by overreaching themselves, that systems make bonfires of their own postulates, and fall into ruins.

To put it another way: has there ever been any 'economy', in the sense of an organization of value that is stably coherent and has a universal purpose and meaning? In absolute terms, the answer is no. Has there ever even been a 'real'? In this chasm of uncertainty, the real, value and the law are exceptions, exceptional phenomena. Illusion is the fundamental rule.

Everything which sets out to exchange itself for something runs up, in the end, against the Impossible Exchange Barrier. The most concerted, most subtle attempts to make the world meaningful in value terms, to endow it with meaning, come to grief on this insuperable obstacle. And that which cannot be exchanged for anything else proliferates wildly. The most structured systems cannot but be thrown out of kilter by the reversion of this Nothing which haunts them. And not in the aftermath of some future catastrophe, but right now. Here and now, the whole edifice of value is exchangeable for Nothing.

The true formula of contemporary nihilism lies here, rather than in any philosophical or moral considerations: it is the nihilism of value itself. This is our fate, and from this stem both the happiest and most baleful consequences. This book might be said to be the exploration, first, of the 'fateful' consequences, and subsequently – by a poetic turnabout – of the fortunate, happy consequences, of impossible exchange.

Behind the exchange of value and, in a sense, serving as an invisible counterpart to it, behind this mad speculation which reaches a peak in the virtual economy, behind the exchange of Something, we have, then, always, the exchange of the Nothing.

Death, illusion, absence, the negative, evil, the accursed share are everywhere, running beneath the surface of all exchanges. It is even this continuity of the Nothing which grounds the possibility of the Great Game of Exchange. All current strategies boil down to this: passing around the debt, the credit, the unreal, unnameable thing you cannot get rid of. Nietzsche analysed the stratagem of God in these terms: in redeeming man's debt by the sacrifice of His son, God, the great Creditor, created a situation where the debt could never be redeemed by the debtor, since it has already been redeemed by the creditor. In this way, He created the possibility of an endless circulation of that debt, which man will bear as his perpetual sin. This is the ruse of God. But it is also the ruse of capital, which, at the same time as it plunges the world into ever greater debt, works simultaneously to redeem that debt, thus creating a situation in which it will never be able to be cancelled or exchanged for anything. And this is true also of the Real and the Virtual: the endless circulation of the Virtual will create a situation where the Real will never be able to be exchanged for anything.

If it is the forgetting and denial of the Nothing which brings about the catastrophic deregulation of systems, there is no way of warding off this process by the magical addition of some *ex machina* corrective – the kind of regulation we see at work in the physical, biological and economic sciences, where new hypotheses, new forces and new particles are constantly being invented to shore up the equations. If it is the Nothing whose absence is missing, it is the Nothing which must be brought (or returned) into play, with the attendant risk of internal catastrophe being constantly present.

The irruption of radical uncertainty into all fields and the end of the comforting universe of determinacy is not at all a negative fate, so long as uncertainty itself becomes the new rule of the game. So long as we do not seek to correct that uncertainty by injecting new values, new certainties, but have it circulate as the basic rule. It is the same here as with the will: you can resolve the problem of the will only by a (poetic) transference into the play of otherness, without ever claiming to resolve the question of its ends and its object. It is on the continuity and reciprocal exchange of the Nothing, of illusion, of absence, of non-value, that the continuity of Something is founded.

Uncertainty in this sense becomes the very precondition for the divided nature of thought. Just as uncertainty in physics arises in the end from the fact that the object, in its turn, analyses the subject, so the uncertainty of thought comes from the fact that I am not alone in thinking the world – that the world, in its turn, thinks me.

The Nothing is the only ground – or background – against which we can apprehend existence. It is existence's potential of absence and nullity, but also of energy (there is an analogy here with the quantum void). In this sense, things only ever exist *ex nihilo*. Things only ever exist out of nothing.

The Nothing does not cease to exist as soon as there is something. The Nothing continues (not) to exist just beneath the surface of things. This is Macedonio Fernandez's 'perpetual continuation of the Nothing'. Everything which exists continues, then, not to exist at the same time. This antinomy is beyond the imagining of our critical understanding.

Ex nihilo in nihilum: this is the cycle of the Nothing. It is also – against a thinking based on origins and ends, on evolution and continuity – a discontinuity-based thinking. Only the consideration of an end allows us to conceive a continuity, and our sciences and technologies have accustomed us to see everything in terms of a continuous evolution, which is never anything other than our own – the theological form of our superiority. The essential form, however, is that of discontinuity.

Everywhere in the universe, discontinuity alone is probable. The Big Bang itself is the absolute model. Might it not be the same for living things, events, language? Infinitesimal as is the passage from one form to another, it is always a jump, a catastrophe – from which the strangest, most anomalous forms ensue unexpectedly, with no regard for the end result. Closer to home, languages also provide a fine example of this singular discontinuity (from one signifier to the other, one language to the other), developing in largely random manner, without any continuous progress or superiority of one over another.

For analytical thought, the evolution and advance of living forms is the only possible hypothesis. If the world has a history, then we can aspire to a final explanation of it. But, as Cioran says, 'if life has a meaning, we are all failures'. In other words, the finalistic hypothesis is a despairing one. It emphasizes our failure, and plunges us into an unhappy uncertainty. On the other hand, if the world emerged at a single stroke, it cannot have any determinate meaning or end. We are protected from its end by this non-meaning which assumes a force of poetic illusion. The world, admittedly, then becomes wholly enigmatic, but this uncertainty, like that of appearances, is a happy uncertainty. Illusion, being *per excellence* the art of appearing, of emerging out of nothing, protects us from *being*. As the art of disappearance, it protects us from death. The world is protected from its end by its diabolical indeterminacy.

According to this other hypothesis, the biomass emerged at a stroke. It has been here in its entirety from the beginning: the subsequent history of its complex forms changes nothing about the Big Bang of life. Things here are exactly as they are with the universe, where everything was present in the primal instant. Exactly as it is for language in Lévi-Strauss's thinking: the logomass, the mass of language, emerges in its entirety at a stroke. There will be no addition to it in terms of potential information. There is even too much information – an excess of signifier, which will (we hope) never be reduced. Once it has appeared, it is indestructible. As indestructible as the material substance of the world, or – closer to us – as the material substance of the sociological masses, whose equally sudden appearance is also irreversible (until their eventual collapse, which is as unpredictable, from our limited standpoint, as was their appearance).

Astromass, biomass, logomass, sociomass, semiomass – all are doubtless destined to end one day. Yet they will end not gradually, but suddenly, the way they appeared. Like cultures, which are also invented at a stroke. Their emergence is inexplicable in evolutionary terms, and they sometimes disappear for no visible reason, like living species.

As for our mental universe, it no doubt functions according to this same catastrophic rule: everything is there from the beginning; it is not negotiated by stages. It is like a set of rules: perfect in itself; any idea of progress or change is absurd. It emerges *ex nihilo*; it can disappear only *ex abrupto*. This suddenness, this emergence out of the void, this non-anteriority of things to themselves continue to affect the event of the world at the very heart of its historical unfolding. What constitutes an event is what breaks with all prior causality. The event of language is what makes it re-emerge miraculously every day, as finished form, outside of all prior significations, even outside its current meaning – as though it had never existed. Gosse's hypothesis and Russell's paradox.[1]

And, in the end, we prefer the *ex nihilo*. We prefer something which draws its magic from arbitrariness, from the absence of causes and history. Nothing gives us greater pleasure than something emerging or disappearing at a stroke, than plenitude giving way to the void. Illusion is made of this magic portion, this accursed share, which creates a kind of absolute gain by removing causes, or by distorting effects and causes.

The fundamental uncertainty lies in this machination of the Nothing, in this parallel machinery of the Nothing.

The illusion of having 'overcome' this uncertainty is a mere phantasm of the understanding – a phantasm which lurks behind all value systems and representations of an objective world, including the traditional philosophical question: 'Why is there Something rather than Nothing?' Whereas the true question should, rather, be: 'Why is there Nothing rather than Something?'

But, then, if Nothing is the underlying fabric of all things, it is safely there for eternity, and it profits us 'nothing' to concern ourselves overmuch either with it or with the apparent hegemony of an objective world. Come what may, the Nothing will recognize its own. But the Nothing is precisely not a state of things. It is the product of the dramatic illusion of appearances. And it is the pre-destined target of the truth enterprise, the enterprise of verifying and objectifying the world – a gigantic homeopathic treatment of the world with the single reality-principle – putting an end to that dramatic illusion, putting an end, with a definitive coherence, to the divine incoherence of the world, an incoherence which is not measured against its own end, and which, indeed, is measured against Nothing.

Not to mention the fact that if this 'dark matter' did not exist, our universe would long ago have vanished into thin air. And this is, indeed, the most likely outcome if we succeed in eliminating it. Wherever this void – this antagonistic parallel universe, this radical illusion irreducible to the facts of the real and the rational – is eliminated, the real meets with immediate catastrophe. For matter in itself is delusion, and the material universe is supported only by the missing mass, whose absence is decisive. The real divested of the anti-real becomes hyperreal, more real than the real, and vanishes into simulation. Matter divested of anti-matter is doomed to entropy. By elimination of the void, it is condemned to gravitational collapse. The subject deprived of all otherness collapses into itself, and sinks into autism. The elimination of the inhuman causes the human to collapse into odium and ridicule (this we see in the pretension and vanity of humanitarianism).

There is a very fine parable for this situation in the story of Ishi. Ishi, the last Indian of his tribe, who was taken to San Francisco, was stupefied by the sight of the vast crowds there. He could think only that the dead – all the previous generations – were also there among the living. And the dead, indeed, shield us from being continually present one to another. If you eliminate the dead, then, by dint of sheer overcrowding, the living become strangers to one another. This is what happens in our state of urban overpopulation, overinformation, overcommunication: the whole space is suffocated by this hyper-presence. This is the mass state, where only the living dead remain.

However, the question remains: why are we so intent on ferreting out and destroying the void, absence and death? Why this fantasy of expelling the dark matter, making everything visible, making it real, and forcibly expressing what has no desire to be expressed, forcibly exhuming the only things which ensure the continuity of the Nothing and of the secret? Why are we so lethally tempted into transparency, identity and existence at all costs? An unanswerable question. But perhaps this tendency to be done with all secrets has itself a secret purpose?

In the past, through Creation and Nature, God was quite naturally the instigator of Good, as a providential transcendence worked itself out. God being naturally good, and mankind, in its modern, Rousseauist version, being basically good too, we did not have to transform the world to make it positive, and Evil was only ever an accident.

It is only since God died that the destiny of the world has become our responsibility. Since it can now no longer be justified in another world, it has to be justified here and now. The equivalent of the Kingdom of God – that is to say, the immanence of an entirely positive world (not the transcendence of an ideal world) – has to be brought about by technical means. And to create such an equivalent is, from the theological viewpoint, a total heresy. It is a diabolic temptation to wish for the Reign of Good, since to do so is to prepare the way for absolute Evil. If Good has a monopoly of this world, then the other will be the monopoly of Evil. We shall not escape the reversal of values, and the world will become the field of the metastases of the death of God.

Another explanation for our fall from grace is that the world is given to us. Now, what is given we have to be able to give back. In the past we could give thanks for the gift, or respond to it by sacrifice. Now we have no one to give thanks to. And if we can no longer give anything in exchange for the world, it is unacceptable.

So we are going to have to liquidate the given world. To destroy it by substituting an artificial one, built from scratch, a world for which we do not have to account to anyone. Hence this gigantic technical undertaking for eliminating the natural world in all its forms. All that is natural will be rejected from top to bottom as a consequence of this symbolic rule of the counter-gift and impossible exchange.

But, by this same symbolic rule, we are going to have to pay the price for this artificial creation, and settle this new debt towards ourselves. How are we to be absolved of this technical world and this artificial omnipotence if not by destruction, which is the only possible decompensation for this new situation – the only future event which will leave us with nothing to answer for?

So, all our systems are converging in a desperate effort to escape radical uncertainty, to conjure away the inevitable, fateful fact of impossible exchange. Commercial exchange, exchange of meaning, sexual exchange – everything has to be exchangeable. With all things, we have to find their ultimate equivalence, have to find a meaning and an end for them. When we have that end, that formula, that purpose, then we shall be quits with the world; all will be 'redeemed', the debt will be paid, and radical uncertainty will come to an end. Up to now, all systems have failed. The magical, metaphysical, religious systems which worked in the past are now a dead letter. *But this time we seem to have the final solution, the definitive equivalent: Virtual Reality in all its forms* – the digital, information, universal computation, cloning. In short, the putting in place of a perfect virtual, technological artefact, so that the world can be exchanged for its artificial double. A much more radical solution than all the others, this, since it will no longer have to be exchanged for some transcendence or finality from elsewhere, but for itself, by the substitution of a double which is infinitely 'truer', infinitely more real than the real world – thus putting an end to the question of reality, and to any inclination to give it a meaning. An automatic writing of the world in the absence of the world. Total equivalence, total screen, final solution. Absolutely consolidating the idea of the network as niche, into which it is so easy to disappear. The Internet thinks me. The Virtual thinks me. My double is wandering through the networks, where I shall never meet him. For that parallel universe has no relation to this one. It is an artificial transcription of it, a total echoing of it, but it does not reflect it. The Virtual is no longer the potentially real, as once it was. Non-referential – orbital and exorbital – it is never again intended to meet up with the real world. Having absorbed the original, it produces the world as undecidable.

But is not this parallel universe, which is based on the disappearance of the other, itself doomed to disappear, and is it not itself prey to undecidability? Perhaps it is simply an outgrowth of this world, playfully duplicating itself, in which case this world continues to exist as it is, and we are merely play-acting the Virtual? In the same way as, with the religious 'ulterior worlds', we were play-acting transcendence, though this time we would be play-acting immanence, operational power, play-acting *la pensée unique* and the automatic writing of the world. In other words, here again, a system doomed to fail, a phantasmagoria without the power to ward off the uncertainty and deregulation which ensued from impossible exchange.

In our general anthropology, there is meaning only in what is Human. The story has meaning only when it fits into some unfolding of events, some rational purpose. There is no reason in history, no reason in Reason, except as part of this triumphant evolutionism.

Measuring life by its meaning.
Measuring the world by the Human.
Measuring the event by History.
Measuring thought by the Real.
Measuring the sign by the thing, and so on.

Instead of *measuring oneself* against the world, measuring oneself against the event, measuring oneself against thought. . . .

We are moving everywhere towards an elimination of the Inhuman, towards an anthropological integrism which aims to submit everything to the jurisdiction of the Human. This is an enterprise of hominization which has been extended to animals, nature, and all other species under the banner of human rights, a moral anthropology and a universal ecology – this latter spearheading a campaign to annex the Inhuman to the *pensée unique* of the Human. A planetary project to exterminate the Inhuman in all its forms, an integrist project to domesticate any reality from outside our own sphere – the extreme turn of an imperialism by which, ironically and paradoxically, we deprive ourselves of any idea of the Human as such. For this can come to us only from the Inhuman. It is only on the basis of a radical alteration of our viewpoint that we can have a vision of ourselves and the world – not to fall into a universe of non-meaning, but to recover the potency and originality of the world before it assumes force of meaning and becomes, in that same movement, the site of all powers.

Thought itself must play its part in this process. It must register a leap, a mutation, an intensification. The point is no longer to throw the system into internal contradiction (we know that it regenerates in this spiral of contradiction), but to destabilize it by the infiltration of a viral – or, in other words, inhuman – thought, a thought which lets itself be thought by the Inhuman.

Ultimately, is not thought already a form of the Inhuman, a luxurious dysfunction which contravenes the evolution of life in general by taking stock of that evolution and trapping it in its own image? Does not the neuronal development of the brain already constitute a critical threshold from the point of view of evolution and the species? Then why not speed up the process and precipitate other concatenations, other forms – forms of an objective fate of which we simply have no inkling?

This exclusion of the Inhuman means that from now on it is the Inhuman which thinks us. We can grasp the world only from an omega point external to the Human, from objects and hypotheses which play, for us, the role of strange attractors. Thought has already run up against these kinds of objects at the margins of the inhuman in the past – as, for example, when it came up against primitive societies. Today, however, we have to look further than this critical thinking, a derivative of Western humanism, to far stranger objects which are bearers of a radical uncertainty, and on which we can no longer impose our perspectives in any way whatever.

The convergence of thought is no longer a convergence with truth, but a collusion with the object and a convergence with a set of rules in which the subject is no longer in control.

And what of all these hypotheses themselves which are advanced here? Do they have an equivalent, a use-value, an exchange-value? Absolutely not; it is impossible to exchange them. They can only strike at the chinks in the world's defences, and thought cannot but destroy itself in the object which thinks it, at the same time as it destroys the object it thinks. This is how it escapes truth. Now we have, at the very least, to escape truth. And to escape truth, you must not, whatever you do, trust the subject. You have to leave matters to the object and its strange attraction, the world and its definitive uncertainty.

The whole problem is one of abandoning critical thought, which is the very essence of our theoretical culture, but which belongs to a past history, a past life.

The conventional universe of subject and object, ends and means, true and false, good and evil, no longer matches up to the state of our world. The 'normal' dimensions – of time, space, determination, representation, and hence also of critical, reflexive thought – are deceptive. The discursive universe of psychology, sociology and ideology in which we move is a trap. It is still functioning in a Euclidean dimension. Now, we have almost no theoretical intuition of what has, without realizing it, become a quantum universe – just as we have never had anything but a dim theoretical awareness of the order of simulation into which our modern world long ago unwittingly passed, while retaining a blind faith in the idea of an objective reality. I would even say that it is this superstitious belief in – this hysteresis of – the 'real' and the reality principle that is the true imposture of our times.

We analysed a deterministic society deterministically Today we have to analyse a non-deterministic society non-deterministically – a fractal, random, exponential society, the society of the critical mass and extreme phenomena, a society entirely dominated by relations of uncertainty.

Everything in this society stands under the sign of uncertainty. As a consequence, we can no longer approach it in terms of social determinacy, even if we were to do so critically. Crisis always brought with it its share of tensions and contradictions; it is the natural movement of our history. But we are no longer in crisis; we are in a catastrophic process – not in the sense of a material apocalypse, but in the sense of an overturning of all rules. Catastrophe is the irruption of something which no longer functions according to the rules, or functions by rules we do not know, and perhaps never will. Nothing is simply contradictory or irrational in this state; everything is paradoxical. To pass beyond the end – into the excess of reality, the excess of positivity, the excess of events, the excess of information – is to enter a paradoxical state, a state which can no longer be content with a rehabilitation of traditional values, and demands a thinking that is itself paradoxical: a thinking that no longer obeys a truth principle, and even accepts the impossibility of verification.

We have passed beyond a point of no-return, and beyond this things develop along quite other lines. Ideas of linear development no longer apply. Everything is cast into a turbulence which makes control impossible, including the control of time, for the simultaneity of world information – that transparency of all places brought together in a single moment – is not unlike a perfect crime perpetrated on time.

The uncertainty principle, which states that it is impossible to calculate the speed of a particle and its position simultaneously, is not confined to physics. It applies also to the impossibility of evaluating both the reality and the meaning of an event as it appears in the information media, the impossibility of distinguishing causes and effects in a particular complex process – of distinguishing the terrorist from the hostage (in the Stockholm syndrome), the virus from the cell (in viral pathology). This is just as impossible as isolating subject from object in experiments in sub-atomic physics. Each of our actions is at the same erratic stage as the microscopic particle: you cannot evaluate both its end and its means. You can no longer calculate both the price of a human life and its statistical value. Uncertainty has seeped into all areas of life. And this is not a product of the complexity of parameters (we can always cope with that); it is a definitive uncertainty linked to the irreconcilable character of the data. If we cannot grasp both the genesis and the singularity of the event, the appearance of things and their meaning, then two courses are open to us: either we master meaning, and appearances escape us; or the meaning escapes, and appearances are saved. By the very play of appearances, things are becoming further and further removed from their meaning, and resisting the violence of interpretation.

However this may be, we live in the real and in the order of rational determination, but we do so as though these things represented a 'state of exception'. We live in a double bind: with a dual allegiance, a dual obligation. We live, for the most part, in a Newtonian universe, but we are governed basically by non-determinist equations. Is there no getting over this disparity? Things are the same in social physics as in the physics of nature: macroscopic phenomena still conform to a deterministic analysis, but microscopic phenomena do not behave in any such way. At the level of physical processes, no flagrant contradictions occur: we get along very well in a Newtonian universe. But in the social and historical world, the world of relationships, the mismatch between behaviour and analysis is becoming blatant. A whole area of social functioning still corresponds to a deterministic analysis, a 'realist' sociology (Marxist, empiricist, behaviourist or statistical), and we operate in large measure in this register of the 'real'. But, simultaneously, another kind of functioning – probabilistic, relativistic, aleatory – is gaining the upper hand, and the 'realist' area is secretly immersed in this. In this de-polarized social space (is it still a social or historical space?), traditional analysis no longer has any purchase, and solutions worked out at this level come to grief on a general uncertainty in the same way as classical calculations come to grief in quantum physics.

There is no longer any social determinism. The increase in speed renders all positions improbable. In a field of exclusion, you cannot calculate both the current position of an individual and his or her velocity of exclusion. With a particular type of work or status (or particular kinds of stocks and shares), you cannot calculate both the real value and the rate of devaluation. With entire categories, you cannot calculate both their advancement and their virtual downgrading (as if by chance, the advancement of women is accompanied by a creeping disqualification of the occupations concerned, which cancels out the social advantage gained). With signs, you cannot calculate both their sense and their obsolescence. And with anything in general, you cannot calculate both its effect in real time and its duration. So it is with the indeterminacy of the social.

Hitherto, priority has been given to the analysis of determinate historical forms, in terms of distinct oppositions, such as capital and labour. Today, however, the sphere of labour has become hazy, and the concept itself has lost its definition. As Canetti says of history, we have passed beyond the 'blind point' of the social, and also imperceptibly beyond capital and labour and their antagonistic dynamic. The social machine now moves in a general cycle or, rather, on a Moebius strip, and the social actors are always on both sides of the contract.

The term 'social fracture' is itself part of an attempt to rehabilitate the old objective conditions of capital and labour. Just as the nineteenth-century utopians tried, in a period of industrial boom, to revive values associated with the land and with craft work, so we are trying, in an age of information technology and virtual reality, to revive the social conflicts and relations associated with the industrial era. The same utopia, the same optical illusion. And if the golden age of relations of force and dialectical contradictions has to go, that is just too bad. Marx's analysis itself was of the order of a deterministic simplification of conflicts and history, but it was linked to an ascending curve, and to the possibility of a determinate negation: the social and the proletariat were still concepts destined to surpass and negate themselves. They bore no relation to the positivistic mystification of the social and of labour in our current context. What is lost in our 'interactivist' sociality is precisely the negative element, and the possibility of a determinate negation of the objective conditions. There are no 'objective conditions' any more. More generally, the virtuality of information no longer offers the possibility of a determinate negation of reality. There is no 'objective' reality any more. We may as well accept this, and stop dreaming of a situation that is long dead. We are no longer in the negative and in history, we are in a state where relations of force and social relations have more or less yielded their vitality to a virtual interface and a diffuse collective performance at the point where all speculative flows intersect – flows of employment, capital flows, information flows. But we have to regard this situation as an unprecedented one, and if history has become – as Marx put it – a farce, it might well be that that farce, by reproducing itself, may become our history.

A painful revision of the reality principle, a painful revision of the principle of knowledge. This latter assumes the existence of a dialectic between subject and object, with the subject in control, since he invents it.

Now, the rules of the game have only to change, or become uncertain, or we have only to lose control of the principles, or the object has only to refuse to allow itself to be decoded in the terms we have laid down, for knowledge to become metaphysically impossible. And this is not simply a *metaphysical* impossibility: right now, the sciences are incapable of according a definite status to their object.

The object is not what it was. In all areas it evades us. It now appears only as a fleeting trace on computer screens. At the end of their experimenting, the most advanced sciences can only register its disappearance. Are we not faced here with an ironic revenge of

the object, a strategy of deterrence, flouting experimental proto-
cols and divesting the subject itself of its subject position?

Ultimately, science has never stopped churning out a reassuring scenario in which the world is being progressively deci-
phered by the advances of reason. This was the hypothesis with
which we 'discovered' the world, atoms, molecules, particles,
viruses, and so forth. But no one has ever advanced the hypothesis that things may discover us at the same time as we discover
them, and that there is a dual relationship in discovery. This is
because we do not see the object in its originality. We see it as
passive, as waiting to be discovered – a bit like America being discovered by the Spaniards. But things are not like that. When the
subject discovers the object – whether that object is viruses or
primitive societies – the converse, and never innocent, discovery
is also made: the discovery of the subject by the object. Today,
they say that science no longer 'discovers' its object, but 'invents'
it. We should say, then, that the object, too, does more than just
'discover' us; it invents us purely and simply – it thinks us. It
seems that we have victoriously wrenched the object from its
peaceful state, from its indifference and the secrecy which
enshrouded it. But today, before our very eyes, the enigmatic
nature of the world is rousing itself, resolved to struggle to retain
its mystery. Knowledge is a duel. And this duel between subject
and object brings with it the subject's loss of sovereignty, making
the object itself the horizon of its disappearance.

At any rate, it seems that reality, indifferent to any truth, cares
not one jot for the knowledge to be derived from observing and
analysing it. A docile – if not, indeed, hyper-docile – reality
bends to all hypotheses, and verifies them all without distinction.
For reality, it is all merely a superficial and provisional 'enfram-
ing' [*Gestell*] in the Heideggerian sense. Reality itself has become
simulative, and leaves us with a sense of its fundamental unintel-
ligibility, which has nothing mystical about it, but would seem,
rather, to be ironic. Having reached the paroxystic state (which
is, as the name implies, the state just before the end), reality slips
over of its own accord into the parodic – irony and parody being
the last glimmer reality sends out to us before disappearing, the
last sign the object sends out to us from the depths of its mystery.

Critical thought sees itself as holding up a mirror to the world, but the world knows no mirror stage. Thought must, then, go beyond this critical stage and reach the ulterior stage of the object which thinks us, the world which thinks us. That object-thought is no longer reflective, but reversible. It is merely a special case in the succeeding states of the world, and no longer has the privilege of universality. It has no privilege whatsoever in respect of the incomparable event of the world (though it doubtless has the charm of singularity). It is, in any event, irreducible to the consciousness of the subject. In the disorder of the world, thought, as an exceptional attribute and destiny of the species, is too precious to be reduced to the consciousness of the subject. There could be said, then, to be an interplay between thinking and the world which has nothing to do with the exchange of truth – and which, indeed, might even be said to suppose such exchange impossible.

Object-thought, thought become inhuman, is the form of thinking which actually comes to terms with impossible exchange. It no longer attempts to interpret the world, nor to exchange it for ideas; it has opted for uncertainty, which becomes its rule. It becomes the thinking of the world thinking us. In so doing, it changes the course of the world. For though there is no possible equivalence between thought and the world, there does occur, beyond any critical point of view, a reciprocal alteration between matter and thought. So the situation is reversed: if, once, the subject constituted an event in the world of the object, today the object constitutes an event in the universe of the subject. If the sudden emergence of consciousness constituted an event in the course of the world, today the world constitutes an event in the course of consciousness, in so far as it now forms part of its material destiny, part of the destiny of matter, and hence of its radical uncertainty.

   Physical alteration of the world by consciousness, metaphysical alteration of consciousness by the world: there is no cause to ask where this begins, or 'who thinks whom'. Each is simultaneously in play, and each deflects the other from its goal. Has not humanity, with its inborn consciousness, its ambiguity, its symbolic order and its power of illusion, ended up altering the universe, affecting or infecting it with its own uncertainty? Has it not ended up contaminating the world (of which it is, nevertheless, an integral part) with its non-being, its way of not-being-in-the-world?

This raises many questions regarding the pertinence of knowledge – and not only classical knowledge but quantum, probabilistic science too, since, above and beyond the experimentation which alters its object – now cited as a commonplace example – man is faced in all registers with a universe altered and destabilized by thought. The hypothesis has even been advanced (Diran) that, if there were objective laws of the universe, it is because of humankind that they could neither be formulated nor operate in fact. Rather than humanity bringing reason into a chaotic universe, it would be the bringer of disorder, by its act of knowledge, of thought, which constitutes an extraordinary *coup de force*: establishing a point (even a simulated one) outside the universe from which to see and reflect (on) the universe. If the universe is what does not have a double, since nothing exists outside it, then the mere attempt to make such a point exist is tantamount to a desire to put an end to it.

Note

1. Here Baudrillard is referring not to what is commonly termed 'Russell's paradox' (a proposition in set theory), but to Russell's argument in *The Analysis of Mind*: 'There is no logical impossibility in the hypothesis that the world sprang into being five minutes ago, exactly as it then was, with a population that "remembered" a wholly unreal past.' The nineteenth-century English naturalist P. H. Gosse actually contended that all geological and fossil findings were merely a simulation contemporaneous with the creation of the world by God five thousand years ago – a contention clearly designed to rescue the biblical account.

CHAPTER ELEVEN

The Millennium, or the Suspense of the Year 2000

In 1999 Baudrillard was asked to give the annual Wellek Library Lectures in Critical Theory at the University of California, Irvine in the USA. A subsequent book, *The Vital Illusion* published by Columbia University Press in 2000 and edited by Julia Witwer, contains the English text of the three lectures by Baudrillard. The 'Vital Illusion' in the title is taken from Friedrich Nietzsche's concept of the vital illusion. Nietzsche is an ever-present influence on Baudrillard's work throughout his life. The first lecture, 'The Final Solution', saw Baudrillard discussing the question of cloning and in the third lecture, 'The Murder of the Real', he considered the accelerating virtual world and the disappearance of the Real, after Nietzsche's 'Death of God'. The extract here is the second of the talks for the Annual Lectures, delivered on 27 May 1999. As the eve of the third millennium was rapidly approaching Baudrillard was seen here announcing 'the great end-of-the-century sale' where 'everything must go' and that 'modernity is over (without ever having happened)'. As in many cities around the world in the 1990s, the Pompidou Centre in Paris (the 'Beaubourg' which Baudrillard had analysed in the 1970s) had a digital clock counting down the time to 31 December 1999. Apparently, as Baudrillard later found out, the authorities in Paris moved the clock from the building before its task was completed! In much of Baudrillard's writing about the end-of-the-millennium party there was a feeling of claustrophobia and things being put on hold, where history is endlessly an instant replay of all that has occurred before. Further Baudrillard wrote here of 'the event strike' where the work of history is over. It must have been a blessed relief to eventually be beyond the limit of the year 2000 when *The Vital Illusion* was actually published. Within a year the 9/11 'accident' (as Baudrillard's friend Paul Virilio would put it) in the US gave Baudrillard a new angle for his thinking in a period where 'events' were once again on the move.

'The Millenium, or the Suspense of the Year 2000', from
***The Vital Ilusion*, trans. Julia Witwer, New York:**
Columbia University Press, 2000.

How can we jump over our shadows when we no longer have any? How can we pass out of the old century (not to speak of the millennium) if we do not make up our minds to put an end to it, engaged as we are in an indefinite work of mourning for all the incidents, ideologies, and violence that have marked it? The – more or less hypocritical – commemorations and recantations give the impression that we are trying to run the events of the century back through the filter of memory, not in order to find a meaning for them – they have clearly lost that meaning somewhere along the way – but in order to whitewash them, or to launder them. Cleansing is the prime activity of this fin de siècle – the laundering of a dirty history, of dirty money, of corrupt consciousnesses, of the polluted planet – the cleansing of memory being indissolubly linked to the (hygienic) cleansing of the environment or to the (racial and ethnic) cleansing of populations. We are turning away from history 'in progress,' with none of the problems it poses having been resolved, and plunging into a regressive history, in the nostalgic hope of making something politically correct out of it. And in this retrospective, necrospective obsession, we are losing any chance of things coming to their term. This is why I advanced the idea that the Year 2000 would not take place – quite simply, because the history of this century had already come to an end, because we are remaking it interminably and because, therefore, metaphorically speaking, we shall never pass on, into the future.[1]

Our millenarianism – for we have reached, all the same, a millenarian deadline – is a millenarianism with no tomorrow. Whereas the coming of the Year 1000, even though it was experienced with dread, was a prelude to *parousia* and to the advent of the Kingdom of God, and hence the prelude to an infinite promise, our own deadline remains a closed, involuted one. All we have left of the millenarian dateline is the countdown to it. A perfect symbol for the century – which could do nothing more than count the seconds separating it from its end – is the digital clock on the Beaubourg Center in Paris that showed the countdown in millions of seconds. It illustrates the reversal of our modern relation to time. Time is no longer counted progressively, by addition, starting from an origin – but by subtraction, starting from the end. This is what happens with rocket launches and time bombs. And that end is no longer the symbolic endpoint of a history but the mark of a zero sum, of a potential exhaustion. Time is viewed from a perspective of entropy – the exhausting of all possibilities – the perspective of a counting down . . . to infinity. We no longer possess a forward-looking, historical, or providential vision, which was the vision of a world of progress or production. The final illusion of history, the final utopia of time no longer exists, since it is already registered there as something potentially accounted for, calculated in digital time, just as the finalities of the human cease to exist at the point where they come to be registered in a genetic capital and are looked at solely from the biological perspective of the exploitation of the genome. When you count the seconds separating you from the end, it means that everything is already at an end, that moreover we are already beyond the end.

By the way: something happened to this digital clock. It was removed from the front of the Beaubourg, relegated to a storehouse at the Parc de la Villette without anyone knowing about it. For a long time it was there ticking in the dark – a very heavy symbol of the destiny of Time at the end of the twentieth century. Then it was displaced again to the Place de la Bastille (the story of the inventor and the EDF: time doesn't work anymore). This is a truly illuminating emblem of Y2K's failure to take place. Even the sign of it was removed in anticipation. It seems that no right place is to be found for the end.

Was it for fear of this deadline? Growing anxiety about this deadline? Or did it mean, as we said, that this end had already occurred, secretly, furtively – perhaps at the very beginning of the countdown? – and that it now lay behind us? And then the registration of it would be useless. The same thing goes for the Apocalypse. The real event of the Apocalypse is behind us, among us, and we are instead confronted with the virtual reality of the Apocalypse, with the posthumous comedy of the Apocalypse. Maybe it was already the same with the first millennium, with the Apocalypse of Y1K. 'The writers of the Apocalypse send letter after letter to one another, instead of questioning the Antichrist himself.' Then, even they were already dealing with the virtual reality of the Apocalypse.

In the countdown, the time remaining is already past, and the maximal utopia of life gives way to the minimal utopia of survival. We are experiencing time and history in a kind of deep coma. This is the hysteresis of the millennium, which expresses itself in interminable crisis. It is no longer the future that lies before us, but an anorectic dimension – the impossibility of anything's being over and, at the same time, the impossibility of seeing beyond the present. Prediction, the memory of the future, diminishes in exact proportion to the memory of the past. When there is overall transparence, when everything can be seen, nothing can be *foreseen* anymore.[2]

What is there beyond the end? Beyond the end extends virtual reality, the horizon of a programmed reality in which all our functions – memory, emotions, sexuality, intelligence – become progressively useless. Beyond the end, in the era of the transpolitical, the transsexual, the transaesthetic, all our desiring machines become little spectacle machines, then quite simply bachelor machines, before trailing off into the countdown of the species. The countdown is the code of the automatic disappearance of the world, and all our little charitable machines, by way of which we anticipate that disappearance – the Telethons, Sidathons, and all kinds of Thanathons – are merely the promotional sales events for the misery of this fin de siècle.[3]

But – and this is even more paradoxical – what are we to do when nothing really comes to an end anymore, that is to say, when nothing ever really takes place, since everything is already calculated, audited, and realized in advance (the simulacrum preceding the real, information preceding the event, etc.)? Our problem is no longer: What are we to make of real events, of real violence? Rather, it is: What are we to make of events that do not take place? Not: What are we to do after the orgy? But: What are we to do when the orgy no longer takes place – the orgy of history, the orgy of revolution and liberation, the orgy of modernity? Little by little, as the hands of the clock move around (though, sadly, digital clocks no longer even have hands), we tell ourselves that, taking everything into account – taking everything into a 'countdown' – modernity has never happened. There has never really been any modernity, never any real progress, never any assured liberation. The linear tension of modernity and progress has been broken, the thread of history has become tangled: the last great 'historic' event – the fall of the Berlin Wall – signified something closer to an enormous repentance on the part of history. Instead of seeking fresh perspectives, history appears rather to be splintering into scattered fragments, and phases of events and conflicts we had thought long gone are being reactivated.

All that we believed over and done, left behind by the inexorable march of universal progress, is not dead at all; it seems to be returning to strike at the heart of our ultra-sophisticated, ultravulnerable systems. It's a bit like the last scene of *Jurassic Park*, in which the modern (artificially cloned) dinosaurs burst into the museum and wreak havoc on their fossilized ancestors preserved there, before being destroyed in their turn. Today we are caught as a species in a similar impasse, trapped between our fossils and our clones.

So, the countdown extends in both directions: not only does it put an end to time in the future but it also exhausts itself in the obsessional revival of the events of the past. A reversed recapitulation, which is the opposite of a living memory – it is fanatical *memorization*, a fascination with commemorations, rehabilitations, cultural museification, the listing of sites of memory, the extolling of heritage. In fact this obsession with reliving and reviving everything, this obsessional neurosis, this forcing of memory is equivalent to a vanishing of memory – a vanishing of actual history, a vanishing of the event in the information space. This amounts to making the past itself into a clone, an artificial double, and freezing it in a sham exactitude that will never actually do it justice. But it is because we have nothing else, now, but objects in which not to believe, nothing but fossilized hopes, that we are forced to go down this road: to elevate everything to the status of a museum piece, an item of heritage. Here again, time reverses: instead of things first passing through history before becoming part of the heritage, they now pass directly into the heritage. Instead of first existing, works of art now go straight into the museum. Instead of being born and dying, beings are 'born' as virtual fossils. Collective neurosis. As a result, the ozone layer that was protecting memory becomes frayed; the hole through which memories and time are leaking out into space expands, prefiguring the great migration of the void to the periphery.[4]

Closing down, closing down! It's the end-of-the-century sale. Everything must go! Modernity is over (without ever having happened), the orgy is over, the party is over – the sales are starting. It's the great end-of-the-century sale. But the sales don't come after the festive seasons any longer; nowadays the sales start first, they last the whole year long, even the festivals themselves are on sale everywhere . . . The stocks have to be used up, time-capital has to be used up, life-capital has to be used up. Everywhere, we have the countdown; what we are living through in this symbolic end of the old millennium is a sort of fatal prescription, whether it be that of the planet's resources or of AIDS, which has become the collective symptom of the prescribed term of death. It is all these things that hang over us in the shadow of the Year 2000, together with the delicious, yet terrifying enjoyment of the lag time left to us. But, ultimately, perhaps the Year 2000 will not have taken place? Perhaps, on the occasion of the Year 2000, we are to be granted a general amnesty?

The concept of countdown evokes once again Arthur C. Clarke's 'The Nine Billion Names of God.'[5] A community of Tibetan monks has been engaged from time immemorial in listing and copying out the names of God, of which there are nine billion. At the end of this, the world will end. So runs the prophecy. But the monks are tired and, in order to hasten the work, they call in the experts at IBM, who come along with their computers and finish the job in a month. It is as if the operation of the virtual dimension were to bring the history of the world to an end in an instant. Unfortunately, this also means the disappearance of the world in real time, for the prophecy of the end of the world associated with this countdown of the names of God is fulfilled. As they go back down into the valley, the technicians, who did not actually believe the prophecy, see the stars vanishing from the firmament, one by one.

This parable depicts our modern situation well: we have called in the IBM technicians and they have launched the code of the world's automatic disappearance. As a result of the intervention of all the digital, computing, and virtual-reality technologies, we are already beyond reality; things have already passed beyond their own ends. They cannot, therefore, come to an end any longer, and they sink into the interminable (interminable history, interminable politics, interminable crisis).

And, in effect, we persevere, on the pretext of an increasingly sophisticated technology, in the endless deconstruction of a world and of a history unable to transcend and complete itself. Everything is free to go on infinitely. We no longer have the means to end processes. They unfold without us now, beyond reality, so to speak, in an endless speculation, an exponential acceleration. But, as a result, they do so in an indifference that is also exponential. What is endless is also desire-less, tension-less, passionless; it is bereft of events. An anorectic history, no longer fueled by real incidents and exhausting itself in the countdown. Exactly the opposite of the end of history, then: *the impossibility of finishing with history.* If history can no longer reach its end, then it is, properly speaking, no longer a history. We have lost history and have also, as a result, lost the end of history. We are laboring under the illusion of the end, under the posthumous illusion of the end. And this is serious, for the end signifies that something has really taken place. Whereas we, at the height of reality – and with information at its peak – no longer know whether anything has taken place or not.

Perhaps the end of history, if we can actually conceive such a thing, is merely ironic? Perhaps it is merely an effect of the ruse of history, which consists in its having concealed the end from us, in its having ended without our noticing it. So that it is merely the end of history that is being fueled, whereas we believe we are continuing to make it. We are still awaiting its end, whereas that end has, in fact, already taken place. History's ruse was to make us believe in its end, when it has, in fact, already started back in the opposite direction.

Whether we speak of the end of history, the end of the political or the end of the social, what we are clearly dealing with is the end of *the scene of the political*, the end of *the scene of the social*, the end of *the scene of history*. In other words, in all these spheres, we are speaking of the advent of a specific era of *obscenity*. Obscenity may be characterized as the endless, unbridled proliferation of the social, of the political, of information, of the economic, of the aesthetic, not to mention the sexual. Obesity is another of the figures of obscenity. As proliferation, as the saturation of a limitless space, obesity may stand as a general metaphor for our systems of information, communication, production, and memory. Obesity and obscenity form the contrapuntal figure for all our systems, which have been seized by something of an Ubuesque distension.[6] All our structures end up swelling like red giants that absorb everything in their expansion. Thus the social sphere, as it expands, absorbs the political sphere entirely. But the political sphere is itself obese and obscene – and yet at the same time it is becoming increasingly transparent. The more it distends, the more it virtually ceases to exist. When everything is political, that is the end of politics as destiny; it is the beginning of politics as culture and the immediate poverty of that cultural politics. It is the same with the economic or the sexual spheres. As it dilates, each structure infiltrates and subsumes the others, before being absorbed in its turn.

Such are the extreme phenomena: those that occur beyond the end (extreme = *ex terminis*). They indicate that we have passed from growth (*croissance*) to outgrowth (*ex-croissance*), from movement and change to stasis, *ek*-stasis, and metastasis. They

countersign the end, marking it by excess, hypertrophy, proliferation, and chain reaction; they reach critical mass, overstep the
critical deadline, through potentiality and exponentiality.

Ecstasy of the social: the masses. More social than the social.
Ecstasy of the body: obesity. Fatter than fat.
Ecstasy of information: simulation. Truer than true.
Ecstasy of time: real time, instantaneity. More present than the
    present.
Ecstasy of the real: the hyperreal. More real than the real.
Ecstasy of sex: porn. More sexual than sex.
Ecstasy of violence: terror. More violent than violence . . . .

All this describes, by a kind of potentiation, a raising to the
second power, a pushing to the limit, a state of unconditional
realization, of total positivity (every negative sign raised to
the second power produces a positive), from which all utopia, all
death, and all negativity have been expunged. A state of extermination, cleansing of the negative, as corollary to all the other
actual forms of purification and discrimination. Thus, freedom
has been obliterated, liquidated by liberation; truth has been
supplanted by verification; the community has been liquidated
and absorbed by communication; form gives way to information
and performance. Everywhere we see a paradoxical logic: the idea
is destroyed by its own realization, by its own excess. And in this
way history itself comes to an end, finds itself obliterated by the
instantaneity and omnipresence of the event.

This kind of acceleration by inertia, this exponentiality of
extreme phenomena, produces a new kind of event: now we
encounter strange, altered, random, and chaotic events that
Historical Reason no longer recognizes as its own. Even if, by
analogy with past events, we think we recognize them, they no
longer have the same meaning. The same incidents (wars, ethnic
conflicts, nationalisms, the unification of Europe) do not have the
same meaning when they arise as part of a history in progress as
they do in the context of a history in decline. Now, we find ourselves in a vanishing history, and that is why they appear as ghost
events to us.

But is a ghost history, a spectral history, still a history?

Not only have we lost utopia as an ideal end, but historical time itself is also lost, in its continuity and its unfolding. Something like a short-circuit has occurred, a switch shift of the temporal dimension – effects preceding causes, ends preceding origins – and these have led to the paradox of achieved utopia. Now, achieved utopia puts paid to the utopian dimension. It creates an impossible situation, in the sense that it exhausts the possibilities. From this point on, the goal is no longer life transformed, which was the maximal utopia, but rather life-as-survival, which is a kind of minimal utopia.

So today, with the loss of utopias and ideologies, we lack objects of belief. But even worse, perhaps, we lack *objects in which not to believe*. For it is vital – maybe even more vital – to have things in which not to believe. Ironic objects, so to speak, dis-invested practices, ideas to believe or disbelieve as you like. Ideologies performed this ambiguous function pretty well. All this is now jeopardized, vanishing progressively into extreme reality and extreme operationality.

Other things are emerging: retrospective utopias, the revival of all earlier or archaic forms of what is, in a sense, a retrospective or necrospective history. For the disappearance of avant-gardes, those emblems of modernity, has not brought the disappearance of the rearguard as well. Just the opposite is true. In this process of general retroversion (was history perhaps infected with a retro-virus?), the rearguard finds itself in point position.

Quite familiar by now is the parodic, palinodic event, the event Marx analyzed when he depicted Napoleon III as a grotesque copy of Napoleon I. In this second event – a cheap avatar of the original – we have a form of dilution, of historical entropy: history self-repeating becomes farce. The fake history presents itself as if it were advancing and continuing, when it is actually collapsing. The current period offers numerous examples of this debased, extenuated form of the primary events of modernity. Ghostevents, clone-events, *faux*-events, phantom-events – such as phantom limbs, those missing legs or arms that hurt even when they are no longer there. Spectrality, of communism in particular.

Events that are more or less ephemeral because they no longer have any resolution except in the media (where they have the 'resolution' images do, where they are 'resolved' in high definition) – they have no political resolution. We have a history that no longer consists of action, of acts, but instead culminates in a virtual acting-out; it retains a spectral air of déjà-vu. Sarajevo is a fine example of this unreal history, in which all the participants were just standing by, unable to act. It is no longer an event, but rather the symbol of a specific impotence of history. Everywhere, virtuality – the media hyperspace and the hyperspace of discourses – develops in a way diametrically opposed to what one might call, if it still existed, the real movement of history.

In the past the virtual was intended to become actual: actuality was its destination. Today the function of the virtual is to proscribe the actual. Virtual history is here in place of real history; the information-replica stands for, stands *in* for, the definitive absence of that real history. Hence our lack of responsibility – both individual and collective – since we are already, by virtue of information, beyond the event, which has not taken place.

We might speak here of a kind of 'event strike,' to use Macedonio Fernandez's expression.[7] What does this mean? That the work of history is over. That the work of mourning is beginning. That the system of information has been substituted for that of history and is starting to produce events in the same way that Capital is starting to produce Work. Just as labor, under these circumstances, no longer has any significance of its own, the event produced by information has no historical meaning of its own.

This is the point where we enter the transhistorical or transpolitical – that is to say, the sphere where events do not really take place precisely because they are produced and broadcast 'in real time,' where they have no meaning because they can have all possible meanings. We have, therefore, to grasp them now not politically but transpolitically – that is to say, *at the point where they become lost in the void of information*. The sphere of information is like a space where, after events are deprived of their meaning, they receive an artificial gravity, where, after being flash-frozen politically and historically, they are restaged transpolitically, in real – that is to say, perfectly virtual – time. We might speak in the same way of the transeconomic sphere – in other words, the sphere where classical economics gets lost in the void of speculation, just as History gets lost in the void of information.

But, in the end, perhaps we have to frame all these problems in terms other than the obsolete ones of alienation and the fatal destiny of the subject. And it is precisely the Ubuesque side of this technological outgrowth, of this proliferating obscenity and obesity, of this unbridled virtuality, which induces us to do so. Our situation is a wholly pataphysical one – that is to say, everything around us has passed beyond its own limits, has moved beyond the laws of physics and metaphysics. Now, pataphysics is ironic, and the hypothesis that suggests itself here is that, *at the same time that things have reached a state of paroxysm, they have also reached a state of parody.*

Might we advance the hypothesis – beyond the heroic stage, beyond the critical stage – of an ironic stage of technology, an ironic stage of history, an ironic stage of value? This would at last free us from the Heideggerian vision of technology as the effectuation and final stage of metaphysics; it would free us from all retrospective nostalgia for being, and we would have, instead, a gigantic, objectively ironic vision of the entire scientific and technological process that would not be too far removed from the radical snobbery, the post-historical Japanese snobbery Kojève spoke of.[8]

An ironic reversal of technology, similar to the irony of the media sphere. The common illusion about the media is that they are used by those in power to manipulate, seduce, and alienate the masses. A naive interpretation. The more subtle interpretation, the ironic one, is just the opposite. Through the media, it is the masses who manipulate those in power (or those who believe themselves to be). It is when the political powers think they have the masses where they want them that the masses impose their clandestine strategy of neutralization, of destabilization of a power that has become paraplegic. Finally undecidable; yet both hypotheses are valid, for any interpretation of the media is reversible. It is precisely in this reversibility that the objective irony lies.

Let us put the same hypothesis regarding the object of science – of the most sophisticated of current sciences. Through the most subtle procedures we deploy to capture it, isn't the scientific object itself playing with us, presenting itself as an object and mocking our objective pretension to analyze it? Scientists are not far from admitting this point today, and this irony of the object is the very form of a radical illusion of the world – an illusion no longer physical (illusion of the senses) or metaphysical (illusion of the mind) but pataphysical, in the sense Jarry gave the word when he spoke of pataphysics as 'the science of imaginary solutions.'[9]

And we can extend the hypothesis to all our technologies, to the technical universe in general. It is becoming the ironic instrument of a world that we only imagine is ours to transform and dominate. It is the world, it is the object itself, that asserts itself, makes itself felt through all the interposing technologies – a process in which we are merely operators. Here again, we see the form of the illusion. Illusion, not error (we are not wrong about technology – there is no human fatality about technology, as is often pretended): the illusion is not an error or deception but a game, a big game whose rules we just don't know and perhaps will never know.

Since the ironic hypothesis – that of a transcendental irony of the technological – is by definition unverifiable, let us take it as undecidable. We are in fact faced with two incompatible hypotheses: that of the perfect crime or, in other words, of the extermination by technology and virtuality of all reality – or that of the ironic game of technology, of an ironic destiny of all science and all knowledge by which the world, and the illusion of the world, are saved and perpetuated. Let us take up both of these irreconcilable and simultaneously 'true' perspectives. Nothing allows us to decide between them. 'The world is everything which is the case,' as Wittgenstein says.[10]

In the *Critique of Political Economy*, Marx writes: 'Therefore mankind always sets itself only such tasks as it can solve; since, looking at the matter more closely, it will always be found that the task itself arises only when the material conditions for its solution already exist or are at least in the process of formation.'[11] But this no longer holds – precisely because of our world's precipitation into the virtual, which overturns all those 'material conditions' Marx was talking about and overturns all those historical conditions that would make it possible to resolve the problems dialectically. The virtual is a form of final solution of history and of all real conflicts. It succeeds so well that today, humanity (or those who would think for humanity) will only set itself problems when they have already been virtually overcome or once the system has successfully displaced and absorbed them. But was this not already the case in the time of Marx? The emergence of the concept of class, and of class struggle, the emergence of the idea of class consciousness marks the moment when class begins progressively to lose its violent, irreducible character. Likewise, if Foucault can analyze power, it is because power no longer has a definition that can be properly called political; it has already become in some sense a lost object. When ethnology turns its attention to primitive societies, it is the sign that they are in the process of disappearing – and what is more, the analyses themselves help to speed their disappearance.

Critical consciousness, thought in general, perhaps, always comes after the fact, a day too late, like Kafka's Messiah – or it comes at the close of the day, like Hegel's owl. It is nothing but retrospective prophecy, or some platonic shadow dancing on the wall of events, in the cavern of history. 'If speak of time,' Queneau wrote, 'it is because we are already out of time.'[12] History doesn't offer a second seating (*L'histoire ne repasse pas les plats*) – only critique does.

Is there space for another kind of thought? An *other* thought – a paradoxical thought that would, in an inversion of the words of Marx, pose only insoluble, definitively insoluble problems? The material conditions for the resolution of such problems are nowhere to be found and never will be found. Is there room for a kind of thought that would instead reproblematize all the old solutions and help to hold the world in enigmatic tension? No one is certain. This may be the risk thought has to take: it must risk falling victim to its own prophecies, just as history risks getting caught in its own snare.

Notes

1. *'This is why I advanced the idea that the Year 2000 would not take place . . .'* The lecture was delivered on May 27, 1999, and in its original form it was an artifact of its time, balanced on the leading edge of the millennium, pointing 'ahead' to a nonevent which we, of course, did not experience. Some of the tenses have been altered to reflect our new position vis-à-vis the end, but many of them have been left as they were written, in a 'suspended' present.

2. *'When there is overall transparence, when everything can be seen, nothing can be* foreseen *anymore.'* 'Transparence' is Baudrillard translator Chris Turner's rendering of the French *'transparence,'* and is meant to help distinguish the term from everyday 'transparency.'

3. *'The countdown is the code of the automatic disappearance of the world, and all our little charitable machines, by way of which we anticipate that disappearance – the telethons, Sidathons, and all kinds of Thanathons – are merely the promotional sales events for the misery of this fin de siècle.'* 'SIDA' is the French acronym for Acquired Immune System Deficiency; a 'Sidathon' is a benefit held to raise money for the victims of AIDS (see, for example, the 1997 Sidathon organized by the group Sid'Afrique to benefit AIDS victims on the Ivory Coast).

4. *'As a result, the ozone layer that was protecting memory becomes frayed; the hole through which memories and time are leaking out into space expands, prefiguring the great migration of the void to the periphery.'* This is an allusion to Alfred Jarry's inversion of the law of falling bodies: 'Contemporary science is founded upon the principle of induction: most people have seen a certain phenomenon precede or follow some other phenomenon most often, and conclude therefrom that it will ever be thus . . . Instead of formulating the law of the fall of a body toward a center, how far more apposite would be the law of the ascension of a vacuum toward a periphery, a vacuum being considered a unit of non-density, a hypothesis far less arbitrary than the choice of a concrete

unit of positive density such as *water*?' (*Selected Works of Alfred Jarry*, ed. Roger Shattuck and Simon Watson Taylor [New York: Grove Press, 1965], p. 193).

5. '*The concept of countdown evokes once again Arthur C. Clarke's "The Nine Billion Names of God."*' In Arthur C. Clarke, *The Nine Billion Names of God* (New York: Harcourt Brace World, 1967).

6. '*Obesity and obscenity form the contrapuntal figure for all our systems, which have been seized by something of an Ubuesque distension.*' Baudrillard here and elsewhere is alluding to Alfred Jarry's notorious invention Père Ubu, around whom Jarry wrote several satirical, highly scatalogical plays and vignettes. Depicted as monstrously obese, Ubu wreaks havoc everywhere he goes (in Ubu's earliest appearance, Jarry has him flush his conscience down the toilet). Of Ubu, Roger Shattuck writes: 'We are all Ubu, still blissfully ignorant of our destructiveness and systematically practicing the soul-devouring "reversal" of flushing our conscience down the john. Ubu, unruffled king of tyrants and cuckolds, is more terrifying than tragedy' ('Introduction,' in *Selected Works of Alfred Jarry*, ed. Roger Shattuck and Simon Watson Taylor [New York: Grove Press, 1965], p. 10).

7. '*We might speak here of a kind of "event strike," to use Macedonio Fernandez's expression.*' The Argentine writer and metaphysician Macedonio Fernandez (1874–1952). His works strongly influenced Jorge Luis Borges, and are today considered to be important precursors of the contemporary Latin American novel. Macedonio's concept of the event strike can be found in his *Papeles de Recienvenido. Continuación de la nada* (Buenos Aires: Editorial Losada, S.A., 1944).

8. '*We would have, instead, a gigantic, objectively ironic vision of the entire scientific and technological process that would not be too far removed from the radical snobbery, the post-historical Japanese snobbery Kojève spoke of.*' This reference can be found in Alexandre Kojève's 'Note to the Second Edition' in 'Interpretation of the Third Part of Chapter VIII of *Phenomenology of Spirit*' in *Introduction to the Reading of Hegel* (ed. Allan Bloom, trans. James H. Nichols, Jr.

[New York: Basic 1969] [orig. publ. as *Introduction à la lecture de Hegel* (2nd edn, Paris: Gallimard, 1947)], pp. 159–62). In this note, the 'natural' post-historical society of America is (unfavorably) compared with what Kojève calls the 'snobbism' of post-historical Japan. For Kojève, Japanese 'snobbism' – the production of purely arbitrary social and cultural forms, of an artifical, 'empty' symbolic ordering of human society – is a compelling alternative approach to the problem of the end of history (and the concomitant loss of tensions, of 'necessary' cultural forms, implicit in that ending). This 'snobbism,' by virtue of its very emptiness, has striking affinities with the arbitrary creativity of the pataphysical response to a 'world without limits' that for Baudrillard would characterize an ironic stage of history.

9. '*Scientists are not far from admitting this point today, and this irony of the object is the very form of a radical illusion of the world – an illusion no longer physical (illusion of the senses) or metaphysical (illusion of the mind) but pataphysical, in the sense Jarry gave the word when he spoke of pataphysics as "the science of imaginary solutions."*' This phrase can be found in Roger Shattuck's 'Superliminal Note' on pataphysics, published originally in *Evergreen Review* 4, no. 2 (May–June 1960); the line was also used by the Collège de Pataphysique in their pamphlet, 'On the Threshhold of "Pataphysics"' (Paris: 'XC,' 1963?).

10. '*Nothing allows us to decide between them. "The world is everything which is the case," as Wittgenstein says.*' *Tractatus Logico-Philosophicus*, trans. D. F. Pears and B. F. McGuinness (London: Routledge & Kegan Paul, 1961), 1:7; orig. publ. as *Logisch-philosophische Abhandlung* in *Annalen der Naturphilosophie*, ed. Wilhelm Ostwald, 1921.

11. '*In the* Critique of Political Economy, *Marx writes: "Therefore mankind always sets itself only such tasks as it can solve; since, looking at the matter more closely, it will always be found that the task itself arises only when the material conditions for its solution already exist or are at least in the process of formation."*' In Karl Marx and Frederick Engels, *Selected Works*, vol. 2 (Moscow: Lawrence and Wishart, 1935), pp. 361 ff.

12. ' "*If I speak of time,*" *Queneau wrote,* "*it is because we are already out of time.*" ' Baudrillard is probably quoting a line from Raymond Queneau's poem, 'L'Explication des métaphores,' in the collection *Les Ziaux*: 'Si je parle d'un lieu, c'est qu'il a disparu / Si je parle du temps, c'est qu'il n'est déjà plus' (*Les Ziaux*: Paris, Gallimard, Métamorphoses, 1948).

CHAPTER TWELVE

Truth or Radicality? The Future of Architecture

In 1999 the influential London-based architecture magazine *Blueprint* published Baudrillard's thinking on what he saw as 'radical thought' on the one hand and the 'future of architecture' on the other, translated into English by Chris Turner. Baudrillard, who never practised architecture, wrote and spoke frequently about architecture as a practice during his life, stressing that his focus was really the 'radicality of space'. Baudrillard and his world-famous countryman, the architect Jean Nouvel, had engaged with other architects and philosophers in a conference sponsored by University of Paris VI and La Villette School of Architecture in Paris in 1997 and 1998. The project was entitled Urban Passages and consisted of six encounters, each between a writer and an architect. In conversation, on the topic of 'architecture et philosophie', with Jean Nouvel in two wide-ranging and creative interviews Baudrillard admitted that he had 'never been interested in architecture' and that he had 'no specific feelings about it one way or another'. Baudrillard insisted that he was most interested in buildings like the Beaubourg and the World Trade Center. However, it was the 'world they translate' not their status as 'architectural wonders' that fascinated Baudrillard. The *Blueprint* 'essay' is made up of translated pieces from Baudrillard's part of the conversation with Nouvel. This piece was published at a time when architecture practitioners like Rem Koolhaas, Jean Nouvel and Daniel Libeskind were much in demand, not though so much as architects for hire but rather as celebrity social and cultural theorists. The extract here is the original article in full. In it Baudrillard warned against the increasingly repetitive nature of buildings, or in other words their cloning, which was likely to lead to the death of architecture. Furthermore, Baudrillard discussed both Nouvel's architecture, including his buildings in Paris such as the Fondation Cartier, and the World Trade Centre in New York about which he would have much more to say after 9/11.

'Truth or Radicality? The Future of Architecture',
***Blueprint*, No. 157, trans. Chris Turner, London: Blueprint, 1999.**

Let us start out from space, which is after all the primal scene of architecture, and from the radicality of space, which is the void. Is it necessary, and is it possible, to structure or organise that space in any other way than by indefinite horizontal or vertical extension? In other words, when confronted with the radicality of space, is it possible to invent a truth of architecture?

Is there nothing more to architecture than its reality – its references, procedures, functions and techniques? Or does it exceed all these things and ultimately involve something quite different, which might be its own end or something which would allow it to pass beyond its end? Does architecture continue to exist once it has passed beyond its own reality, beyond its truth, in a kind of radicality, a sort of challenge to space (and not simply a management of space), challenge to this society (and not simply a respect for its constraints and a mirroring of its institutions), challenge to architectural creation itself, and challenge to creative architects or the illusion of their mastery? That is the question.

I would like to examine the issue of architectural illusion in two completely opposing senses of the term: on the one hand, to look at architecture insofar as it generates illusion, including illusions about itself, and, on the other, to look at it insofar as it invents a new illusion of urban space and space in general, another scene which exceeds its own grasp.

Personally, I have always been interested in space, and my interest in so-called 'built' objects has been in all those features which give me back the dizzying sense of space. Hence I've found myself interested in such objects as the Pompidou Centre, the

World Trade Center and Biosphere 2 – objects which were not exactly (in my view) architectural marvels. It wasn't their architectural significance which captivated me. The question for me was: what is the truth of these objects which – as is the case with most of our great contemporary architectural objects – seem to have been parachuted in from some other world? If, for example, I consider the truth of a building like the World Trade Center, I see that even in the 1960s architecture was already generating the profile of a society and a period which was hyperreal, if not yet actually computerised, with the twin towers resembling nothing so much as two strips of punched tape. In their twinness we might say today that they were already cloned, and were indeed something like a presentiment of the death of 'the original'. Are they, then, an anticipation of our time? Do architects inhabit not the reality, but the fiction of a society? Do they live in an anticipatory illusion? Or are they quite simply expressing what is already there? It is in this sense that I ask the question 'Is there a truth of architecture?' – by which I mean, is there some suprasensible intended purpose for architecture and space?

Let us try and see how things stand with this 'creative' illusion, with this 'beyond' of architectural reality. The architect's adventure takes place in a world which is eminently real. He or she is in a very particular situation which is not that of an artist in the traditional sense. Architects are not people who sit poring over blank pages or working at canvases. Working to a precise timetable, to a set budget, and for specified persons, they have an object to produce (though one which is not necessarily specified in advance). They work with a team and are in a situation in which they are going to be limited, directly or indirectly, by considerations of safety and finance and by their own professional organisation. Given this situation, where is the scope for freedom, how can they get beyond these constraints? The problem is one of articulating each project to a prior concept or idea (with a very particular strategy in terms of perception and intuition), which is going to define a place of which they have as yet no clear knowledge. We are in the area of invention here, the area of nonknowledge, in the area of risk, and this can in the end become a place where we do not have total control – where things happen secretly, things which are of the order of fate and the voluntary surrender of control. This is where overt illusion enters the picture, the illusion of a space which is not merely visible, but might be said to be the mental prolongation of what one sees, the basic hypothesis here being that architecture is not what fills up a space, but what generates space. This may be achieved through internal visual 'feedback' effects, through the (mis)appropriation of other elements or spaces, through an almost unconscious conjuring. But it is here that the mind kicks in. Take Japanese gardens. There is always a vanishing point, a point where you can't say whether the garden comes to a stop or carries on. Or, again, Jean Nouvel's attempt, with the projected Tour sans Fin at La Défense outside Paris, to go beyond the logic of Albertian perspective (in other words, to organise all the elements so that they are read in an ascending order of scale and thus generate an awareness of space). Though Nouvel's building disappears into the sky, and, being at the outer reaches of sensory perception, verges upon the immaterial, this is not an architecture which is in any sense virtual (though the building has remained virtual in the sense that it has never been built), but one which knows how to create more than merely what one sees.

We have here a mental space of seduction for the eye and the mind. If I look at the façade of the Fondation Cartier building, also by Jean Nouvel, then because that façade is larger than the building, I don't know whether I'm seeing through glass to the sky or seeing the sky directly. If I look at a tree through three panes of glass, I never know if I'm seeing through to a real tree or seeing a reflection. And when two trees are by chance standing parallel to a pane of glass, I never know whether there's a second tree or whether that, too, is a reflection. This form of illusion is not gratuitous: by the destabilisation of perception, it enables a mental space to be created and a scene to be established – a scenic space – without which buildings would merely be constructions and the city itself would merely be an agglomeration of buildings. It is, indeed, from this loss of the scene, with the concomitant thwarting of the viewer's gaze – and, consequently, from the loss of a whole dramaturgy of illusion and seduction – that our cities suffer, being condemned as they are to the saturation of space by an architecture of (both useful and useless) functions.

The most recent presentation of Issey Miyake designs at the Fondation Cartier was a fine illustration of this mise en scéne, in which the living transparency of the architectural object gave it an active role in the spectacle. Scene one: the Issey Miyake creations, moving around in the inner space. Then the guests gallery (the women for the most part already dressed in Issey Miyake clothes), unwitting extras in the same mise en scéne. Then the building itself, reflecting all this – all of it together, seen from outside, presented as one overall event – so that the exhibition site itself became an exhibited object and in the end made itself invisible.

This capacity to be there and at the same time to be invisible seems to me a fundamental quality. This form of what one might call secret (in)visibility is the most effective counter to the currently hegemonic regime of visibility – that dictatorship of transparency in which everything must make itself visible and interpretable, in which the whole aim is to invest mental and visual space, space which is then no longer a space of seeing, but of showing, of making-seen. The antidote to this is an architecture capable of creating both place and non-place, and retaining the charms of transparency without its dictatorship.

The products of such an architecture are unidentified, unidentifiable objects which are a challenge to the surrounding order and stand in a dual – and potentially 'duelling' – relation with the order of reality. It is in this sense that we can speak not of their truth, but of their radicality. If this duel does not take place, if architecture has to be the functional and programmatic transcription of the constraints of the social and urban order, then it no longer exists as architecture. A successful object is one which exists beyond its own reality, which creates a dual (and not merely interactive) relation (with its users also), a relation of contradiction, misappropriation and destabilisation.

The problem is the same in the register of writing and thought and in the political and social orders. Everywhere, whatever you do, you have no choice of events. You merely have a choice of concepts. But that choice is one we hold on to.

Concepts necessarily come into conflict with contexts, with all the (positive, functional) meanings a building or a theory – or anything else – may take on. The concept is something which, in relation to the event as it presents itself, as it is interpreted and over-interpreted by the media and the information system, creates the non-event. To the allegedly 'real' event, it opposes a theoretical and fictional non-event. I can see how this can work with writing. It is much less clear how it works with architecture, but in some architectural objects I sense a kind of extrapolation from another space, another scene, there being here an inspiration running counter to any project or functional constraint. This is the only solution to the impossible exchange between space and the city, a solution which is clearly not to be found in the artificial spaces of freedom created in the city. It brings us to the very question of the destiny of architecture when it aspires to some truth. What happens to the project of truth (by which I mean the determined ambition to fulfil a programme, to respond to needs, to be a transformer of social or political situations, with a cultural and pedagogic mission, etc. – in short, everything that goes into the official discourse and relates to the conscious will of the architect himself)? For better or for worse, what one finds is that these programmatic intentions are always hijacked by the very people at whom they were aimed. They are reformulated by the users, by that mass of people whose original – or perverse – response can never be written into the project. There is no 'automatic writing' of social relations or of mass needs, either in politics or in architecture. Here too there is always a duel, and the reaction is unpredictable. The reaction in question is that of a fully fledged participant in the process, a participant who tends most often to be included as a passive element, but does not necessarily play by the rules of the game or respect the rules of dialogue. The masses take over the architectural object in their own way and if the architect has not already been diverted from his programmatic course himself, the users will see to it that the unpredictable final destination of that programme is restored. There is another form of radicality here, though in this case it is an involuntary one.

This is how all the intentions which initially shaped the project of the Pompidou Centre were thwarted by the actual object. That project, which was based on positive perspectives of culture and communication, in the end entirely succumbed to the reality – nay, hyperreality – of the object. Instead of being contextual, it created a void all around it. With its flexible, dispersed spaces and its transparency, it ran up against the action of the masses, who rendered it opaque and misused it as only they can. Contradiction came in here in a sort of spontaneous way, and for the Pompidou Centre the effect was something akin to a destiny. The object, the true object, bears within it a kind of fate and it would doubtless be a mistake to attempt to escape this. This calls into question the control exerted by the creator, but it is right that it should: wherever one is tempted to assign a function to a place, everyone else will take it upon themselves to make a non-place of it, to invent another set of rules. This is, in a sense, immoral, but, as we know, societies do not progress by their moralities or their positive value-systems, but by their vices and their immorality. And there must surely be a kind of ineluctable curvature to the imagination, as there is to space, which runs counter to any kind of planning, linearity or programming.

In this situation, the architect himself can play at thwarting his own plans, but he cannot aspire to control the object as event, the symbolic rule being that the player is never greater than the game itself. We are all players, gamblers. In other words, our most fervent hope is that rational sequences of events will unravel every now and again and be replaced, if only for a short time, by an unprecedented sequence of a different order, an extraordinary, apparently predestined build-up of events, in which things which have until then been artificially kept apart will suddenly appear not to occur randomly, but to be converging, spontaneously and with equal intensity, by the very fact of their being interconnected.

Our world would not be bearable without this innate power of détournement, this 'strange attraction', this radicality originating elsewhere – originating in the object (for radicality comes now not from the subject, but from the object). And there is something attractive in this for architects themselves: to imagine that the buildings they construct, the spaces they invent are the site of secret, random, unpredictable and, in a sense, poetic behaviour, and not merely of official behaviour that can be represented in statistical terms.

Having said this, we are confronted in our contemporary world with quite another dimension. A dimension in which the issues of truth and radicality no longer even arise, because we have already passed into virtuality. And there is here a major danger: the danger that architecture no longer exists, that there is no longer any architecture at all.

There are various ways for architecture not to exist. There is a kind of architecture which goes on, and has gone on for millennia, without any 'architectural' conception. People have designed and built their environments by spontaneous rules, and the spaces generated in this way were not made to be contemplated. They had no value as architecture, nor even, properly speaking, any aesthetic value. Even today, what I like about some cities particularly American ones, is that you can move around them without any thought of architecture. You can travel through them as though travelling through a desert, without indulging in any fine notions of art, history of art, aesthetics or architecture. They are, admittedly, structured to fulfil a multitude of purposes, but, in the way one comes across them, they resemble pure events, pure objects: they enable us to get back to a primal scene of space. In this sense, this is an architecture which serves as anti-architecture (and we can see from Rem Koolhaas' book *Delirious New York* how Manhattan was initially built up on something which had no architectural pretensions, the Coney Island Amusement Park). In my view, perfect architecture is the kind which covers over its own tracks, architecture in which the space is the thought itself. This goes for art and painting too. There are no finer works than those that cast aside all the trappings of art, the history of art and aesthetics. The same goes for thought: the only truly powerful thought is the kind which casts aside the trappings of meaning, profundity and the history of ideas, the trappings of truth . . .

With the coming of the virtual dimension, we lose that architecture which plays on the visible and the invisible, that symbolic form which plays both with the weight and gravity of things and with their disappearance. Virtual architecture is an architecture which no longer has any secret, which has become a mere operator in the field of visibility, a screen-architecture. It has become, as it were, in every sense of these terms, not the natural, but the artificial intelligence of the city and space (I have nothing against artificial intelligence, except when it claims, with its universal calculation, to absorb all the other forms and reduce mental space to a digital one). In order to assess this danger, which is at the same time the danger of the end of the architectural adventure, I shall take an example from another register which I know better: photography.

According to Wilhelm Flusser's hypothesis, the immense majority of current photographic images do not express the photographer's choice or vision, but merely deploy the technical resources of the camera. The equipment is in control, pushing itself to the limits of its potential. The human being is merely the technical operator of the programme. This is what 'the virtual' means: the exhaustion of all the technical potentialities of the machine. You can extend this analysis to computers or to artificial intelligence where thought is mostly a mere combinatorial procedure on the part of the software, the virtual and infinite operation of the machine. In this way, everything which takes the technological route, with its immense possibilities for producing diversity, opens on to an 'automatic writing' of the world and it is the same with architecture, which is now exposed to the full range of its technical possibilities.

This is not simply a matter of materials and building techniques; it is also a question of models. Just as all images are possible using the camera, which asks nothing more than to function, so all architectural forms can be revived out of a virtual stock of forms, arranged either conventionally or in some other way. As a result, architecture no longer refers to a truth or originality of some sort, but to the mere technical availability of forms and materials. The truth that emerges is no longer even the truth of objective conditions. Still less is it the truth of the architect's subjective will. It is quite simply the truth of the technical apparatus and its operation. We may still choose to call this 'architecture', but it is not at all clear that it genuinely is so. Let us take, for example, the Guggenheim Museum in Bilbao, a virtual object if ever there was one, the prototype of virtual architecture. It was put together on a computer out of optional elements or modules, so that a thousand similar museums could be constructed merely by changing the software or the scale of the calculations. Its very relation to its contents – art works and collections – is entirely virtual. The museum, as surprising in its unstable structure and illogical lines as it is unsurprising – and almost conventional – in its exhibition spaces, merely symbolises the performance of a machinery, an applied mental technology. Now, admittedly, it is not just any old technology and the object is a marvel, but it is an experimental marvel, comparable to the bio-genetic exploration of the body which will give rise to a whole host of clones and chimeras. The Guggenheim is a spatial chimera, the product of machinations which have gained the upper hand over architectural form itself.

It is, in fact, a 'ready-made'. And under the impact of technology and sophisticated equipment everything is becoming 'ready-made'. All the elements to be combined are there already; they merely have to be rearranged on the stage, like most post-modern forms. Duchamp did this with his bottle-rack, with a real object which he turned into a virtual one merely by displacing it. Today, they do it with computer programs and strings of code, but it's the same thing. They take them as they find them and put them on the architectural stage, where they may possibly become works of art. Now one may ask oneself whether this sort of acting-out of Duchamp's, which consists in transposing any old object into the sphere of art by mere displacement (an aesthetic displacement which puts an end to aesthetics, but which opens up at the same time on to a generalised aestheticisation) – this revolution of the 'ready-made', which consists in taking real objects and the real world as a pre-given programme for an automatic and infinite aesthetic operation (since all objects are susceptible of entering into this virtual performance), this radical intervention which took place in the field of art and painting – has its equivalent somewhere in the architectural sphere. Is there a break of a similar kind in the history of architecture? Something like a sudden, stark levelling of the sublime sense of aesthetics, as a result of which everything which follows in the field of art will no longer have the same meaning: everything will occur, so to speak, beyond the end, on the basis of the disappearance of art as such. I should like to ask the same question in relation to architecture: hasn't something occurred in architecture which means that all that has happened since has taken place against a background of the disappearance of architecture as such (as history, as the symbolic configuration of a society)? This hypothesis – the hypothesis of something 'beyond' their discipline – ought to be attractive even to architects. The question arises for politics too: doesn't everything which happens today on the so-called political scene actually take place against a background of the disappearance of the real – its disappearance, in effect, into the virtual? This hypothesis is by no means a dispiriting one: it may be more exciting to see what happens beyond the end than purely and simply to prolong the history of art. It gives an original and exceptional character to everything which can come into being beyond that disappearance. If we accept the disappearance hypothesis, it is still possible for anything whatever to appear. I like the radicalism of this hypothesis because I would like architecture, the architectural object to remain something exceptional and not to sink into that state which threatens us today on all sides: the virtual reality of architecture.

But we are in that state. Architecture is to a large extent doomed today merely to serve culture and communication. In other words, it is doomed to serve the virtual aestheticisation of the whole of society. It functions as a museum of the packaging of a social form known as culture, a museum of the packaging of immaterial needs which have no other definition than their being inscribed in numerous buildings designated for cultural ends. When people are not being turned into museum pieces on the spot (in heritage centres, where they become the virtual extras in their own lives, this too being a form of 'ready-made'), they are siphoned off to the huge, more or less interactive warehousing spaces that are the world's cultural and commercial centres, or to places of transit and circulation which have rightly been described as sites of disappearance (at Osaka in Japan they are already building a Memorial to Twenty-First Century Communications). Today architecture is enslaved to all these functions of circulation, information, communication and culture. There is a gigantic functionalism in all this and it is no longer a functionalism based in a mechanical world of organic needs, a real social relation, but a functionalism of the virtual. In other words, it is a functionalism relating, in the main, to useless functions, in which architecture itself is in danger of becoming a useless function. The danger is that we shall see a world-wide proliferation of an architecture of clones, a proliferation of transparent, interactive, mobile playful buildings, built in the image of the networks and of virtual reality, by way of which an entire society will deck itself out with the empty trappings of culture, communication and the virtual, much as it is already decked out with the empty trappings of politics. Can there be an architecture of real time, an architecture of flows and networks, an architecture of the virtual and the operational, an architecture of absolute visibility and transparency, an architecture of space restored to its indeterminacy in all dimensions? A polymorphous, multi-purpose architecture (an example might be the delightful little museum built at Nice by Kenzo Tange, which has been left empty for several years now – a Museum of the Void, in a sense, but also a craft centre or body-building centre or who knows what else). Most current public buildings, which are often oversized, give the impression not of space, but of emptiness. And the works or people moving around in them seem like virtual objects themselves, there being no apparent need for their presence. Empty functionality, the functionality of the useless space (the Centro Cultural de Belém in Lisbon, the National Library of France, etc.).

Everything is caught up in this metastasis of culture today, and architecture is not spared. It is very difficult now to distinguish between what remains of that secret register, of that singularity I was speaking of – and I do not think it has completely disappeared because I believe it to be indestructible – and what has passed over into the register of culture, which is itself a mental technology involving the ascendancy of all available models. There are of course urban and geographical constraints upon the architect, constraints imposed by financial pressures and by the commission. But, above all, there are models: the models which are in the contractor's or the client's head and all those, too, which

circulate in the architectural journals and in the history of architectural forms themselves. All these models impose a certain
number of parameters, which means that what is built in the end
is most often a collage of objects representing a compromise solution. The tragedy of contemporary architecture is this endless
cloning of the same type of living space the world over, as a function of parameters of functionality, or the cloning of a certain
type of typical or picturesque architecture. The end result is an
(architectural) object which not only fails to reach beyond its own
project, but fails even to reach beyond its own programme.

Might we not say, then, that architecture has lost its shadow,
to employ an analogy with Albert Chamisso's novella, *Peter
Schlemihl*, in which the hero sells his shadow to the devil?
Architecture, having become the transparent medium for all the
models running through it, might now be in a situation where it
can only repeat itself to infinity, or work its way through all the
possible variations of a pre-programmed code, that code trotting
out its generic stock of conventional forms in some pale imitation
of the genetic code?

Take the twin towers of the World Trade Center (and I'm not
objecting in any sense to the architectural event they constitute,
which I find admirable). One might see the one tower as the
other's shadow, its exact replica. But the point is that there no
longer is any shadow; the shadow has become a clone. The aspect
of otherness, secrecy and mystery, for which the shadow is a
metaphor, has disappeared, leaving an identical genetic copy in
its stead. Now, loss of a shadow means the disappearance of the
sun, without which, as we know, things would merely be what
they are. And indeed, in our virtual universe, our universe of
clones, our shadowless universe, things are merely what they are.
And they are so in innumerable copies, multiplied indefinitely,
since the shadow in a sense set bounds upon a being; it marked
out its individual limit: it was the shadow which prevented it
from reproducing itself to infinity.

But the situation is not, in my view, entirely hopeless. Though
architecture is no longer the invention of a world, we may hope
for it to be something other than a more or less kitsch repetition
of itself, something other than a geological layer of concrete – that

new sedimentation of the quaternary period. The field of photography offers the possibility of wresting some exceptional images from the automatic working of the camera, which has infinite technical potentialities and tends to produce an uncontrollable flow of images. As we know, 'automatic writing' is never truly automatic, and there is always a chance of hasard objectify, a chance that an unforeseeable series of events will occur. In the visual profusion of images that is currently submerging us, there is still a chance of recreating the primal, primitive scene of the image. In a sense, any image whatever retains something savage and fantastical, and intuition can recover this punctum (Barthes), this secret of the image, if it is taken literally. But we have to want that literalness: we have to secrete that secret, we have to want to thwart the general aestheticisation and the mental technology of culture which are now upon us.

And so we may believe that in architecture too, starting out from the spirit of place, the pleasure of place, and taking account of what are often chance factors, one can invent other strategies other dramaturgies. We may believe that, against this universal cloning of human beings, places and buildings, against this irruption of universal virtual reality, we can effect what I shall term a poetic transference of situation or a poetic situation of transference – towards a poetic architecture, a dramatic architecture, a literal architecture, a radical architecture – which, naturally, we all still dream of.

Truth and transcendent aesthetic value have no place here. Nothing is to be had from the function, the meaning, the project or the programme. Literalness is all. An example of this? Take the Pompidou Centre. What does that building speak of? Art, aesthetics, culture? No, it speaks of circulation, storage and flow, whether of individuals, objects or signs. And the architecture of the Pompidou Centre says these things well, says them literally. It is a cultural object, a cultural memorial to the obscure disaster of culture. The fantastic thing about it – even if this is involuntary – is that it shows both culture and the fate culture has succumbed to, and is succumbing to increasingly: the perfusion, superfusion and confusion of all signs. The same goes for the World Trade Center: the wonder of that building is that it puts on a fantastic urban show, a marvellous show of verticality, and is, at the same time, the glaring symbol of the fate the city has succumbed to; it is the symbol of what the city died of as a historical form. This is what gives such architecture its power: it is a form of extreme anticipation of a lost object and, at the same time, of retrospective nostalgia for that object.

Here, then, are some fragments of a primal scene of architecture, seen through the imagination of an outsider to the profession. You can interpret them literally and in all senses, as Rimbaud put it, one of the possible senses being that there still exists, beyond any illusion or disillusionment, a future of architecture in which I believe, even if that future of architecture is not necessarily architectural. There is a future of architecture for the simple reason that no one has yet invented the building or architectural object that would put an end to all others, that would put an end to space itself. Nor has anyone yet invented the city which would end all cities or the body of thought which would end all thought. Now, at bottom, this is everyone's dream. So long as it does not become a reality, there is still hope.

CHAPTER THIRTEEN

The Art Conspiracy

In 2000 Editions Galilée published a collection of Baudrillard's 'jour-
nalistic' articles in the Paris-based radical newspaper *Libération*,
written between June 1987 and May 1997. The title was *Ecran Total*.
Verso published an English translation by Chris Turner in 2002 as
Screened Out. Topics for Baudrillard's dissection included La
Cicciolina, President Jacques Chirac, Formula One motor racing, Walt
Disney, AIDS, the Holocaust, the West and Bosnia, genetic cloning,
mad cow disease, Jean-Marie Le Pen, Silvio Berlusconi and Salman
Rushdie, all of which had constituted current 'events' in contemporary
culture sometime in the decade between the late 1980s and the late
1990s. The extract here is entitled 'The Art Conspiracy', originally an
article first published in *Libération* on 20 May 1996, which had
spawned much debate and controversy. It effectively marked the end
of Baudrillard's honeymoon with the US art world which had extended
from the early 1980s until the mid 1990s. Sylvère Lotringer of
Semiotext(e) republished the article in book form in America, with a
different English translation, as 'The Conspiracy of Art' in 2005, collected alongside diverse interviews with Baudrillard and rare writings
on art, including his first text – a fragment of a few hundred words
dating from 1952 when Baudrillard was only twenty-three years old
which runs for only four pages and finds the young Jean 'rapping' on
pataphysics, Antonin Artaud and Albert Jarry. In 'The Art Conspiracy'
Baudrillard was taken by the 'shocked' critics as saying that art is dead.
The critics, and his former supporters among the global artistic community, responded to Baudrillard's article by criticising him for biting
the hand that had been, apparently, feeding him well for over a
decade. In fact Baudrillard was not writing anything in particular
he had not said before. Andy Warhol was just about the only artist

Baudrillard had consistently praised during his life but Warhol was 'outside the limits of art'. 'Art' for Baudrillard was indeed always on 'the periphery'.

'The Art Conspiracy', from *Screened Out*, trans. Chris Turner, London: Verso, 2002.

Just as, amid all the pornography which surrounds us, we have lost the illusion of desire, so in contemporary art we have also lost the desire for illusion. In porn, there is no longer any room for desire. After the orgy and the liberation of all desires, we have moved into the transsexual, in the sense of a transparency of sex, into signs and images which obliterate the whole secret, the ambiguity of sex. Transsexual in the sense that sex now has nothing to do with the illusion of desire, but relates solely to the hyperreality of the image.

So it is with art, which has also lost the desire for illusion – preferring the elevation of everything to aesthetic banality – and has consequently become transaesthetic. For art, the orgy of modernity consisted in the exhilaration of deconstructing the object and representation. During that period, the aesthetic illusion was still very powerful, as is, for sex, the illusion of desire. The energy of sexual difference, which passes into all the figures of desire, has as its counterpart in art the energy of dissociation from reality (Cubism, abstraction, Expressionism), though each of these corresponds to a desire to pierce the secret of desire and the secret of the object. To the point where these two strong configurations, the scene of desire and the scene of illusion, disappear, giving way to the same transsexual, transaesthetic obscenity – the obscenity of visibility and of the inexorable transparency of everything. In reality, there is no longer any pornography identifiable as such, because the essence of the pornographic has passed into all the technologies of the visual and televisual spheres.

But perhaps, deep down, we are merely playing out the comedy of art, as other societies have played out the comedy of ideology, as Italian society, for example (though it is not the only one), plays out the comedy of power, as we play out the comedy of porn in the obscene advertising of the images of the female body. This perpetual striptease, these phantasies *à sexe ouvert*, this sexual blackmail – if it were all true, it would be genuinely unbearable. But fortunately it is all too obvious to be true. Transparency is too good to be true. As for art, it is too superficial to be really useless. There must be an underlying mystery. As with anamorphosis, there must be an angle from which all this useless orgy of sex and signs makes complete sense but, for the moment, we can only adopt an attitude of ironic indifference towards it. In this unreality of porn, this insignificance of art, there is something of the order of an underlying enigma, an inherent mystery. An ironic form of our destiny perhaps? If everything becomes too obvious to be true, perhaps there is still a chance for illusion. What lurks behind this falsely transparent world? Another sort of intelligence or a definitive lobotomy?

(Modern) art was able to be part of the *part maudite*, the 'accursed share', by being a sort of dramatic alternative to reality, by expressing the irruption of unreality into reality. But what can art mean now in a world that is hyperrealist from the outset, a world that is cool, transparent, image-conscious? What can porn mean in a world that is pornographied from the outset? What can they do but tip us a last paradoxical wink – that of reality mocking itself in its most hyperrealistic form, that of sex mocking itself in its most exhibitionistic form, that of art mocking itself and its own disappearance in its most artificial form: irony. The dictatorship of images is, in any event, an ironic dictatorship. But that irony itself is no longer part of the accursed share; it is, rather, party to insider-trading, to that hidden, shameful complicity which binds the artist, playing on his/her aura of derision, to the stupefied, incredulous masses. Irony, too, is a part of the art conspiracy.

Art playing on its own disappearance and the disappearance of its object was still an art of great works. But art playing at re-cycling itself indefinitely by helping itself to reality? Most contemporary art is engaged in just this: appropriating banality, the throwaway, mediocrity as value and as ideology. In these innumerable installations and performances, what is going on is merely a compromise with the state of things – and simultaneously with all the past forms of the history of art. An admission of unoriginality, banality and worthlessness, elevated into a perverse aesthetic value, if not indeed a perverse aesthetic pleasure. Admittedly, it is claimed that all this mediocrity is sublimated in the transition to the level of art, which is distanced and ironic. But it is just as worthless and insignificant at that level as before. Transition to the aesthetic level rescues nothing. In fact the opposite is true: it is mediocrity raised to the second power. It claims to be worthless: '*I'm worthless, I'm worthless!*' and it really is worthless!

We have here the whole duplicity of contemporary art: laying claim to worthlessness [*la nullité*], insignificance and non-meaning; aiming for worthlessness, when it is already worthless; aiming for non-meaning, when it already signifies nothing; claiming to achieve superficiality in superficial terms. Now, nullity is a secret quality which not everyone can aspire to. Insignificance – true insignificance, the victorious defiance of meaning, the stripping away of meaning, the art of the disappearance of meaning – is an exceptional quality possessed by a few rare works – works which never claim that quality.

There is an initiatory form of nullity, just as there is an initiatory form of the nothing, or an initiatory form of evil. And then there is insider-trading, the fakers of nullity, the snobbery of nullity, of all those who prostitute the Nothing for value, who prostitute Evil for useful ends. We must not let these fakers get away with it. When the Nothing shows up in signs, when Nothingness emerges at the very heart of the system of signs, that is the fundamental event of art. It is the proper task of poetry to raise the Nothing to the power of the sign – not the banality or indifference of the real, but the radical illusion. In this way, Warhol truly is a 'zero', in the sense that he reintroduces nothingness into the heart of the image. He turns nullity and insignificance into an event which he transforms into a fatal strategy of the image.

The others merely have a commercial strategy of nullity, to which they give a promotional form, the sentimental form of the commodity, as Baudelaire put it. They hide behind their own nullity and the metastases of the discourse on art, which works generously to promote this nullity as a value (among other things, a value on the art market, of course). In a sense, this is worse than nothing, because it means nothing and yet it exists all the same, giving itself every reason to exist. With this paranoia colluding with art, there is no room for critical judgement any more, but merely for an amicable, and inescapably convivial, participation in nullity. This is the art conspiracy and its primal scene, carried forward by all the private shows, hangings, exhibitions, restorations, collections, donations and speculations. It is a conspiracy which cannot be 'unhatched' in any known universe, since, behind the mystification of images, it has put itself beyond the reach of thought.

The other side of this trickery is the way people are bluffed into according importance and credence to all this, on the grounds that it is not possible that it should be so worthless and empty and there must be something to it. Contemporary art plays on this uncertainty, on the impossibility of a reasoned aesthetic value-judgement, relying on the guilt of those who simply cannot understand, or have not understood that there is nothing to understand. Here again, this is insider-trading. But we may also take the view that these people, whom art keeps at bay, have indeed fully understood, since, by their very stupefaction, they show an intuitive understanding that they are victims of an abuse of power; that they are not being let in on the rules of the game; that the wool is being pulled over their eyes. In other words, art has made its entry into the general process of insider-trading (and not merely from the financial point of view of the art market, but in the very management of aesthetic values). In this it is not alone: the same kind of collusion is to be found in politics, the economy and information, with the same ironic resignation on the part of the 'consumers'.

'Our admiration for painting is the consequence of a long process of adaptation which has gone on over centuries, and exists for reasons which very often have nothing to do either with art or the mind. Painting created its receptor. It is, at bottom, a relationship of convention' (Gombrowicz to Dubuffet). The only question is how such a machine can continue to function in a situation of critical disillusionment and commercial frenzy. And if it can, how long will this illusionism, this occultism last? A hundred years? Two hundred? Will art have a second, interminable existence, like the secret services, which, though we know they have long had no secrets to steal or exchange, still thrive amid a superstitious belief in their usefulness, and continue to generate a mythology?

CHAPTER FOURTEEN

Requiem for the Twin Towers

Apart from his views on the first Gulf War nothing has made Baudrillard more notorious than his outspoken writings on the 9/11 events in the USA, not even him turning his back on the New York art world in the 1990s. Baudrillard saw 9/11 as the end of the 'event strike' of the 1990s where world events like the soccer World Cup or Diana's death had occurred but nothing which challenged 'globalisation'. The extract here was originally Baudrillard's spoken contribution, later written up with slight alterations, to a debate in New York about the 9/11 events. The debate included, among others, the Althusserian theorist Jacques Ranciére and was mainly conducted in French. It was broadcast by France Culture on 23 February 2002, six months after 9/11 at a time when anti-French propaganda in the US was still high as a result of France's perceived lack of support for America in the so-called 'war on terror'. Verso books published the written piece in translation by Chris Turner as part of the book *The Spirit of Terrorism* in 2002 and then expanded the volume with two more essays in a second edition in 2003. The original book was published in 2002 as part of a three-book mini series by Verso on 9/11 which also included books by Slavoj Žižek and Paul Virilio. In the second edition of the book Baudrillard considered 'conspiracy' theories about the air attack on the Pentagon and by extension the Twin Towers of the World Trade Center but although he did not necessarily reject them he maintained that his thesis about 9/11 was not dependent on their 'truth'. Jean Baudrillard's fundamental argument, which brought new howls of derision down upon him after 9/11, was that 'the worst thing for global power is not to be attacked or destroyed, but to be humiliated'. The events of 9/11 made sure it was humiliated 'because the terrorists inflicted on it something that it cannot return'. On 9/11 in Washington and New York, for

Baudrillard, and for that matter 7/7 in London, 'global power was defeated symbolically'.

'Requiem for the Twin Towers', from *The Spirit of Terrorism*, 3rd edn, trans. Chris Turner, London: Verso, 2003.

The September 11 attacks also concern architecture, since what was destroyed was one of the most prestigious of buildings, together with a whole (Western) value-system and a world order.[1] It may, then, be useful to begin with a historical and architectural analysis of the Twin Towers, in order to grasp the symbolic significance of their destruction.

First of all, why the *Twin* Towers? Why *two* towers at the World Trade Center?

All Manhattan's tall buildings had been content to confront each other in a competitive verticality, and the product of this was an architectural panorama reflecting the capitalist system itself – a pyramidal jungle, whose famous image stretched out before you as you arrived from the sea. That image changed after 1973, with the building of the World Trade Center. The effigy of the system was no longer the obelisk and the pyramid, but the punch card and the statistical graph. This architectural graphism is the embodiment of a system that is no longer competitive, but digital and countable, and from which competition has disappeared in favour of networks and monopoly.

Perfect parallelepipeds, standing over 1,300 feet tall, on a square base. Perfectly balanced, blind communicating vessels (they say terrorism is 'blind', but the towers were blind too – monoliths no longer opening on to the outside world, but subject to artificial conditioning[2]). The fact that there were two of them signifies the end of any original reference. If there had been only one, monopoly would not have been perfectly embodied. Only the doubling of the sign truly puts an end to what it designates.

There is a particular fascination in this reduplication. However tall they may have been, the two towers signified, none the less, a halt to verticality. They were not of the same breed as the other buildings. They culminated in the exact reflection of each other. The glass and steel façades of the Rockefeller Center buildings still mirrored each other in an endless specularity. But the Twin Towers no longer had any façades, any faces. With the rhetoric of verticality disappears also the rhetoric of the mirror. There remains only a kind of black box, a series closed on the figure two, as though architecture, like the system, was now merely a product of cloning, and of a changeless genetic code.

New York is the only city in the world that has, throughout its history, tracked the present form of the system and all its many developments with such prodigious fidelity. We must, then, assume that the collapse of the towers – itself a unique event in the history of modern cities – pre-figures a kind of dramatic ending and, all in all, disappearance both of this form of architecture and of the world system it embodies. Shaped in the pure computer image of banking and finance, (ac)countable and digital, they were in a sense its brain, and in striking there the terrorists have struck at the brain, at the nerve-centre of the system.

The violence of globalization also involves architecture, and hence the violent protest against it also involves the destruction of that architecture. In terms of collective drama, we can say that the horror for the 4,000 victims of dying in those towers was inseparable from the horror of living in them – the horror of living and working in sarcophagi of concrete and steel.

These architectural monsters, like the Beaubourg Centre, have always exerted an ambiguous fascination, as have the extreme forms of modern technology in general – a contradictory feeling of attraction and repulsion, and hence, somewhere, a secret desire to see them disappear. In the case of the Twin Towers, something particular is added: precisely their symmetry and their twin-ness. There is, admittedly, in this cloning and perfect symmetry an aesthetic quality, a kind of perfect crime against form, a tautology of form which can give rise, in a violent reaction, to the temptation to break that symmetry, to restore an asymmetry, and hence a singularity.

Their destruction itself respected the symmetry of the towers: a double attack, separated by a few minutes' interval, with a sense of suspense between the two impacts. After the first, one could still believe it was an accident. Only the second impact confirmed the terrorist attack. And in the Queens air crash a month later, the TV stations waited, staying with the story (in France) for four hours, waiting to broadcast a possible second crash 'live'. Since that did not occur, we shall never know now whether it was an accident or a terrorist act.

The collapse of the towers is the major symbolic event. Imagine they had not collapsed, or only one had collapsed: the effect would not have been the same at all. The fragility of global power would not have been so strikingly proven. The towers, which were the emblem of that power, still embody it in their dramatic end, which resembles a suicide. Seeing them collapse themselves, as if by implosion, one had the impression that they were committing suicide in response to the suicide of the suicide planes.

Were the Twin Towers destroyed, or did they collapse? Let us be clear about this: the two towers are both a physical, architectural object and a symbolic object[3] (symbolic of financial power and global economic liberalism). The architectural object was destroyed, but it was the symbolic object which was targeted and which it was intended to demolish. One might think the physical destruction brought about the symbolic collapse. But in fact no one, not even the terrorists, had reckoned on the total destruction of the towers. It was, in fact, their symbolic collapse that brought about their physical collapse, not the other way around.

As if the power bearing these towers suddenly lost all energy, all resilience; as though that arrogant power suddenly gave way under the pressure of too intense an effort: the effort always to be the unique world model.

So the towers, tired of being a symbol which was too heavy a burden to bear, collapsed, this time physically, in their totality. Their nerves of steel cracked. They collapsed vertically, drained of their strength, with the whole world looking on in astonishment.

The symbolic collapse came about, then, by a kind of unpredictable complicity – as though the entire system, by its internal fragility, joined in the game of its own liquidation, and hence joined in the game of terrorism. Very logically, and inexorably, the increase in the power of power heightens the will to destroy it.

But there is more: somewhere, it was party to its own destruction. The countless disaster movies bear witness to this fantasy, which they attempt to exorcize with images and special effects. But the fascination they exert is a sign that acting-out is never very far away – the rejection of any system, including internal rejection, growing all the stronger as it approaches perfection or omnipotence. It has been said that 'Even God cannot declare war on Himself.' Well, He can. The West, in the position of God (divine omnipotence and absolute moral legitimacy), has become suicidal, and declared war on itself.

Even in their failure, the terrorists succeeded beyond their wildest hopes: in bungling their attack on the White House (while succeeding far beyond their objectives on the towers), they demonstrated unintentionally that that was not the essential target, that political power no longer means much, and real power lies elsewhere. As for what should be built in place of the towers, the problem is insoluble. Quite simply because one can imagine nothing equivalent that would be worth destroying – that would be worthy of being destroyed. The Twin Towers were worth destroying. One cannot say the same of many architectural works. Most things are not even worth destroying or sacrificing. Only works of prestige deserve that fate, for it is an honour. This proposition is not as paradoxical as it sounds, and it raises a basic issue for architecture: one should build only those things which, by their excellence, are worthy of being destroyed. Take a look around with this radical proposition in mind, and you will see what a pass we have come to. Not much would withstand this extreme hypothesis.

This brings us back to what should be the basic question for architecture, which architects never formulate: is it normal to build and construct? In fact it is not, and we should preserve the absolutely problematical character of the undertaking. Undoubtedly, the task of architecture – of good architecture – is to efface itself, to disappear as such. The towers, for their part, have disappeared. But they have left us the symbol of their disappearance, their disappearance as symbol. They, which were the symbol of omnipotence, have become, by their absence, the symbol of the possible disappearance of that omnipotence – which is perhaps an even more potent symbol. Whatever becomes of that global omnipotence, it will have been destroyed here for a moment.

Moreover, although the two towers have disappeared, they have not been annihilated. Even in their pulverized state, they have left behind an intense awareness of their presence. No one who knew them can cease imagining them and the imprint they made on the skyline from all points of the city. Their end in material space has borne them off into a definitive imaginary space. By the grace of terrorism, the World Trade Center has become the world's most beautiful building – the eighth wonder of the world![4]

Notes

1. In the New York debate, Baudrillard prefaced his talk with the following comments: 'There is an absolute difficulty in speaking of an absolute event. That is to say, in providing an analysis of it that is not an explanation – as I don't think there is any possible explanation of this event, either by intellectuals or by others – but its *analogon*, so to speak; an analysis which might possibly be as unacceptable as the event, but strikes the . . . let us say, symbolic imagination in more or less the same way.'
2. In New York, Baudrillard here glossed: 'Air conditioning, but mental conditioning too'.
3. In New York, Baudrillard added: 'symbolic in the weak sense, but symbolic, for all that'.
4. After delivering a slightly modified version of this last paragraph in New York, Baudrillard closed with the comment: 'So I set out to produce a Requiem, but it was also, in a way, a Te Deum.'

CHAPTER FIFTEEN

Pornography of War

Baudrillard had written controversially about the first Gulf War in the early 1990s. In 2004 when the news of US military torture in Iraq broke his views on the scandalous images of Abu Ghraib prison in Iraq, originally published in French, were eagerly awaited. His brief 'war porn' article, translated into English by Chris Turner, was published in the first issue of a new academic journal in the theoretical humanities and social sciences called *Cultural Politics* published by Berg in 2005, including on its editorial board Baudrillard's compatriot Paul Virilio. Although Baudrillard's very brief contribution is certainly not 'academic' or 'political' in any conventional sense, it is a fascinating cultural reflection on the immediate impact of the obscene acts at Abu Ghraib with allusions to Albert Jarry's Pére Ubu figure as well as his own earlier work on the images of the destruction of the Twin Towers in 2001. The extract here is Turner's masterly translation. Baudrillard had seemingly been enervated by the 9/11 events and the boost to his thesis about symbolic exchange and the counter-gift and the end of the 'event strike' at the beginning of the twenty-first century. He had already written about the US and its allies responding to the 9/11 'terrorist' by 'bombing him to smithereens or locking him up like a dog at Guantanamo'. But his constant question was 'who can thwart the global system?' Photographic images had always intrigued Baudrillard and it is significant that the 'abject tableaux' of Abu Ghraib are made up of still photographs, rapidly transmitted globally by newspapers and the twenty-four hour news mass media for all to see and view again and again. For Baudrillard the photographic images of the post-occupation events at the Baghdad prison of Abu Ghraib, already regularly used under the Saddam regime for torture, return humiliation on power (or America), a self-inflicted lethal counter-gift. The 'pornography of war' is not so much the pictures of the soldiers' sadistic sexual and physical torture of the Iraqis but the urge to make 'everything visible'.

'Pornography of War', *Cultural Politics*, Vol. 1, No. 1, trans. Chris Turner, Oxford: Berg, 2005.

The World Trade Center: the electric shock to power, the humiliation inflicted on power – but from the outside. With the Baghdad prison images it is worse. This is the humiliation, just as lethal symbolically, which world power – in the form of the Americans, as it happens – inflicts on itself. The electric shock of shame and bad conscience. This is how the two events are linked.

To the two events, a violent reaction throughout the world: in the first instance, a sense of momentousness, in the second, a sense of abjection.

In the case of 9/11, the thrilling images of a major event; in the other, the shaming images of something that is the opposite of an event, a non-event of obscene banality, the atrocious but banal degradation not merely of the victims but also of the amateur stage managers of this parody of violence. For the worst thing about this is that here we have a parody of violence, a parody of war itself, pornography becoming the ultimate form of abjection of a war that is incapable of being merely war, of merely killing, and that is being drawn out into an infantile, Ubuesque 'reality show,' a desperate simulacrum of power.

These scenes are the illustration of a power that, having reached its extreme point, no longer knows what to do with itself, of a power now aimless and purposeless since it has no plausible enemy and acts with total impunity. All it can do now is inflict gratuitous humiliation, and, as we know, the violence we inflict on others is only ever the expression of the violence we do to ourselves. And it can only humiliate itself in the process, demean and deny itself in a kind of perverse relentlessness. Ignominy and sleaze are the last symptoms of a power that no longer knows what to do with itself.

September 11th was like a global reaction of all those who no longer know what to do with – and can no longer bear – this world power. In the case of the abuse inflicted on the Iraqis, it is worse still: it is power itself that no longer knows what to do with itself and can no longer bear itself, other than in inhuman self-parody.

These images are as lethal for America as the pictures of the World Trade Center in flames. Yet it is not America in itself that stands accused, and there is no point laying all this at the Americans' door: the infernal machine generates its own impetus, freewheeling out of control in literally suicidal acts. The Americans' power has in fact become too much for them. They no longer have the means to exorcize it. And we are party to that power. It is the whole of the West whose bad conscience crystallizes in these images; it is the whole of the West that is present in the American soldiers' sadistic outburst of laughter; just as it is the whole of the West that is behind the building of the Israeli wall.

This is the truth of these images; this is their burden: the excess of a potency designating itself as abject and pornographic. The truth of the images, not their veracity, since, in this situation, whether they are true or false is beside the point. We are hence-forth – and forever – in a state of uncertainty where images are concerned. Only their impact counts, precisely insofar as they are embedded in war. There isn't even a need for 'embedded' journalists any more; it's the military itself that is embedded in the image; thanks to digital technology, images are definitively integrated into warfare. They no longer represent; they no longer imply either distance or perception or judgement. They are no longer of the order of representation, or of information in the strict sense and, as a result, the question of whether they should be produced, reproduced, broadcast or banned, and even the 'essential' question of whether they are true or false, is 'irrelevant.'

For images to constitute genuine information they would have to be different from war. But they have become precisely as virtual as war today and hence their own specific violence is now superadded to the specific violence of war. Moreover, by their omnipresence, by the rule that everything must be made visible, which now applies the world over, images – our present images – have become in substance pornographic; they therefore cleave spontaneously to the pornographic dimension of war.

There is in all this, and particularly in the last Iraqi episode, a justice immanent in the image: he who stakes his all on the spectacle will die by the spectacle. If you want power through the image, be prepared to die by the image playback.

The Americans are learning this, and will continue to learn it, by bitter experience. And this despite all the 'democratic' subterfuge and despite a despairing simulacrum of transparency commensurate with the despairing simulacrum of military power. Who committed these acts and who is really responsible for them? The military higher-ups? Or human nature, which is, as we know, brutish – 'even in a democracy'? The real scandal lies not in the torture but in the perfidy of those who knew and remained silent (or of those who revealed it?). At any rate, the whole of the real violence is diverted on to the question of openness, democracy finding a way to restore its virtue by publicizing its vices.

Leaving all that aside, what is the secret of these abject tableaux? Once again, they are a response, beyond all the vicissitudes of strategy and politics, to the humiliation of 9/11 and an attempt to respond to it by a humiliation that is worse, much worse, than death. Not even counting the hoods, which are in themselves a form of beheading (to which the beheading of the Americans obscurely corresponds), and not counting the piled-up bodies and the dogs, enforced nudity is in itself a violation. We have, for example, seen GIs walking naked Iraqis through the streets in chains, and in Patrick Dekaerke's short story 'Allah Akhbar' we see Franck, the CIA's man on the ground, make the Arab strip naked, force him to put on a basque and fishnet stockings and finally have him buggered by a pig, all the while taking photographs that he will send to the village and to the man's family and friends. In this way the 'other' will be exterminated symbolically. It is here we see that the aim of war is not to kill or to win but to abolish the enemy, to black out (the expression is, I think, Canetti's) the light from his sky.

And what is it, in fact, that we want to make these men confess? What secret are we trying to force out of them? We quite simply want them to tell us how it is – and in the name of what – that they are unafraid of death. This explains the 'zero-death' soldier's deep jealousy of – and the revenge he takes on – those who are not afraid of death. For which reason they will have visited on them something worse than death . . . In the radical shaming, the dishonor of nudity, the ravaging of all veils, we are back at the same problem of openness and transparency: tearing off the women's veils or hooding the men to make them seem more naked, more obscene . . . This whole masquerade that tops off the ignominy of war, going so far as the literal travestying – in what is the most ferocious image (the most ferocious for America), because it stirs up most phantoms and is the most 'reversible' – of the prisoner threatened with electrocution who has been turned completely into a hood, into a Ku Klux Klan member, crucified by his own kind. This really is America having electrocuted itself.

CHAPTER SIXTEEN

Contemporary Art: Art Contemporary with Itself

In 2004 Editions Galilée published *Le Pacte de Lucidité ou l'Intelligence du Mal*, a familiar 'late' Baudrillardian tract. In 2005 Berg published Chris Turner's English translation as *The Intelligence of Evil or The Lucidity Pact* with a contextualised summation of Baudrillard's life and work by the translator published as the introduction to the English edition. The book encapsulates many of the themes Baudrillard had been writing about since the mid 1980s and is as good an example of his 'theory-fiction' writing style as any of his books. The unreferenced name checks are familiar (McLuhan, Nietzsche, Borges) but the 'shadow' of 9/11 falls everywhere. It is demonstrably a post 2001 book. The extract here is a representative piece from the book. In 2003 Baudrillard gave a lecture entitled 'Art Contemporary with Itself' at the Venice Biennale in Italy. The majority of this lecture (minus the ending which comprised two disembodied quotations from Saul Bellow and Guido Ceronetti) is the text extracted here. It appeared in full in written-up form as the chapter entitled 'Contemporary Art' in the book. The subject is modern, or contemporary, art. By the early years of the 2000s Baudrillard's spat with the art world had to some extent been forgotten but Baudrillard reignites it here, mentioning the art conspiracy which he had written about in the mid 1990s. He begins by declaiming that 'the adventure of modern art is over' and continues with the observation that the art market is the modern charnel house of culture, hardly endearing himself to his former art world supporters. The provocateur in Baudrillard was just as strong at the end of his life as in his early years when he first encountered, and embraced, pataphysics. As he contracted cancer and neared the end of his life the irony that Baudrillard himself was increasingly regarded as an 'artist' (as a photographer, but also, as Sylvère Lotringer has described him, 'a practicing artist of his own concepts') would not have been lost on the philosopher/sociologist.

'Contemporary Art: Art Contemporary with Itself', from *The Intelligence of Evil or The Lucidity Pact*, trans. Chris Turner, Oxford: Berg, 2005.

The adventure of modern art is over. Contemporary art is contemporary only with itself. It no longer knows any transcendence either towards past or future; its only reality is that of its operation in real time and its confusion with that reality.

Nothing now distinguishes it from the technical, promotional, media, digital operation. There is no transcendence, no divergence any more, nothing of another scene: merely a specular play with the contemporary world as it takes place. It is in this that contemporary art is worthless: between it and the world, there is a zero-sum equation.

Quite apart from that shameful complicity in which creators and consumers commune wordlessly in the examination of strange, inexplicable objects that refer only to themselves and to the idea of art, the true conspiracy lies in this complicity that art forges with itself, its collusion with the real, through which it becomes complicit in that Integral Reality, of which it is now merely the image-feedback.

There is no longer any differential of art. There is only the integral calculus of reality. Art is now merely an idea prostituted in its realization.

Modernity was the golden age of a deconstruction of reality into its simple elements, of a detailed analytics, first of impressionism, then of abstraction, experimentally open to all the aspects of perception, of sensibility, of the structure of the object and the dismemberment of forms.

The paradox of abstraction is that, by 'liberating' the object from the constraints of the figural to yield it up to the pure play of form, it shackled it to an idea of a hidden structure, of an objectivity more rigorous and radical than that of resemblance. It sought to set aside the mask of resemblance and of the figure in order to accede to the analytic truth of the object. Under the banner of abstraction, we moved paradoxically towards more reality, towards an unveiling of the 'elementary structures' of objectality, that is to say, towards something more real than the real.

Conversely, under the banner of a general aestheticization, art invaded the whole field of reality.

The end of this history saw the banality of art merge with the banality of the real world – Duchamp's act, with its automatic transference of the object, being the inaugural (and ironic) gesture in this process. The transference of all reality into aesthetics, which has become one of the dimensions of generalized exchange . . .

All this under the banner of a simultaneous liberation of art and the real world.

This 'liberation' has in fact consisted in indexing the two to each other – a chiasmus lethal to both.

The transference of art, become a useless function, into a reality that is now integral, since it has absorbed everything that denied, exceeded or transfigured it. The impossible exchange of this Integral Reality for anything else whatever. Given this, it can only exchange itself for itself or, in other words, repeat itself *ad infinitum*.

What could miraculously reassure us today about the essence of art? Art is quite simply what is at issue in the world of art, in that desperately self-obsessed artistic community. The 'creative' act doubles up on itself and is now nothing more than a sign of its own operation – the painter's true subject is no longer what he paints but the very fact that he paints. He paints the fact that he paints. At least in that way the idea of art remains intact.

This is merely one of the sides of the conspiracy.

The other side is that of the spectator who, for want of under-standing anything whatever most of the time, consumes his own culture at one remove. He literally consumes the fact that he understands nothing and that there is no necessity in all this except the imperative of culture, of being a part of the integrated circuit of culture. But culture is itself merely an epiphenomenon of global circulation.

The idea of art has become rarefied and minimal, leading ultim-ately to conceptual art, where it ends in the non-exhibition of non-works in non-galleries – the apotheosis of art as non-event. As a corollary, the consumer circulates in all this in order to experience his non-enjoyment of the works.

At the extreme point of a conceptual, minimalist logic, art ought quite simply to fade away. At that point, it would doubtless become what it is: a false problem, and every aesthetic theory would be a false solution.

And yet it is the case that there is all the more need to speak about it because there is nothing to say. The movement of the democratization of art has paradoxically merely strengthened the privileged status of the *idea* of art, culminating in this banal tau-tology of 'art is art', it being possible for everything to find its place in this circular definition.

As Marshall McLuhan has it, 'We have now become aware of the possibility of arranging the entire human environment as a work of art.'[1]

The revolutionary idea of contemporary art was that any object, any detail or fragment of the material world, could exert the same strange attraction and pose the same insoluble questions as were reserved in the past for a few rare aristocratic forms known as works of art.

That is where true democracy lay: not in the accession of everyone to aesthetic enjoyment, but in the transaesthetic advent of a world in which every object would, without distinction, have its fifteen minutes of fame (particularly objects without distinction). All objects are equivalent, everything is a work of genius. With, as a corollary, the transformation of art and of the work itself into an object, without illusion or transcendence, a purely conceptual acting-out, generative of deconstructed objects which deconstruct us in their turn.

No longer any face, any gaze, any human countenance or body in all this – organs without bodies, flows, molecules, the fractal. The relation to the 'artwork' is of the order of contamination, of contagion: you hook up to it, absorb or immerse yourself in it, exactly as in flows and networks. Metonymic sequence, chain reaction.

No longer any real object in all this: in the ready-made it is no longer the object that's there, but the idea of the object, and we no longer find pleasure here in art, but in the idea of art. We are wholly in ideology.

And, ultimately, the twofold curse of modern and contemporary art is summed up in the 'ready-made': the curse of an immersion in the real and banality, and that of a conceptual absorption in the idea of art.

> '. . . that absurd sculpture by Picasso, with its stalks and leaves of metal; neither wings, nor victory, just a testimony, a vestige – the idea, nothing more, of a work of art. Very similar to the other ideas and vestiges that inspire our existence – not apples, but the idea, the reconstruction by the pomologist of what apples used to be – not ice-cream, but the idea, the memory of something delicious, made from substitutes, from starch, glucose and other chemicals – not sex, but the idea or evocation of sex – the same with love, belief, thought and the rest . . .'[2]

Art, in its form, signifies nothing. It is merely a sign pointing towards absence.

But what becomes of this perspective of emptiness and absence in a contemporary universe that is already totally emptied of its meaning and reality?

Art can now only align itself with the general insignificance and indifference. It no longer has any privileged status. It no longer has any other final destination than this fluid universe of communication, the networks and interaction.

Transmitter and receiver merging in the same loop: all transmitters, all receivers. Each subject interacting with itself, doomed to express itself without any longer having time to listen to the other.

The Net and the networks clearly increase this possibility of transmitting for oneself in a closed circuit, everyone going at it with their virtual performances and contributing to the general asphyxia.

This is why, where art is concerned, the most interesting thing would be to infiltrate the spongiform encephalon of the modern spectator. For this is where the mystery lies today: in the brain of the receiver, at the nerve centre of this servility before 'works of art'. What is the secret of it?

In the complicity between the mortification 'creative artists' inflict on objects and themselves, and the mortification consumers inflict on themselves and their mental faculties.

Tolerance for the worst of things has clearly increased considerably as a function of this general state of complicity.

Interface and performance – these are the two current leitmotifs.

In performance, all the forms of expression merge – the plastic arts, photography, video, installation, the interactive screen. This vertical and horizontal, aesthetic and commercial diversification is henceforth part of the work, the original core of which cannot be located.

A (non-) event like *The Matrix* illustrates this perfectly: this is the very archetype of the global installation, of the total global fact: not just the film, which is, in a way, the alibi, but the spin-offs, the simultaneous projection at all points of the globe and the millions of spectators themselves who are inextricably part of it. We are all, from a global, interactive point of view, the actors in this total global fact.

Photography has the selfsame problem when we undertake to multi-mediatize it by adding to it all the resources of montage, collage, the digital and CGI, etc. This opening-up to the infinite, this deregulation, is, literally, the death of photography by its elevation to the stage of performance.

In this universal mix, each register loses its specificity – just as each individual loses his sovereignty in interaction and the networks – just as the real and the image, art and reality lose their respective energy by ceasing to be differential poles.

Since the nineteenth century, it has been art's claim that it is useless. It has prided itself on this (which was not the case in classical art, where, in a world that was not yet either real or objective, the question of usefulness did not even arise).

Extending this principle, it is enough to elevate any object to uselessness to turn it into a work of art. This is precisely what the 'ready-made' does, when it simply withdraws an object from its function, without changing it in any way, and thereby turns it into a gallery piece. It is enough to turn the real itself into a useless function to make it an art object, prey to the devouring aesthetic of banality.

Similarly, old objects, being obsolete and hence useless, automatically acquire an aesthetic aura. Their being distant from us in time is the equivalent of Duchamp's artistic act; they too become 'ready-mades', nostalgic vestiges resuscitated in our museum universe.

We might extrapolate this aesthetic transfiguration to the whole of material production. As soon as it reaches a threshold where it is no longer exchanged in terms of social wealth, it becomes something like a giant Surrealist object, in the grip of a devouring aesthetic, and everywhere takes its place in a kind of virtual museum. And so we have the museification, like a 'ready-made', of the whole technical environment in the form of industrial wasteland.

The logic of uselessness could not but lead contemporary art to a predilection for waste, which is itself useless by definition. Through waste, the figuration of waste, the obsession with waste, art fiercely proclaims its uselessness. It demonstrates its non-use-value, its non-exchange-value at the same time as selling itself very dear.

There is a misconception here. *Uselessness has no value in itself.* It is a secondary symptom and, by sacrificing its aims to this negative quality, art goes completely off track, into a gratuitousness that is itself useless. It is the same scenario, more or less, as that of nullity, of the claim to non-meaning, insignificance and banality, which attests to a redoubled aesthetic pretension.

Anti-art strives, in all its forms, to escape the aesthetic dimension. But since the 'ready-made' has annexed banality itself, all that is finished. The innocence of non-meaning, of the non-figurative, of abjection and dissidence, is finished.

All these things, which contemporary art would like to be, or return to, merely reinforce the inexorably aesthetic character of this anti-art.

Art has always denied itself. But once it did so through excess, thrilling to the play of its disappearance. Today it denies itself by default – worse, it denies its own death.

It immerses itself in reality, instead of being the agent of the symbolic murder of that same reality, instead of being the magical operator of its disappearance.

And the paradox is that the closer it gets to this phenomenal confusion, this nullity as art, the greater credit and value it is accorded, to the extent that, to paraphrase Canetti, we have reached a point where nothing is beautiful or ugly any more; we passed that point without realizing it and, since we cannot get back to that blind spot, we can only persevere in the current destruction of art.

Lastly, what purpose does this useless function serve?

From what, by its very uselessness, does it deliver us?

Like politicians, who deliver us from the wearisome responsibility of power, contemporary art, by its incoherent artifice, delivers us from the ascendancy of meaning by providing us with the spectacle of non-sense. This explains its proliferation: independently of any aesthetic value, it is assured of prospering by dint of its very insignificance and emptiness. Just as the politician endures in the absence of any representativeness or credibility.

So art and the art market flourish precisely in proportion to their decay: they are the modern charnel-houses of culture and the simulacrum.

It is absurd, then, to say that contemporary art is worthless and that there's no point to it, since that is its vital function: to illustrate our uselessness and absurdity. Or, more accurately, to make that decay its stock in trade, while exorcizing it as spectacle.

If, as some have proposed, the function of art was to make life more interesting than art, then we have to give up that illusion. One gets the impression that a large part of current art participates in an enterprise of deterrence, a work of mourning for the image and the imaginary, a – mostly failed – work of aesthetic mourning that leads to a general melancholia of the artistic sphere, which seems to survive its own demise by recycling its history and its relics.

But neither art nor aesthetics is alone in being doomed to this melancholy destiny of living not beyond their means, but beyond their ends.

Notes

1. In English in the original.
2. This passage is cited from an unidentified work by Saul Bellow, and I have not been able to trace the original. As a result, I can only offer here a retranslation of the French.

CHAPTER SEVENTEEN

The Pyres of Autumn

In late 2005 the outlying estates of Paris, and twenty other towns and cities, were burning. The suburbs were rising that November and global media attention was rife. Youths rioted and set cars and property alight for many consecutive nights. Government dithered and politicians, especially on the right, ranted. Not exactly May 68 which Baudrillard, influenced at the time by Herbert Marcuse, had witnessed alongside situationist contemporaries but not insignificant as an 'event' either. Baudrillard had long since given up on the 'left' to come to the rescue in such 'situations' but he was acutely aware of the damage Le Pen and the far right could do as the 'immigrant' question was raised nightly on the news as images of riot torn France proliferated. Baudrillard's views, as an instant pundit, were as usual eagerly awaited in France and around the globe. Chris Turner's English translation of Baudrillard's short commentary on the riots of the 'banlieues' was published in the journal *New Left Review* in 2006. The extract here is the article in full. Baudrillard made reference to the Watts riots in the US in the late 1960s, immigration and asylum seeking in Europe and the 'No' vote in the European Union Constitutional referendum in the mid 2000s. He contemptuously denigrated contemporary sociology's 'integrationist' social policy recommendations for the long-term 'solution' to the social problem of the riots in France. Appropriately for one of his last commentaries on contemporary events as his illness grew more serious, Baudrillard was scathing about the supposed superiority of Western culture. France in particular, and Europe in general, was seen by Baudrillard as part of the global problem, whereby symbolic exchange, with its duality and reciprocity, is in a deadly challenge with the semiotic or simulated order. Even though its seductive appeal remained, for Baudrillard the hyperconsumerism of the West was manifestly in flames as the motor car, still its most potent symbol of affluence, was burnt instead of driven.

'The Pyres of Autumn', *New Left Review*, No. 37, January/February, trans. Chris Turner, London: New Left Review, 2006.

Fifteen hundred cars had to burn in a single night and then, on a descending scale, nine hundred, five hundred, two hundred, for the daily 'norm' to be reached again, and people to realize that ninety cars on average are torched every night in this gentle France of ours. A sort of eternal flame, like that under the Arc de Triomphe, burning in honour of the Unknown Immigrant. Known now, after a lacerating process of revision – but still in *trompe l'oeil*.

The French exception is no more, the 'French model' collapsing before our eyes. But the French can reassure themselves that it is not just theirs but the whole Western model which is disintegrating; and not just under external assault – acts of terrorism, Africans storming the barbed wire at Melilla – but also from within. The first conclusion to be drawn from the autumn riots annuls all pious official homilies. A society which is itself disintegrating has no chance of integrating its immigrants, who are at once the products and savage analysts of its decay. The harsh reality is that the rest of us, too, are faced with a crisis of identity and disinheritance; the fissures of the *banlieues* are merely symptoms of the dissociation of a society at odds with itself. As Hélé Béji[1] has remarked, the social question of immigration is only a starker illustration of the European's exile within his own society. Europe's citizens are no longer integrated into 'European' – or 'French' – values, and can only try to palm them off on others.

'Integration' is the official line. But integration into what? The sorry spectacle of 'successful' integration – into a banalized, technized, upholstered way of life, carefully shielded from self-questioning – is that of we French ourselves. To talk of 'integration' in the name of some indefinable notion of France is merely to signal its lack.

It is French – more broadly, European – society which, by its very process of socialization, day by day secretes the relentless discrimination of which immigrants are the designated victims, though not the only ones. This is the change on the unequal bargain of 'democracy'. This society faces a far harder test than any external threat: that of its own absence, its loss of reality. Soon it will be defined solely by the foreign bodies that haunt its periphery: those it has expelled, but who are now ejecting it from itself. It is their violent interpellation that reveals what has been coming apart, and so offers the possibility for awareness. If French – if European – society were to succeed in 'integrating' them, it would in its own eyes cease to exist.

Yet French or European discrimination is only the micro-model of a worldwide divide which, under the ironical sign of globalization, is bringing two irreconcilable universes face to face. The same analysis can be reprised at global level. International terrorism is but a symptom of the split personality of a world power at odds with itself. As to finding a solution, the same delusion applies at every level, from the *banlieues* to the House of Islam: the fantasy that raising the rest of the world to Western living standards will settle matters. The fracture is far deeper than that. Even if the assembled Western powers really wanted to close it – which there is every reason to doubt – they could not. The very mechanisms of their own survival and supe-riority would prevent them; mechanisms which, through all the pious talk of universal values, serve only to reinforce Western power and so to foment the threat of a coalition of forces that dream of destroying it.

But France, or Europe, no longer has the initiative. It no longer controls events, as it did for centuries, but is at the mercy of a suc-cession of unforeseeable blow-backs. Those who deplore the ide-ological bankruptcy of the West should recall that 'God smiles at those he sees denouncing evils of which they are the cause'. If the explosion of the *banlieues* is thus directly linked to the world situation, it is also – a fact which is strangely never discussed – connected to another recent episode, solicitously occluded and misrepresented in just the same way: the No in the EU Constitutional referendum. Those who voted No without really knowing why – perhaps simply because they did not wish to play the game into which they had so often been trapped; because they too refused to be integrated into the wondrous Yes of a 'ready for occupancy' Europe – their No was the voice of those jettisoned by the system of representation: exiles too, like the immigrants themselves, from the process of socialization. There was the same recklessness, the same irresponsibility in the act of scuppering the EU as in the young immigrants' burning of their own neighbourhoods, their own schools; like the blacks in Watts and Detroit in the 1960s. Many now live, culturally and politically, as immigrants in a country which can no longer offer them a definition of national belonging. They are disaffiliated, as Robert Castel[2] has put it.

But it is a short step from disaffiliation to *desafío* – defiance. All the excluded, the disaffiliated, whether from the *banlieues*, immigrants or 'native-born', at one point or another turn their disaffiliation into defiance and go onto the offensive. It is their only way to stop being humiliated, discarded or taken in hand. In the wake of the November fires, mainstream political sociology spoke of integration, employment, security. I am not so sure that the rioters want to be reintegrated on these lines. Perhaps they consider the French way of life with the same condescension or indifference with which it views theirs. Perhaps they prefer to see cars burning than to dream of one day driving them. Perhaps their reaction to an over-calculated solicitude would instinctively be the same as to exclusion and repression.

The superiority of Western culture is sustained only by the desire of the rest of the world to join it. When there is the least sign of refusal, the slightest ebbing of that desire, the West loses its seductive appeal in its own eyes. Today it is precisely the 'best' it has to offer – cars, schools, shopping centres – that are torched and ransacked. Even nursery schools: the very tools through which the car-burners were to be integrated and mothered. 'Screw your mother' might be their organizing slogan. And the more there are attempts to 'mother' them, the more they will. Of course, nothing will prevent our enlightened politicians and intellectuals from considering the autumn riots as minor incidents on the road to a democratic reconciliation of all cultures.

Everything indicates that on the contrary, they are successive phases of a revolt whose end is not in sight.

Notes

1. Tunisian writer, author of *L'Imposture culturelle* (1997).
2. Sociologist, author of *L'Insécurité sociale* (2003).

CHAPTER EIGHTEEN

We Have Never Been Postmodern: Reading Jean Baudrillard
by Steve Redhead

The Jean Baudrillard Reader comprises a majority of his own words in relatively short extracts from the writings of Baudrillard over a five-decade period and a series of explanatory, introductory commentaries on each chapter as well as an editorial introduction. All the sections have been written in an accessible style for students across many different courses and levels, but are detailed and rigorous enough for long-time Baudrillard followers who wish to put Jean Baudrillard's entire life and work into a better context. The strong assumption behind this book is that it is instructive to read Baudrillard in his own words, in chronological order, if necessary over and over, before settling down with his many intrepreters. Interpretations of Baudrillard are, however, necessary in coming to an understanding of Baudrillard's significance. This bibliographical overview is intended to be a guide through the morass of Baudrillard interpretations and the whole of the extensive bibliography he himself produced. Once the texts in this *Reader* are absorbed, what else can anyone in search of a rounded view on Baudrillard read? The Recommended Reading list here is intended as a way into this dense and often contradictory and difficult body of literature. The commentary following it should help to chart the way.

Recommended Reading: What to read next

Baudrillard, Jean (2006a) *Utopia Deferred: Writings for* Utopie *(1967–1978)*. Los Angeles and New York: Semiotext(e).

Baudrillard, Jean (2006b) *Cool Memories V*. London: Polity.

Baudrillard, Jean (2004) *Fragments: Conversations with François L'Yvonnet*. London: Routledge.

Baudrillard, Jean (2003a) *Cool Memories IV*. London: Verso.

Baudrillard, Jean (2003b) *Passwords*. London: Verso.

Baudrillard, Jean (1999) *Photographies 1985–1998*. Ostfildem-Ruit: Hatje Cantz.

Baudrillard, Jean (1998) *Paroxysm: Interviews with Philippe Petit*. London: Verso.

Baudrillard, Jean (1997) *Fragments: Cool Memories III, 1990–1995*. London: Verso.

Baudrillard, Jean (1996a) *Cool Memories II*. London: Verso.

Baudrillard, Jean (1996b) *The System of Objects*. London: Verso.

Baudrillard, Jean (1996c) *The Perfect Crime*. London: Verso.

Baudrillard, Jean (1993) *The Transparency of Evil: Essays on Extreme Phenomena*. London: Verso.

Baudrillard, Jean (1990a) *Cool Memories*. London: Verso.

Baudrillard, Jean (1990b) *Fatal Strategies*. New York: Semiotext(e).

Baudrillard, Jean (1990c) *Revenge of the Crystal: Selected Writings on the Modern Object and Its Destiny 1968–1983*. London: Pluto Press.

Baudrillard, Jean (1988) *America*. London: Verso.

Baudrillard, Jean (1986) *The Ecstasy of Communication*. New York: Semiotext(e).

Baudrillard, Jean (1983a) *Simulations*. New York: Semiotext(e).

Baudrillard, Jean (1983b) *In the Shadow of the Silent Majorities, Or, The End of the Social and other essays*. New York: Semiotext(e).

Baudrillard, Jean and Lotringer, Sylvère (2005) *The Conspiracy of Art: Manifestos, Interviews, Essays*. Los Angeles and New York: Semiotext(e).

Baudrillard, Jean and Lotringer, Sylvère (1987) *Forget Foucault*. New York: Semiotext(e).

Baudrillard, Jean and Nouvel, Jean (2002) *The Singular Objects of Architecture*. Minneapolis, MN: University of Minnesota Press.

Butler, Rex (1999) *Jean Baudrillard: The Defence of the Real*. London: Sage.

Gane, Mike (2003) *French Social Theory*. London: Sage.

Gane, Mike (ed.) (1993) *Baudrillard Live: Selected Interviews*. London: Routledge.

Gane, Mike (1991a) *Baudrillard: Critical and Fatal Theory*. London: Routledge.

Gane, Mike (1991b) *Baudrillard's Bestiary: Baudrillard and Culture*. London: Routledge.

Genosko, Gary (ed.) (2001) *The Uncollected Baudrillard*. London: Sage.

Hegarty, Paul (2004) *Jean Baudrillard: Live Theory*. London: Continuum.

Horrocks, Christopher (1999) *Baudrillard and the Millennium*. Cambridge: Icon.

Horrocks, Christopher and Jevtic, Zoran (1996) *Baudrillard for Beginners*. Cambridge: Icon.

Kamper, Dietmar and Wulf, Christoph (eds) (1989) *Looking Back on the End of the World*. New York: Semiotext(e).

Kellner, Douglas (ed.) (1994) *Baudrillard: A Critical Reader*. Oxford: Basil Blackwell.

Kellner, Douglas (1989) *Jean Baudrillard: From Marxism to Postmodernism and Beyond*. Cambridge: Polity.

Lane, Richard J. (2000) *Jean Baudrillard*. London: Routledge.

Merrin, William (2005) *Baudrillard and the Media: A Critical Introduction*. Cambridge: Polity.

Poster, Mark (ed.) (2001) *Jean Baudrillard: Selected Writings*, 2nd edn. Cambridge: Polity Press.

Poster, Mark (ed.) (1988) *Jean Baudrillard: Selected Writings*. Stanford, CA: Stanford University Press.

Proto, Francesco (ed.) (2006) *Mass, Identity, Architecture: The Architectural Writings of Jean Baudrillard*, 2nd edn. London: John Wiley.

Rojek, Chris and Turner, Bryan (eds) (1993) *Forget Baudrillard?* London: Routledge.

The starting point for Baudrillard completists would be his first book from 1968 *The System of Objects* (Baudrillard 1996b) and two later works *The Transparency of Evil* and *The Perfect Crime* (Baudrillard 1993; Baudrillard 1996c) none of which are directly represented in this *Reader*.

There are three books which are useful jumping off points for those interested in following Baudrillard's long trajectory. Firstly, Douglas Kellner's 'reader' (Kellner 1994) is a collection of useful essays on Baudrillard. Secondly, there is Mark Poster's reader (Poster 2001), originally produced in 1988, a book which is genuinely a collection of selected writings by Baudrillard, alongside interview material. However, the selected writings were first chosen in 1988, the date of the first edition, and the second edition is a revised and expanded version – essentially adding five more selected writings. Because it also includes interview material as well as original essays, the unfolding of Baudrillard's thought is not always clear. Thirdly, there is *The Uncollected Baudrillard* (Genosko 2001), Gary Genosko's excellent collection of 'obscure' Baudrillard texts from various eras which is by far the most interesting of the diverse books seeking to 'represent' Baudrillard, but by definition, because it seeks to collect the 'uncollected Baudrillard', the book does not reflect the whole of Baudrillard's career.

One way of reading Baudrillard is to seek out what he has written in particular magazines and journals. For example, he wrote for much of his later life for *Libération* and between the mid 1970s and the early 1990s for *Traverses*. In the 1960s and 1970s he was a prominent author in the group which produced the ultra-leftist journal *Utopie*. Semiotext(e) in the US has collected the entire body of Baudrillard's writings for *Utopie*, where he worked with the likes of Henri Lefebvre, in a large volume alongside an interview with Baudrillard by Jean-Louis Voileau from 1997 (Baudrillard 2006a). Another way of reading Baudrillard is to group his writings and conversations by topic – cinema, art, architecture, the media, the object and so on. Baudrillard's essays and interviews on art (Baudrillard and Lotringer 2005) were collected together by Sylvère Lotringer for Semiotext(e) in 2005 together with a fascinating, previously unpublished 1996 interview with Baudrillard by Lotringer on Antonin Artaud. Baudrillard's writings on architecture have similarly been selected and collected by Francesco Proto (Proto 2006). The conversations on architecture and philosophy between Jean Baudrillard and his countryman Jean Nouvel, in the unique Urban Passages project from 1997–8 which involved pairs of philosophers and architects, are simply riveting (Baudrillard and Nouvel 2002) and are highly recommended. Baudrillard's enduring, pervasive connection to the media is superbly caught by the astute, radical Durkheimian viewpoint of William Merrin's critical introduction to Baudrillard and the media (Merrin 2005). In 1990 Paul Foss and Julian Pefanis edited a selected writings collection of Baudrillard's texts on the subject of 'the object' ranging from publications in 1968 through to 1983 (Baudrillard 1990c).

Both Mark Poster (1988) and Douglas Kellner (Kellner 1989) have a particular neo-Marxist reading of Baudrillard, initially at least in the 1980s branding him a postmodernist, which determines the particular selection of Baudrillard's output to be discussed or presented. Poster translated some of Baudrillard's Marxist-oriented writings from the early 1970s for the journal and publishing house *Telos* and tended to carry this 'neo-Marxist' trajectory through to interpretation of later texts. This reading of Jean Baudrillard has been severely discredited over the past decade. Gary Genosko's book has been one of several texts which have helped in this revisionism around Baudrillard. It is now possible to conclude that Jean Baudrillard has 'never been postmodern', and the way of reading him becomes altered in the process. It is also instructive to go back over his many interviews over the years with this altered perspective in mind, in other words to re-read Baudrillard as never having been postmodern.

In the case of the Genosko and Poster books, interviews with Baudrillard are reprinted alongside other material. In fact, Mike Gane's *Baudrillard Live* (Gane 1993) already does an excellent job of collecting Baudrillard's interviews up to the early 1990s. A number of good interviews (Hegarty 2004: 134–49), and books of interviews, with Jean Baudrillard have also been published since *Baudrillard Live*, especially *Fragments* (Baudrillard 2004), consisting of a series of conversations between Baudrillard and François L'Yvonnet on the eve of 9/11, whose English translation by Chris Turner has a succint foreword by Mike Gane as well as additional, very instructive notes. Mike Gane has written extensively about Baudrillard (see particularly Gane 1991a and Gane 199b) but nowhere more pertinently than in his contextualisation of French social theory (Gane 2003: *passim*, especially 152–61). The most revealing interviews with Baudrillard, apart from the above, can be found in the French journalist Phillippe Petit's talks with Baudrillard in *Paroxysm* (Baudrillard 1998) and 'Forget Baudrillard', a wonderful series of conversations with Sylvère Lotringer of Semiotext(e) which took place in Rome and Paris in 1984 and 1985 (Baudrillard and Lotringer 1987).

Baudrillard himself published a short, self-reflexive book on 'keywords' for his oeuvre (Baudrillard 2003b), the concepts ranging from 'the object', 'symbolic exchange' and 'the transparency of evil' through 'the perfect crime' and 'the end' to 'impossible exchange' and 'duality' – a veritable little Baudrillardian dictionary for our times! But there are also three excellent summaries and analyses of Baudrillard's conceptual work which I would strongly recommend for those coming to Baudrillard for the first time: namely the books by Paul Hegarty (Hegarty 2004), Rex Butler (Butler 1999) and Richard Lane (Lane 2000) in the Continuum 'Live Theory', Sage 'Core Cultural Theorists' and Routledge 'Critical Thinkers' series respectively. A provocative collection of essays on Baudrillard, edited by Chris Rojek and Bryan Turner (Rojek and Turner 1993) is well worth reading too. Christopher Horrocks has popularised Baudrillard in two short books (Horrocks and Jevtic 1996; Horrocks 1999), one mainly in cartoon form.

In the 1980s Baudrillard turned distinctively towards the aphorism and the diary form of writing. *Amérique* (in English translation, Baudrillard 1988) was the first, highly controversial example of these projects to be published (in 1986 in France) but the idea had emerged at the beginning of the decade. The period covered by *Cool Memories I* (in English translation, Baudrillard 1990a) ran from 1980 to 1985 though it was not published until 1987 in French, thereby coming out after *Amérique*. This 'aphoristic turn' gave rise to four further volumes of what might loosely be referred to as diaries in French. There are now available in excellent English translation, courtesy of Chris Turner, all five volumes of Baudrillard's aphoristic journals entitled *Cool Memories* (Baudrillard 1990a, 1996a, 1997, 2003a, 2006b), the first four published by Verso, the last, and literally final, one covering the years 2000 to 2004, published by Polity Press.

Alongside Verso in the UK, Semiotext(e) in the US has been Baudrillard's long-time English language publisher. The 'little black books' in the Foreign Agent Series edited by Jim Fleming and Sylvère Lotringer at Semiotext(e) were for many years the only way to discover Baudrillard around the world (Baudrillard 1983a, 1983b, 1987; Baudrillard and Lotringer 1987). Semiotext(e) also published *Fatal Strategies* (Baudrillard 1990b) in a larger format in the Double Agents series. A Baudrillard contribution was also often published in Semiotext(e) edited collections, such as *Looking Back on the End of the World* (Kamper and Wulf 1989).

Baudrillard's photography became an increasingly important part of his own life, art and theoretical work from the mid 1980s and a beautiful coffee table book in German, French and English comprising a collection of his photographic work alongside various Baudrillard texts on photography and the image was published in the late 1990s (Baudrillard 1999). Effectively the catalogue for an exhibition of the photographs at the Neue Galerie in Graz, Austria in 1999, this was the first time all the works of photography had been collectively shown, demonstrating a 'new aspect of Baudrillard' as artist, according to Christa Steinle (in Baudrillard 1999: 17–19). One of his own photographs from 1987, collected in *Photographies* and shown in the exhibition, reappeared to adorn the Semiotext(e) collection of Baudrillard's art interviews and essays a decade later (Baudrillard and Lotringer 2005).

Surfing the Internet will bring many rewards and hundreds of thousands of Baudrillard 'hits' but also much confusion and plain wrong-headedness. In particular, the online *International Journal of Baudrillard Studies*, begun in 2004, is essential reading for all interested in Baudrillard's life and work and connected theorists like Paul Virilio, Slavoj Žižek or Giorgio Agamben – available at http://www.ubishops.ca/BaudrillardStudies. Before the advent of *IJBS*, the web journal *CTHEORY* edited by Arthur and Marilouise Kroker was perhaps the most important online place for Baudrillard's output of articles or interviews – it can be reached at http://www.ctheory.net.

Finally, Baudrillard devotees can still buy, wear and read the special T-shirt made by the Philosophy Football company (London-based 'sporting outfitters of intellectual distinction' at http://www.philosophyfootball.com) – blue, with the number 3 and the name Baudrillard on the back, and the quotation, on the front, 'Power is only too happy to make football bear a diabolical responsibility for stupefying the masses'. The full, original Baudrillard quotation is in fact slightly more unwieldy: 'Power is only too happy to make football bear a facile responsibility, even to take upon itself the diabolical responsibility for stupefying the masses', a typically odd, quirky sentence taken from Baudrillard's volume *In The Shadow of the Silent Majorities* (Baudrillard 1983b: 14) originally published in French in 1978, the year of the soccer World Cup in Argentina. At his wedding to Marine in the late 1990s, when he was well into his sixties, the ushers were kitted out with brand new Baudrillard Philosophy Football T-shirts at Jean Baudrillard's own expense!

Index

European Perspectives
A Series in Social Thought and Cultural Criticism

Lawrence D. Kritzman, Editor